THE
WOMEN'S HERITAGE
SOURCEBOOK

THE
WOMEN'S HERITAGE
SOURCEBOOK

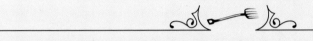

BRINGING HOMESTEADING TO EVERYDAY LIFE

Cooking • Herbalism • Canning • Fermenting
Beekeeping • Natural Beauty • Keeping Chickens
Milking Cows • Raising Pigs

Emma Rollin Moore • Lauren Malloy • Ashley Moore

with Audria Culaciati

RIZZOLI
NEW YORK

New York · Paris · London · Milan

Contents

Introduction

It started with a conversation. While our kids played, we had time to share about our lives, hobbies, and things we'd been learning. There was a shared excitement that caught fire. We discovered a world of knowledge with our combined experiences. Then came the desire to share that knowledge and passion with other women. We started to put on workshops and created an online journal. Apparently, our excitement was infectious, and it was obvious that other women had a thirst for knowledge of traditional skills too.

The skills and crafts we are passionate about have been around for centuries. They are nothing new, and yet they offer a whole new way of living in this modern, technologically advanced society. As they did hundreds of years ago, these hobbies and crafts connect us to a community of like-minded women who continue to inspire and teach us. We've met so many wonderful women who are ignited in a craft, hobby, or lifestyle, and we've witnessed how empowering it is for all of us to come together. We want to keep this momentum alive, and we want more women to be inspired to adopt new interests and try new things.

We do not claim to be homesteaders, or even experts of the crafts and hobbies often associated with that term, which include gardening, owning animals, making beauty products, using herbs as medicine, and preserving food. What we do know is that our quality of life has benefited from the decades we've spent learning and developing such crafts. We've found a relationship between slowing down and giving a certain kind of attention and presence to the everyday, tedious

tasks we do to simply survive—a cause and effect, an input and output—the outcome is a wholeness in our health.

Our hands get a bit dirty with tactile hobbies, and it feels good, whether it's working in the garden, picking herbs, handling a chicken, or making a meal. Studies have shown that being in nature, even for a few minutes at a time, has positive effects on brain chemistry and quality of life. Slowing down and being present with and within an activity reduces stress. Of course, as with anything intended to be "good for you," one can still be absentminded and rush through an action. Gardening with a multitasking, rushed mentality will not relieve stress. On the other hand, surrendering to the simple, physical, and present task of using your hands to complete an activity can ground you.

Whether you live in a small apartment in an urban environment or on hundreds of rural acres, there's something in this book for everyone. Perhaps your family grows most of its food; raises pigs, sheep, chickens, and turkeys; harvests and barrels rainwater and has a greywater system; grows and prepares medicine and toiletries; uses a composting toilet; preserves vegetables in a root cellar; and cans and pickles enough food to last through the lean months of the year.

Or perhaps your family lives in a small apartment in the city, makes your own soap, and has a vertical garden on the balcony. All of the elements described in these pages can be added, removed, or put up on a shelf until the time is right. Maybe you'll incorporate all of the ideas discussed here, or maybe you'll try out just one or two. It's up to you!

In this book, we have brought together our favorite things about our individual crafts and highlighted several other women who inspire us. Ultimately, we hope to encourage readers to consider adopting hobbies or interests that can open them up to a new community and enhance their quality of life.

A NOTE ON EQUIPMENT

In addition to standard kitchen equipment and utensils, here are some items you might want to have on hand when making some of the recipes in this book:

- Kitchen scale
- Immersion blender
- Food processor
- Stand mixer
- Popsicle molds
- Ice cream maker
- Dairy thermometer
- Water bath canner
- Mason jars in various sizes
- Cheesecloth
- Fermentation weights
- Bamboo skewers

FOOD

Seasonal Creativity
and Holistic Cooking

EMMA

I CALL MYSELF A SELF-TAUGHT ENTHUSIASTIC HOME COOK. I GREW UP IN THE CENTRAL Valley of California on a dairy farm. My father raised Holstein Friesian cows and farmed the land around us. At an early age, I found myself doing chores outside on the farm, growing fruits and vegetables in our garden, and cooking in the kitchen with my mother. I loved to watch her prepare dinner. I would pore over the stack of her dog-eared cookbooks and plead with her to cook certain recipes. Sometimes I could convince her to try a new seasonal recipe, but most often she prepared meals that were passed down from her mother and grandmother. No matter what, we would always sit down as a family to share dinner and stories from the day. This really left an impression on me.

My interest in health and well-being evolved in my young adult years. I studied human relationships at the University of California, Santa Barbara, and went on to get my master's in Los Angeles on the same topic. I returned to Santa Barbara and taught courses centered on healthy relationships at Santa Barbara City College.

The birth of my first child in 2008 rekindled my love for nutrition and merged all my different interests within food, well-being, and human relationships. Having my own family inspired me to reclaim the lifestyle and principles I experienced as a child. The only catch was that we lived in the city, but that didn't stop me. I adapted, chiseled down my values and priorities, and was determined to live a healthy, homegrown lifestyle.

A great influence during this time, and one of my favorite books in general, was Sally Fallon's *Nourishing Traditions*. It showed me recipes and inspired ideas on how to ferment, soak, and sprout food. The rest is history. I started gardening so we could eat our own fruits and veggies, and then taught myself how to make a sourdough starter, fresh sourdough bread, lacto-fermented veggies, and so on. I read labels and sought to create meals that were seasonal and nourishing without any added preservatives, which meant preparing the food from scratch.

My family and I have made a homegrown lifestyle work for us while living in suburbia. We live on a small plot of land in the foothills of Santa Barbara. We sprout food in our kitchen, have a backyard garden, and preserve and ferment seasonal produce. We raise chickens and ducks for eggs and have bees for honey. We make every space count. I've found that eating real, whole food is at the center of overall health and quality of life, and it is my hope that this book will inspire you to see that anyone can bring elements of the homestead to their daily life—especially when it comes to food.

DAIRY AND NONDAIRY

Growing up on a dairy farm, my family always had an ample supply of fresh milk right from the source. I remember taking the bucket to the milking parlor and filling it up with rich, creamy, and frothy cow's milk. I would bring it home and drink it right away. I still remember how good that fresh milk tasted. It wasn't until I was an adult that I learned about the benefits of fermenting milk. Fermented milk products are rich in probiotics and easier to digest. On a practical note, making yogurt, cheese, and kefir from home means I'm reusing containers, which reduces the number of packages in landfills.

Milk Kefir

Milk kefir is a fermented beverage containing probiotics. It uses kefir grains to ferment the milk, which results in a tangy, delicious beverage. It can be made from any type of animal milk—such as goat, sheep, or cow—or nondairy options such as coconut milk. You can find kefir grains in specialty stores or online. I order mine from a company called Cultures for Health.

1 to 2 tablespoons milk kefir grains

2 cups animal milk, preferably organic, raw, or non-homogenized (never ultra-pasteurized)

1. Place the milk kefir grains and milk in a 1-quart jar or container.
2. Cover lightly (I use cheesecloth), and leave the jar at room temperature (70 to 75°F) for at least 12 hours.
3. After 12 hours, start tasting the kefir every hour until it reaches your desired level of fermentation.
4. Strain out the milk kefir grains using a colander set over a bowl. Do not rinse the kefir grains. Either repeat the process with another 2 cups of milk, or add the milk and then store the kefir grains for later use in the fridge for up to 1 month.
5. For a nondairy option, follow the same procedure but substitute coconut milk for the animal milk. To keep the kefir grains working properly, however, you will need to cycle them through animal milk every couple of batches. So make one or two batches with nondairy milk, then a batch with regular dairy milk, then one or two batches with nondairy, and so on.
6. Store the fermented milk kefir in the fridge until you drink it.

FLAVORING MILK KEFIR AND SECOND FERMENTATION

Once the kefir grains have been strained out and transferred to fresh milk (or stored in the fridge for later use), the liquid that remains is milk kefir. Since the grains have been removed, the kefir can be further cultured and flavored. This culturing period is the second fermentation. A good amount of time for flavoring and creating a second ferment is 2 to 6 hours. This literally means the milk kefir, without grains, can sit for another 2 to 6 hours with the additional flavor and the fermentation will continue to happen. The benefits of this process are additional bacterial content, reduced lactose content, and improved flavor. Some flavor options are:

- Chai spices
- Citrus
- Cocoa powder
- Fresh or frozen fruit
- Herbs de Provence (to make a savory kefir dip)
- Honey
- Maple syrup
- Vanilla and cinnamon

Strawberry Kefir Milkshake

MAKES ABOUT 1¼ CUPS

Homemade strawberry kefir is such a treat. It is one of my son's favorite breakfast foods. This drink is a play on the classic strawberry milk, with a slightly sweeter twist and healthy probiotics.

1. Place the strawberries and maple syrup in a blender and blend until smooth.
2. Add the milk kefir and blend again.
3. Drink immediately, or let sit for 2 to 6 more hours to ferment. Store in the fridge for up to 1 week.

½ cup fresh strawberries (or frozen, defrosted)

1 tablespoon maple syrup

1 cup milk kefir

Peaches and Cream Kefir Popsicles

These slightly tangy and sweet summery popsicles are bursting with flavor and loaded with beneficial probiotics. Make them from scratch with your own milk kefir, or buy your choice of plain, full-fat milk kefir.

2 cups milk kefir

2 cups fresh peaches

¼ cup heavy cream, preferably organic

¼ to ½ cup raw honey (adjust depending on desired sweetness)

Pinch of sea salt

1. Place the milk kefir, peaches, cream, honey, and salt in a blender and blend until smooth.
2. Pour the mixture into popsicle molds or ice cube trays.
3. Place the molds in the freezer for 6 to 8 hours until the popsicles are frozen.

Kefir Cream Cheese

This recipe is a cream cheese upgrade that's easier for your body to digest. Spread it on crackers or bread—just like you'd use traditional cream cheese.

1. Line a colander with cheesecloth and set in a bowl. Add the milk kefir and let it sit for 48 hours.
2. Place the resulting cheese in a small bowl.
3. Season the cheese with salt and herbs to taste.
4. Refrigerate the cheese until ready to serve. Store the cheese in the fridge and use within 1 week.

2 cups milk kefir, grains removed

Sea salt

Herbs of choice, such as herbs de Provence, dried rosemary, sumac, or za'atar

Dairy Yogurt

Store-bought yogurt can be full of added sugars and preservatives. For this reason, I like to make my own homemade rich and creamy yogurt. I either serve it as is or flavor it with a smidge of honey, maple syrup, or my favorite seasonal preserved fruit.

3¾ cups whole milk, preferably organic, raw, or non-homogenized (never ultra-pasteurized)

1 tablespoon kefir or yogurt starter culture

1. Warm the milk in a small saucepan over medium heat until a dairy thermometer reads 160°F.
2. If using kefir as a starter culture, keep the heat between 165 and 185°F for 30 minutes, stirring constantly. If using yogurt, skip this step.
3. Remove the pan from the heat, and let the milk cool to 110°F.
4. Add the yogurt starter culture to ¼ cup of the cooled milk and stir to combine. Add this mixture to the remaining milk and stir until incorporated, being careful to not stir too vigorously.
5. Pour into a jar and incubate for 6 to 12 hours at 110°F in an oven, a cooler with a pot of steaming hot water, or a yogurt maker.
6. Place the set yogurt in the fridge and chill for at least 6 hours (the yogurt will thicken as it chills).
7. Store the yogurt in the fridge and use within 2 weeks.

Raw, Dairy-Free
Coconut Yogurt

MAKES ABOUT 4 CUPS

Most store-bought coconut yogurt has extra fillers, like gums and carrageenan. I like to make my coconut yogurt with fresh young Thai coconuts and no fillers. This recipe is simple—only two ingredients—and tastes incredible.

1. Preheat the oven to 100°F and turn on the oven light to keep the environment warm. (You can also use a yogurt maker, a dehydrator at 100°F, or an insulated camping cooler with a pot of boiling water inside.)
2. Open the coconuts by carefully piercing a large hole in the top of each one, and then pour the coconut water into a blender.
3. Scrape the flesh from the inside of the coconut and place in the blender with the water. Blend on high for about 1 minute until smooth and well combined.
4. Open the probiotic capsules and pour the powder over the coconut mixture; discard the capsule casings. Blend for 30 seconds.
5. Pour the coconut mixture into a 1-quart glass jar and screw on the lid.
6. Place the jar in the oven, yogurt maker, dehydrator, or insulated cooler.
7. Let rest for 12 to 18 hours without disturbing. (The ferment time depends on the temperature of your kitchen. If it is around 74°F, it should be ready after 12 hours, but it can take longer.)
8. Place the set yogurt in the fridge and chill for at least 6 hours (the yogurt will thicken as it chills).
9. Store the coconut yogurt in the fridge and use within 2 weeks.

2 young Thai coconuts

2 probiotic capsules, such as Jarrow Formulas

Homemade Ricotta

Homemade ricotta sounds pretty fancy, right? But it's not complicated. All you need is milk, cream, sea salt, and lemon juice. That's it! Just four simple ingredients and the result is a fresh and creamy ricotta cheese. (I use lemon juice because I like the flavor profile it creates, but white vinegar will do as a substitute.) Spread it on bread and drizzle with honey, or add it to pancakes, a spring salad, or your favorite Italian pasta dish. The possibilities are endless. Once you make this version, you won't buy store-bought ricotta again.

3½ cups whole milk, preferably organic

½ cup heavy cream, preferably organic

½ teaspoon sea salt

3 tablespoons freshly squeezed lemon juice

1. Place the milk, cream, and salt in a small saucepan set over medium heat, and heat the milk to 165°F. This will take 5 to 10 minutes. Stir occasionally to prevent scorching on the bottom of the pan.
2. Remove from the heat and add the lemon juice. Stir once or twice, gently and slowly.
3. Let the pan sit undisturbed for 5 minutes.
4. Line a colander with a few layers of cheesecloth and place in a large bowl.
5. Pour the curds and whey into the colander and let the curds drain for at least 1 hour, after which you'll have a tender, spreadable ricotta. At 2 hours, it will be spreadable but a bit firmer, almost like cream cheese.
6. Eat the ricotta immediately or transfer it to an airtight container and refrigerate for up to 1 week.

Zucchini and Corn Galette with Fresh Ricotta and Herbs

This savory galette is a summertime staple at my house. The filling uses homemade ricotta, corn, and zucchini all wrapped up in a buttery and slightly tangy sourdough pastry crust.

1. Spread the zucchini out on a large cutting board. Sprinkle it with the salt and let stand for 30 minutes. Gently blot with a towel.
2. Preheat the oven to 400°F. Line a baking sheet with parchment paper.
3. On a lightly floured work surface, roll out the pastry dough to a diameter of 12 inches and a thickness of ⅛ inch. Transfer the dough to the prepared baking sheet.
4. Spread the ricotta over the dough, leaving a 2-inch border.
5. Sprinkle with the pepper and 1½ teaspoons each of the basil and thyme.
6. Arrange the zucchini, red onion, and corn kernels in a circular pattern over the ricotta.
7. Drizzle with up to 1 tablespoon of the olive oil and sprinkle on the remaining basil and thyme. Season with salt and pepper.
8. Fold the border to the filling and crimp the edges.
9. Bake in the oven for 55 minutes.
10. Cool for 5 to 10 minutes, cut, and serve with additional herbs if desired.

1 large zucchini, thinly sliced into rounds

½ teaspoon sea salt

Sourdough pastry crust dough (see page 154), or store-bought pie dough

½ cup homemade ricotta (see page 28)

¼ teaspoon freshly ground black pepper

1 tablespoon chopped fresh basil

1 tablespoon chopped fresh thyme

½ red onion, peeled and thinly sliced

Kernels from 1 ear of corn

1 tablespoon extra virgin olive oil

Homemade Mozzarella

When I first started making mozzarella from scratch, I used citric acid and rennet along with cow's milk, water, and sea salt. After a failed attempt or two, I did get the hang of it, and the cheese was yummy. However, when I discovered you could make mozzarella with lemon juice instead of citric acid, I knew I wanted to try, because I love using Mother Nature in her purest form when cooking. It turns out making mozzarella using lemon juice produces a superb flavor. I know it might take a little extra time and care, but try it. It's so worth it.

1 gallon whole milk, preferably organic (never ultra-pasteurized)

⅔ cup freshly squeezed lemon juice

14¼ cups cold filtered water

¼ tablet rennet

¼ cup sea salt

1. Pour the milk into a large stockpot.
2. Dilute the lemon juice in 2 cups of the cold filtered water. Add the lemon juice and water solution to the milk, stirring gently to incorporate.
3. Heat the mixture on medium-low until the temperature reaches 90°F, stirring occasionally. While the milk is heating, dissolve the rennet in ¼ cup of the cold filtered water and set aside.
4. Once the milk has reached 90°F, remove the pot from the heat. Stir in the dissolved rennet and continue stirring for 30 seconds. Cover the milk and set it aside for 15 minutes.
5. Place the pot with the coagulated milk (now curds and whey) back on medium heat, stirring gently until the mixture reaches 110°F.
6. Once the mixture reaches 110°F, remove the pot from the heat. Line a colander with cheesecloth and place it in a bowl. Gently scoop out the curds and transfer to the colander. Let the whey drain (this can take 30 minutes to 1 hour). When drained, fold up the curds in the cheesecloth to squeeze out the remaining whey. When most of the whey is squeezed out, form five or six balls with the curds.
7. Put 6 cups of the cold filtered water in a medium saucepan and heat over medium-high heat. Place the remaining 6 cups of water in a container, add the salt, and stir to dissolve.
8. Once the water on the stove reaches 190°F, place one of the balls of the curds in the water and let it heat for about 5 minutes, until the curds soften.
9. Remove the ball of curds from the water and knead it. Knead for 1 minute or so, form it into another ball, and place it back in the hot water. Leave it for another 5 minutes.
10. Remove the ball, knead it again for 1 minute, then re-form the ball. Submerge the ball in the saltwater brine. Set aside.

11. Repeat this process with the remaining balls of curds.
12. Refrigerate the container with the balls in brine for 1 hour.
13. Drain the brine and eat the cheese immediately, or keep it in an airtight container in the fridge for up to 1 week.

TIP: There is often a lot of whey created when making kefir cream cheese, ricotta, or mozzarella. Instead of tossing it, store it in an airtight container in the fridge for up to 3 months, and use it in place of water when making pizza dough, waffles, or other baked goods.

Mint Ice Cream

I am always looking for something fun to do with the abundance of mint in our garden and eggs from our chickens. This recipe happens to be quite a refreshing treat.

1. Combine the milk and heavy cream in a medium saucepan. Place over medium-low heat and cook until just steaming.
2. Remove from the heat. Tear the mint leaves over the mixture to release oils and flavor and add the torn leaves to the saucepan.
3. Cover with a lid, and allow the fresh mint to infuse in the milk and cream mixture for at least 20 minutes.
4. Strain the mint-milk mixture through a fine-mesh sieve into a medium bowl.
5. In a separate large mixing bowl, whisk together the egg yolks and honey until smooth.
6. Transfer the strained milk mixture back into the same saucepan and warm over medium heat until almost bubbling, but not boiling.
7. Slowly add the hot milk mixture into the egg yolks, whisking constantly.
8. Pour the mixture back into the saucepan and heat on low, stirring constantly, until the ice cream base has thickened considerably and coats the back of a spoon.
9. Once the ice cream base is thick, pour it through a fine-mesh sieve into a large airtight container. Place in the fridge until it is completely chilled, about 6 to 8 hours or overnight.
10. Remove the ice cream base from the fridge. Churn the ice cream in an ice cream maker according to the manufacturer's instructions. Place the ice cream in an airtight container, covering the surface of the ice cream lightly with parchment paper or plastic wrap before putting the lid on.
11. Freeze the ice cream for a minimum of 4 hours, or until it is firm enough to scoop. The ice cream will keep for 2 weeks in the freezer.

1 cup whole milk, preferably organic

2 cups heavy cream, preferably organic

1 bunch (fistful) fresh mint

5 egg yolks, whisked

¼ to ½ cup raw honey (depending on desired sweetness)

½ teaspoon sea salt

PRESERVING

Saving the season's harvest that you or a local farmer has grown is satisfying on many levels, and there's no better way to eat fresh. I am a big believer in eating as close to home as possible. I also am a stickler about not letting things go to waste. I've been known to knock on a neighbor's door to see if I can help them preserve unpicked or freshly fallen fruit.

Canning, jamming, and pickling all serve the same function of preserving food's lifespan, but in very different ways. Canning is the process of placing food in jars and heating them to a temperature that destroys the microorganisms that cause food to spoil. During this heating process, air is driven out of the jar and a vacuum seal forms as it cools. This vacuum seal prevents air, and the microorganisms carried with it, from getting back into the product. Heating for the required period of time also kills any possibly present molds, yeasts, bacteria, and enzymes.

Jamming is the process of reducing the potential bacteria content of fruits and vegetables, which significantly prolongs their shelf life. There are three main options when jamming. One is to cook the fruit into a jam by adding sugar, letting it cool, and then putting it in the freezer until you are ready to use it. The second option is to place the jam directly in the fridge once it cools, and the third is to actually can the jam.

Pickling is the process of preserving the lifespan of food by either anaerobic fermentation in brine or immersion in vinegar. Almost any vegetable or fruit can be pickled, and it's a great way to give your body good nutrition year-round.

Basic Water Bath Canning

Supplies

Here's a list of some essentials to have on hand when canning and preserving:

- ← Water bath canner or large pot
- ← Canning jars, lids, and bands
- ← Jar lifter
- ← Wide-mouth jar funnel
- ← Thermometer
- ← Bubble remover and headspace tool
- ← Dishcloths
- ← Hot pads or gloves
- ← Sharp knife and cutting board

Instructions

For the purposes of this book, all the recipes use the water bath canning method. Essentially, a water bath canner is a large pot big enough to hold at least seven 1-quart jars and allow them to be submerged by 1 to 2 inches of water. The canners usually include a rack with handles to make it easier (and safer) to put the jars in and take them out of boiling water. You can buy a water bath canner at your local hardware store. However, it is not necessary to purchase special cookware. A large, deep stockpot equipped with a lid and rack works just as well. As long as it is large enough to fully immerse the jars in water by 1 to 2 inches—and allow the water to boil rapidly when covered—the pot is adequate. If you don't have a rack designed for home preserving, use a round cake cooling rack or extra bands tied together to cover the bottom of the pot.

1. Fill a water bath canner at least halfway with water. Cover and maintain a simmer (180°F) until the jars are filled and ready to be placed in the canner.
2. Check the jars, lids, and bands for proper functioning. Jars with nicks, cracks, uneven rims, or sharp edges may prevent sealing or cause jar breakage. The underside of the lids should not have scratches or uneven or incomplete sealing compound, as this may prevent sealing. The bands should fit on the jars. Wash everything in hot, soapy water and dry well.
3. To sterilize your canning jars, preheat them in hot (180°F) water for 10 minutes. Keeping the jars hot also prevents them from breaking when filled with hot food. There is no need to sterilize the lids or bands; leave them at room temperature for easy handling.
4. Use a jar lifter to remove the preheated jars. Fill the jars one at a time with prepared food using a jar funnel, leaving the headspace recommended in each recipe. If stated in the recipe, remove air bubbles by sliding a bubble remover and headspace tool between the jar and food to release trapped air. Repeat around the jar two or three times. For successful sealing, you need to leave the correct amount of space between the food and the rim of the jar.
5. Wipe the rim of the jar using a clean, damp cloth to remove any food residue. Center the lid on the jar, allowing the sealing compound to contact the jar rim. Apply the band and adjust until the fit is fingertip-tight. Place the jar in the canner. Repeat steps four and five until all the jars are filled and placed back in the canner. Ensure the water covers the jars by 1 to 2 inches.
6. Place the lid on the water bath canner and bring the water to a rolling boil. Process in the boiling water for the time indicated in each recipe.
7. When complete, shut off the heat and remove the lid. Allow the jars to rest in the canner for 5 minutes to become acclimated to the outside temperature.
8. Transfer the jars from the canner and set them upright on a towel. This will prevent the jar breakage that can occur from temperature differences. Leave the jars undisturbed for 12 to 24 hours. Do not re-tighten the bands, as this may interfere with the sealing process.

Note

For the recipes in this chapter, always process the filled jars according to the water bath instructions described here for the amount of time indicated in each recipe. The water in the canning pot should be warm or hot but not boiling when you add the filled jars. This is to avoid an extreme temperature change when placing them in the water.

Tips

- **Be clean.** Make sure the vessels, jars, and utensils you use to can and pickle are clean. The jars must be sterilized first.

- **Check your altitude.** Similar to baking a cake, a higher altitude can affect your fresh preserving recipes. If you are preserving at an altitude higher than 1,000 feet above sea level, increase your process time accordingly.

- **Start simple, with the freshest produce available.** Use produce from your own garden, a farmers market, or a local market where you can taste and see the freshness.

- **Lacto-ferment, pickle, and can all year long.** Every season has a fresh crop of fruits and veggies to savor and pickle, not just the summer months.

- **Clean fruits or veggies before pickling.** Make it your routine to scrub your produce and check for any bruises. Cut any blemishes out before pickling.

- **Toast spices before adding them to a brine**. This really brings out their flavor.

- **Label your jars.** Before you put your goods away in the pantry, label the jars with the contents and the date they were made. Masking tape will do, or get crafty and design your own custom labels to print.

- **Experiment.** Classic spices are dill seed, celery seed, yellow and brown mustard seeds, garlic, bay leaves, and whole black peppercorns. Also consider fresh ginger, shallots, dried chili peppers, fresh and dried herbs, coriander seeds, allspice berries, star anise, and cinnamon sticks. You get the idea.

- **Consult canning resources.** The National Center for Home Food Preservation (nchfp. uga.edu) is an invaluable source of research-based recommendations for most methods of home food preservation, including canning, fermenting, freezing, curing, and drying.

Vanilla-Rhubarb Compote

Sweet and slightly tart, vanilla-rhubarb compote is a delicious way to use your spring rhubarb. It's perfect for spreading on toast, putting in overnight oats, or serving over ice cream.

1 vanilla bean

4 cups chopped rhubarb

1¼ cups sugar

1 tablespoon bottled lemon juice

Pinch of canning salt (optional)

1. Start heating the water in your canning pot. (See complete canning instructions on page 38 at beginning of chapter.)
2. Using the back of a butter knife, scrape the inside of the vanilla bean. Add the paste (along with the vanilla bean pod), rhubarb, sugar, lemon juice, and salt (if using) in a saucepan set over medium heat.
3. Cook, stirring occasionally, until the mixture becomes the consistency of applesauce.
4. Remove from the heat and fish out the vanilla bean pod. Cut it in half. Funnel the compote into the sterilized jars, leaving ½ inch headspace.
5. Place half of the vanilla bean pod in one jar, and the other half in the other jar. Wipe the jars clean and place the lids on the jars. Process in the water bath for 10 minutes.
6. Store the jars in a cool, dark place for up to 1 year. Once opened, store in the fridge for up to 1 month.

TIP: Bottled lemon juice is used instead of fresh in many canning recipes because it has a consistent and dependable acid level.

Strawberry Jam

MAKES 4 PINTS OR 8 HALF-PINTS

Canned jam and preserves capture the sweet goodness of spring and summer fruits to be enjoyed any time of the year on toast, bread, pancakes, and even yogurt or ice cream. One of my favorites is this simple strawberry jam.

1. Start heating the water in your canning pot. (See complete canning instructions on page 38 at beginning of chapter.)
2. Combine the strawberries, sugar, and lemon juice in a medium saucepan over medium heat. Bring to a simmer and cook for 15 to 20 minutes until the jam reaches 220°F and is the consistency you prefer.
3. Remove from the heat. Funnel the jam into the sterilized jars, leaving ½ inch headspace.
4. Wipe the jars clean and place the lids on the jars. Process in the water bath for 10 minutes.
5. Store the jars in a cool, dark place for up to 1 year. Once opened, store in the fridge for up to 1 month.

3 pounds strawberries

3 cups sugar

6 tablespoons bottled lemon juice

TIP: When making any jam, you can check to see if it is set by removing a spoon from the freezer and dribbling several drops of the jam onto the spoon. Wait a few seconds, and then run a finger through the jam. If it leaves a track in the jam, it is done. If it runs together, keep cooking the jam and test a few minutes later.

Summer Tomatoes

In the heat of summer, my garden overflows with heirloom tomatoes, which means it's canning time! Canned tomatoes are such a treat. I use them for so many recipes—soups, stews, enchilada sauce, and pasta sauce, to name just a few.

21 pounds tomatoes

14 tablespoons bottled lemon juice

7 teaspoons canning salt (optional)

1. Start heating the water in your canning pot. (See complete canning instructions on page 38 at beginning of chapter.)
2. To remove the tomato skins, bring a large pot of water to a boil. Have a bowl of ice water, a cutting board, a knife, and a slotted spoon nearby. Remove the tomato cores and score the bottom of each tomato with a small X. Working in batches, place 4 to 6 tomatoes in the boiling water for 30 to 60 seconds, or until you see the skins split. Remove the tomatoes with the slotted spoon, and place immediately in the bowl of ice water. Slip the skins off, and quarter the tomatoes on your cutting board. Repeat with the remaining tomatoes.
3. Add the tomatoes to the sterilized jars. Press down on the tomatoes, crushing them as you fill the jars and making sure to leave ½ inch headspace.
4. Add 2 tablespoons of lemon juice and 1 teaspoon of salt per quart. Salting the tomatoes is optional, but it adds to the flavor.
5. Remove any air bubbles with a bubble remover. Wipe the jars clean and place the lids on the jars. Process in the water bath for 45 minutes.
6. Store the jars in a cool, dark place for up to 1 year. Once opened, store in the fridge for up to 1 month.

Tomato or Pizza Sauce

This recipe is my favorite when my garden is full of tomatoes and I'm trying to can them before they spoil. You can double, triple, or quadruple the recipe depending on how many tomatoes you have.

1. Start heating the water in your canning pot. (See complete canning instructions on page 38 at beginning of chapter.)
2. To remove the tomato skins, bring a large pot of water to a boil. Have a bowl of ice water, a cutting board, a knife, and a slotted spoon nearby. Remove the tomato cores and score the bottom of each tomato with a small X. Working in batches, place 4 to 6 tomatoes in the boiling water for 30 to 60 seconds, or until you see the skins split. Remove the tomatoes with the slotted spoon, and place immediately in the bowl of ice water. Slip the skins off, and quarter the tomatoes on your cutting board. Core and dice the peeled tomatoes. Repeat with the remaining tomatoes.
3. Heat a large Dutch oven or cast-iron pot over medium-high heat. Add the tomatoes, oil, red bell pepper, salt, onion powder, basil, oregano, pepper, and red pepper flakes. As they heat, use the back of a spoon or fork to mash the tomatoes and help them break down a bit.
4. Bring to a low boil, constantly stirring until the mixture is reduced by half, about 25 to 35 minutes. When the sauce is finished cooking, remove from the heat.
5. Add the lemon juice. Working in batches, place the tomato mixture in a blender and purée until the desired consistency. (Skip this step if you want your sauce to be chunky.)
6. Funnel the mixture into the sterilized jars, leaving ½ inch headspace. Wipe the jars clean and place the lids on the jars. Process in the water bath for 15 minutes.
7. Store the jars in a cool, dark place for up to 1 year. Once opened, store in the fridge for up to 1 week.

4 pounds tomatoes (plum, roma, or beefsteak)

2 teaspoons extra virgin olive oil

¼ cup finely chopped and seeded red bell pepper

2 teaspoons canning salt

½ teaspoon onion powder

½ teaspoon dried basil

½ teaspoon dried oregano

½ teaspoon freshly ground black pepper

Pinch of red pepper flakes

2 tablespoons bottled lemon juice

Tomato Paste

If you have an abundance of summer tomatoes, try turning your tomato sauce into tomato paste. Making tomato paste takes a lot of time and patience, so be prepared. But the result is so rewarding!

2 pints homemade tomato sauce (see page 47)

2 tablespoons bottled lemon juice

1. Preheat the oven to 350°F.
2. Pour the tomato sauce onto a rimmed baking sheet. Place the baking sheet on a wire rack in your oven and bake for 1 hour, stirring every 20 minutes.
3. Start heating the water in your canning pot. (See complete canning instructions on page 38 at beginning of chapter.)
4. Continue baking, checking and stirring often, until the sauce is reduced to a thick paste. Be careful not to burn it. This should take about 1 more hour.
5. Funnel the paste into the sterilized jars, leaving ½ inch headspace. Wipe the jars clean and place the lids on the jars. Process in the water bath for 40 minutes.
6. Store the jars in a cool, dark place for up to 1 year. Once opened, store in the fridge for up to 1 week.

Pickled Red Tomatoes

I love these pickled red tomatoes on a sandwich, pizza, pasta dish, or on their own as a snack. They also make great gifts to showcase your summer harvest.

1. Start heating the water in your canning pot. (See complete canning instructions on page 38 at beginning of chapter.)
2. To remove the tomato skins, bring a large pot of water to a boil. Have a bowl of ice water, a cutting board, a knife, and a slotted spoon nearby. Remove the tomato cores and score the bottom of each tomato with a small X. Working in batches, place 4 to 6 tomatoes in the boiling water for 30 to 60 seconds, or until the skins split. Remove the tomatoes with the slotted spoon, and place immediately in the bowl of ice water. Slip the skins off. Repeat with the remaining tomatoes.
3. To make the brine, combine the vinegar, water, salt, sugar, and ginger in a large pot and bring to a boil over medium-high heat.
4. Gently add the tomatoes and 1 teaspoon of pickling spice to each sterilized half-pint jar (or 2 teaspoons per pint jar), being careful not to crush the tomatoes.
5. Slowly pour the brine over the tomatoes, leaving ½ inch headspace. Remove any air bubbles with a bubble remover. Wipe the jars clean and place the lids on. Process in the water bath for 15 minutes.
6. Store the jars in a cool, dark place for up to 1 year. Once opened, store in the fridge for up to 1 month.

4 pounds tomatoes

2 cups red wine vinegar

2 cups filtered water

2 tablespoons canning salt

6 tablespoons sugar

2-inch piece fresh organic ginger, thinly sliced

6 teaspoons pickling spice

Tomato Jam

Sweet and savory, this jam is the perfect accompaniment to a cheese platter. It also elevates a grilled cheese sandwich to a higher level. It's great to have on hand in your pantry or to give as a gift.

4 pounds tomatoes (plum, roma, or beefsteak)

2¾ cups brown sugar

1 tablespoon grated fresh organic ginger

½ teaspoon red pepper flakes

2 teaspoons sea salt

1 teaspoon ground cumin

½ teaspoon smoked paprika

4 tablespoons bottled lemon juice

1. Start heating the water in your canning pot. (See complete canning instructions on page 38 at beginning of chapter.)
2. To remove the tomato skins, bring a large pot of water to a boil. Have a bowl of ice water, a cutting board, a knife, and a slotted spoon nearby. Remove the tomato cores and score the bottom of each tomato with a small X. Working in batches, place 4 to 6 tomatoes in the boiling water for 30 to 60 seconds, or until the skins split. Remove the tomatoes with the slotted spoon, and place immediately in the bowl of ice water. Slip the skins off, and quarter the tomatoes on your cutting board. Core and dice the peeled tomatoes. Repeat with the remaining tomatoes.
3. Heat a large Dutch oven or cast-iron pot over medium heat. Add the tomatoes, brown sugar, ginger, red pepper flakes, salt, cumin, and paprika. Stir frequently to ensure the mixture is cooking evenly. Continue cooking the mixture until it reaches a thick, jam-like consistency, about 25 minutes, and then remove from the heat.
4. Add the lemon juice and stir. Working in batches, place the tomato mixture in a blender and purée until the desired consistency. (Skip this step if you want your jam to be chunky.)
5. Funnel the mixture into the sterilized jars, leaving ½ inch headspace. Wipe the jars clean, and place the lids on the jars. Process in the water bath for 15 minutes.
6. Store the jars in a cool, dark place for up to 1 year. Once opened, store in the fridge for up to 1 month.

Something Good Organics

CAROLYN GIVENS

I first met Carolyn Givens at our local farmers market. I would often frequent the Givens Family Farm stand for the freshest strawberries, crisp spring greens, and the sweetest snap peas. Her wealth of knowledge and genuine passion for living more sustainably and eating seasonally is what makes Carolyn such an inspiration to me. Most of her canning experience is with fresh produce such as tomatoes, peaches, and beans rather than actual recipes. She thinks it's more convenient to jar tomatoes, which can make a variety of things, instead of canning tomato sauce.

Carolyn was raised in Munich, Germany, but has lived in California for about 20 years. Her relationship with organic farming, sustainability, and the food movement began about a decade ago when she met her husband, Mathew Givens. He propelled her interest in all of these things at high speed. Her mother has always been big into canning as well, and she still helps to this day.

Canning is important to Carolyn for a variety of reasons—one being a zero-waste lifestyle— and making sure she has plenty of homemade food helps keep this idea alive. The ability to reuse jars and throw away as little as possible is a must. It's also become very clear to her that simple, amazing food starts with the best ingredients. And the best ingredients are local, seasonal, and picked at the peak of ripeness. She believes food is truly medicine, and it's a very gratifying experience to be crafting her canning creations in her own kitchen.

Tomatillo Salsa

There is nothing like opening a jar of this salsa in the middle of winter and enjoying a little piece of summer. I make sure to grow tomatillos every year in our garden just so I can make this salsa.

4 pounds tomatillos

2 cups finely chopped onions

2 finely chopped jalapeños

6 garlic cloves, peeled and finely chopped

½ cup finely chopped fresh cilantro

½ cup bottled lime juice

2 teaspoons canning salt

2 teaspoons ground cumin

½ teaspoon freshly ground black pepper

1. Start heating the water in your canning pot. (See complete canning instructions on page 38 at beginning of chapter.)
2. Combine all the ingredients in a large pot set over high heat. Stir frequently until the mixture boils.
3. Reduce the heat and simmer for 20 minutes.
4. Remove from the heat. Working in batches, place the tomatillo mixture in a blender and purée until the desired consistency. (Skip this step if you want your salsa to be chunky.)
5. Funnel the mixture into the sterilized jars, leaving ½ inch headspace. Wipe the jars clean, and place the lids on the jars. Process in the water bath for 15 minutes.
6. Store the jars in a cool, dark place for up to 1 year. Once opened, store in the fridge for up to 1 month.

Stone Fruit Jam

Summer stone fruits make the best jam! Make sure to leave the skins on the fruit for added color, flavor, and ease.

1. Start heating the water in your canning pot. (See complete canning instructions on page 38 at beginning of chapter.)
2. Combine the stone fruit, sugar, lemon juice, and zest in a saucepan over medium heat. Bring to a simmer and cook for 15 to 20 minutes, stirring frequently, until the jam reaches 220°F and is the consistency you prefer.
3. Remove the pan from the heat. Funnel the jam into the sterilized jars, leaving ½ inch headspace. Wipe the jars clean, and place the lids on the jars. Process in the water bath for 10 minutes.
4. Store the jars in a cool, dark place for up to 1 year. Once opened, store in the fridge for up to 1 month.

3 pounds stone fruit, such as peaches, apricots, and nectarines, sliced and pits removed

3 cups sugar

3 tablespoons bottled lemon juice

Zest of 1 organic lemon

Applesauce

Apples are a quintessential autumn fruit. They are easily available year-round, but nothing beats the taste of homegrown or fresh-from-the-farm apples. One of my favorite ways to savor the season of this fall fruit is by canning them. No sugar is needed, and the result is a fruitful sauce that can be eaten on its own for snacking (or added to kids' lunches), paired with yogurt, or used in baking. Empress, Cortland, Gala, Jonagold, Braeburn, Golden Delicious, and Honeygold apples are all great options for this recipe.

4 pounds apples

½ cup filtered water

1 tablespoon ground cinnamon (optional)

1 teaspoon grated nutmeg (optional)

½ teaspoon ground cloves (optional)

1 tablespoon sugar (optional)

1. Start heating the water in your canning pot. (See complete canning instructions on page 38 at beginning of chapter.)
2. Core, quarter, and dice the apples. Put them in a large pot, add the water, cover, and bring to a simmer.
3. Let the fruit cook for approximately 15 to 20 minutes, or until the mixture is soft.
4. Using an immersion blender or food mill, break down the fruit until it has reached the desired consistency.
5. Add the spices (if using). Taste and add sugar if necessary.
6. If you use a food mill, return the smooth applesauce to the pot and heat it back to a simmer. It doesn't require any additional cooking, but it should remain hot.
7. Working quickly and carefully, funnel the hot applesauce into the sterilized jars, leaving ½ inch headspace.
8. Remove any air bubbles with a bubble remover. Wipe the jars clean, and place the lids on the jars. Process in the water bath for 20 minutes.
9. Store the jars in a cool, dark place for up to 1 year. Once opened, store in the fridge for up to 1 month.

TIP: I don't always peel my apples. I've found that the skin breaks down as the apples slowly cook, providing added nutrition. If you don't like the skins on, you can either pick out the peel as the fruit cooks or peel the apples before you start cooking them.

Bourbon–Brown Sugar Apple Butter

Thick, sweet apple butter is always a treat—and the bourbon and brown sugar in this recipe make it all the better. Flavors of caramel and vanilla somehow come through. I have gifted this apple butter to friends and family over the holidays, and it never made it on toast—they just ate it straight from the jar! Empress, Cortland, Gala, Jonagold, Braeburn, Golden Delicious, and Honeygold apples are all great options for this recipe.

1. Start heating the water in your canning pot. (See complete canning instructions on page 38 at beginning of chapter.)
2. Core and cut the apples into quarters, leaving the skin on. Put them in a large pot, and then add the vinegar and water.
3. Cover and bring to a boil over high heat, then reduce the heat to a simmer and cook until the apples are soft, about 20 minutes. Remove from the heat.
4. Working in batches, purée the apple mixture using a blender or a fine-mesh sieve.
5. Return the puréed apple mixture to the pot. Add the sugar, bourbon, spices, and lemon zest and juice.
6. Cook, uncovered, on medium-low heat, stirring constantly to prevent burning. Scrape the bottom and sides of the pot. Cook until thick and smooth, about 1 hour, until the jam reaches 220°F and is the consistency you prefer.
7. Funnel the mixture into the sterilized jars, leaving ½ inch headspace. Wipe the jars clean and place the lids on the jars. Process in the water bath for 20 minutes.
8. Store the jars in a cool, dark place for up to 1 year. Once opened, store in the fridge for up to 1 month.

4 pounds apples

½ cup apple cider vinegar

2 cups filtered water

4 cups brown sugar

2 tablespoons bourbon

1 ½ tablespoons ground cinnamon

½ teaspoon ground cloves

½ teaspoon allspice

Zest and juice of 1 organic lemon

Persimmon Jam

The persimmon is a unique fall fruit that is naturally both tangy and sweet. There are two main persimmon types available: hachiya and fuyu. The hachiya persimmon is more tart than the fuyu due to its higher tannin content. For this recipe, I used hachiya persimmons, but feel free to add a combination of both types if you'd like. This will result in a little less tartness, but the unique flavor of the persimmon will still shine through. Spread this autumnal preserve on toast, or use it to top your favorite ice cream or cake.

3 pounds ripe hachiya persimmons (or a combo of hachiya and fuyu), peeled and seeded

3 cups sugar

6 tablespoons bottled lemon juice

Zest of 1 organic lemon

1. Start heating the water in your canning pot. (See complete canning instructions on page 38 at beginning of chapter.)
2. Combine the persimmons, sugar, lemon juice, and zest in a large saucepan over medium heat. Bring to a simmer and cook for about 30 to 45 minutes, stirring frequently, until the jam reaches 220°F and is the consistency you prefer.
3. Remove from the heat. Funnel the jam into the sterilized jars, leaving ½ inch headspace. Wipe the jars clean and place the lids on the jars. Process in the water bath for 10 minutes.
4. Store the jars in a cool, dark place for up to 1 year. Once opened, store in the fridge for up to 1 month.

Pickled Kabocha Squash

This recipe is worth a try when fall or winter rolls around and you can find squash at the farmers market or in your CSA box. Use these tangy winter-squash pickles to dress up a cheese platter; as an alternative to cranberry sauce at the holiday table; or tossed in a salad with quinoa, arugula, walnuts, and goat cheese. You can also substitute butternut squash or sugar pumpkin for the kabocha.

1. Start heating the water in your canning pot. (See complete canning instructions on page 38 at beginning of chapter.)
2. Peel the squash and remove the inner seeds and strings. Cut the flesh into ½-inch cubes.
3. Place the peppercorns, cloves, allspice berries, and bay leaf in a small muslin bag or cheesecloth and tie securely.
4. In a medium pot over medium-high heat, combine the vinegar, water, sugar, salt, cinnamon stick, and spice bag. Stir to dissolve the sugar.
5. Add the squash chunks to the pot and bring to a boil. Reduce the heat and simmer the squash until the chunks are translucent and fork-tender, 30 to 45 minutes.
6. Funnel the squash into the sterilized jars, and cover with the syrup that remains, leaving ½ inch headspace. Wipe the jars clean and place the lids on the jars. Process in the water bath for 15 minutes.
7. Remove the jars from the pot, place them on a kitchen towel to cool completely, and then store in a cool, dark place. These pickles are best if allowed to rest for 2 weeks to let the flavors meld before eating.
8. Continue storing the jars in a cool, dark place for up to 1 year. Once opened, store in the fridge for up to 1 month.

1 small kabocha squash (about 1½ pounds)

10 black peppercorns

8 whole cloves

5 allspice berries

1 bay leaf

1½ cups apple cider vinegar

1 cup filtered water

1 cup sugar

1 teaspoon canning salt

1 cinnamon stick

TIP: Due to the low acidity and thick texture of pumpkins, they are no longer considered safe to home can. However, it's OK when vinegar, sugar, and spices are added and the dense veggies swim in an acidic brine.

Pickled Kumquats

Kumquats are small citrus fruits that are bursting with a sour and slightly sweet citrus tang. Save a bit of the winter citrus season by pickling kumquats and pairing them with cheese, meat, or even salads, or try adding the pickled fruits to avocado toast (see page 183).

1 pound kumquats

1½ cups apple cider vinegar

½ cup pure cane sugar

½ teaspoon canning salt

6 black peppercorns

6 whole cloves

4 cardamom pods

1 star anise

1. Start heating the water in your canning pot. (See complete canning instructions on page 38 at beginning of chapter.)
2. Slice the kumquats into three or four disks each and pop out any visible seeds.
3. Place the fruit with the remaining ingredients in a medium pot and bring to a boil over medium-high heat. Reduce the heat and simmer for 3 to 5 minutes, until the kumquat pieces are soft but still hold their shape.
4. Funnel the mixture into the sterilized jars and cover with the syrup that remains, leaving ½ inch headspace. Wipe the jars clean and place the lids on the jars. Process in the water bath for 15 minutes.
5. Remove the jars from the pot, place them on a kitchen towel to cool completely, and then store in a cool, dark place. These pickles are best if allowed to rest for 2 weeks to let the flavors meld before eating.
6. Continue storing the jars in a cool, dark place for up to 1 year. Once opened, store in the fridge for up to 1 month.

TIP: Use the syrup too! The syrup from these pickles can be added to sparkling water or champagne for a tangy effervescent drink, or it can be whisked into a salad dressing.

Preserved Lemon

Preserved lemon, or lemon pickle, is a condiment that is popular in North African cooking. The lemons are diced, quartered, halved, or left whole and then pickled in a brine. Occasionally spices are included as well. This preserved lemon recipe uses only lemons and salt. Preserved lemons add so much citrus and umami flavor. Toss them in your favorite salad dressing or hummus recipe, or add to a rice or pasta dish.

1. In a sterilized jar, add 1 teaspoon of salt per one lemon quartered and seeded. Fill the jar and then press down to release the juices. If the juice released from the lemons does not cover them, add more freshly squeezed lemon juice.
2. Close the jar with a tight-fitting lid.
3. Let the lemons sit in the jar on the counter for 1 month before consuming. After that, you can refrigerate preserved lemons for up to 6 months.

Sea salt

Organic lemons

Hummus with Preserved Lemon

Over time, the juice in which preserved lemons have been sitting becomes a thick gel with a lot of citrus notes and a hint of saltiness. This gel, along with the lemon pulp and peel, becomes the perfect base for hummus.

1½ cups cooked chickpeas, rinsed (¼ pound dried or a 15-ounce can)

Juice of 1 lemon

6 tablespoons tahini

½ cup preserved lemon (see page 71), gel, peel, and pulp included

1 garlic clove, peeled and smashed

Pinch of smoked paprika, plus extra for serving

3 tablespoons extra virgin olive oil, plus extra for serving

Slivered fresh mint, for serving

1. In the bowl of a food processor, combine the chickpeas, lemon juice, tahini, preserved lemon, garlic, and paprika. With the motor running, drizzle in the olive oil. Process 2 to 3 minutes, until smooth and airy. Taste and adjust the seasonings.
2. Serve at room temperature, drizzled with a bit of olive oil. Top with smoked paprika and fresh mint.

Basic Salad Dressing

Add a bright citrus flavor to your salad by adding preserved lemons to your basic salad dressing.

1. In a jar, combine the lemon juice, preserved lemon, fresh herbs, honey (if using), garlic, and shallots. Cover and shake until blended.
2. Add the oil, cover, and shake again. Season with salt and pepper.
3. Set aside for 45 minutes to allow the flavors to meld. Shake again before serving.

⅓ cup freshly squeezed lemon juice

1 to 2 teaspoons finely chopped preserved lemon, gel, peel, and pulp included (see page 71)

1 to 2 teaspoons finely chopped fresh herbs (I used thyme and parsley)

½ teaspoon raw honey (optional)

1 garlic clove, peeled and minced

2 tablespoons minced shallots

1 cup extra virgin olive oil

Sea salt and freshly ground black pepper

Fermented Honey Garlic

Some call this "honey-infused garlic" or "garlic-infused honey" because this recipe works much like an infusion in addition to fermentation. Fermented honey garlic can be used to combat a cold or the flu in winter. It can also be used as a condiment. Drizzle it over pizza (our kids' favorite), serve it alongside spicy roasted veggies, or use it in a glaze for grilled pork or fish. It is also the perfect accompaniment to any cheese platter, along with some nuts, dried fruits, and fresh-baked bread.

Garlic cloves, peeled

Raw honey

1. Add enough garlic cloves to fill a sterilized jar about two-thirds full.
2. Add enough honey to completely cover the garlic cloves. Close the jar with a tight-fitting lid.
3. Let the garlic sit in the jar on the counter for 1 month before consuming. There is no need to refrigerate after opening.

Toast with Soft Cheese, Stone Fruit, and Fermented Honey Garlic

This simple dish combines the sweet flavor of summer stone fruit with the pungent taste of a soft, strong-flavored cheese. Drizzle the fermented honey garlic on top to take the toast to an entirely new level. It's good any time of day—eat it for breakfast or serve it as an evening appetizer.

Fresh bread

Semisoft or soft cheese, for spreading

Stone fruit

Fermented honey garlic

1. Cut the bread into ½-inch-thick slices.
2. Toast the bread, and then spread soft cheese on it.
3. Top the bread with stone fruit and drizzle with the fermented honey garlic.

Fermented Honey Cranberries

With a little prep and a lot of patience, these fermented honey cranberries become the perfect addition to a holiday-inspired meal or cocktail. Use the cranberries in your favorite stuffing or rice dish, and use the honey to flavor dressings or drizzle over roasted vegetables.

1. In a sterilized jar, add the cranberries, ginger, cinnamon stick, cloves, and orange zest and juice.
2. Pour the honey over the cranberries so they are completely covered. Close the jar with a tight-fitting lid.
3. Let the cranberries sit in the jar on the counter for 1 month before consuming. There is no need to refrigerate after opening.

2 cups fresh cranberries, rinsed, well drained, and pierced with a fork

4 to 5 slices fresh organic ginger

1 cinnamon stick

¼ teaspoon whole cloves

Zest and juice of 1 organic orange

2½ cups raw honey

MAKING A BEVERAGE

To make a mocktail, pour 1 to 2 ounces of honey into sparkling water and drop in a couple fermented cranberries.

For a cocktail, substitute prosecco or your favorite alcohol for the sparkling water.

FERMENTED LIBATIONS

A shrub is a drinking vinegar that includes vinegar, fruit, and sugar. Once it has been made, bubbly water can be added, or a bit of alcohol and maybe some bitters to spice it up. There are a lot of different ways to make shrubs. Some recipes instruct you to heat all of the ingredients before straining and using. Others require no cooking at all. I prefer the latter, which is called the cold method. I also love to use Bragg apple cider vinegar, which is raw and unfiltered. The ingredients in these beverages can be teeming with probiotics and digestive enzymes. They make for the perfect aperitif, as well as a digestive healer. The recipes included here are some of my favorite summertime drinking vinegars, as well as a variety of other fermented beverages that I love to make throughout the year.

Before fermenting, it is important to ensure your jars are nice and clean in order to avoid contamination. It is not vital that they are sterilized, but if you'd like to do so, add your jars to a large stockpot and cover with water by at least 1 inch. Bring to a low, rolling boil and let simmer for 5 minutes. Remove the jars carefully using tongs, and then place them on towels (cold countertops can shock the jars and break them). Let the jars cool slightly to room temperature, and then proceed with the recipe.

Plum-Thyme Shrub

This shrub is tart and sweet with a touch of earthy thyme, making it the perfect summer sipper.

4 cups sliced red plums

1 tablespoon fresh thyme leaves

2 cups pure cane sugar

1 cup champagne vinegar

1 cup apple cider vinegar, preferably Bragg

1. Combine the plums, thyme, and sugar in a 1-quart jar with a tight-fitting lid. Use the back of a wooden spoon or a muddler to smash the fruit a bit.
2. Close the lid and let the jar sit on the counter for 24 hours.
3. Add the vinegars, stir well, and then close the lid.
4. After 1 week, strain out the fruit with a fine-mesh sieve set over a measuring cup and taste the mixture. If it's to your liking—that is, fruity with a mellow vinegar flavor—pour the syrup into a jar with a tight-fitting lid. If it's too tart, add a touch more sugar, making sure to stir well before pouring the syrup into the jar.
5. Your shrub will keep, covered in the fridge, for 3 weeks.

TIP: A muddler is a bartender's tool, used like a pestle to mash—or muddle—fruits, herbs, and spices in the bottom of a glass to release their flavors.

Watermelon-Mint Shrub

This flavor combination is one of my favorites. It's fresh and is the perfect mix of sweet and tangy.

1. Combine the watermelon, mint, and honey in a 1-quart jar with a tight-fitting lid. Use the back of a wooden spoon or a muddler to smash the fruit a bit.
2. Close with the lid and let the jar sit on the counter for 24 hours.
3. Add the vinegar, stir well, and then close the lid.
4. After 1 week, strain out the fruit with a fine-mesh sieve set over a measuring cup and taste the mixture. If it's to your liking—that is, fruity with a mellow vinegar flavor—pour the syrup into a jar with a tight-fitting lid. If it's too tart, add a touch more sugar, making sure to stir well before pouring the syrup into the jar.
5. Your shrub will keep, covered in the fridge, for 3 weeks.

4 cups coarsely chopped ripe watermelon, seeds and rind removed

¼ cup chopped mint

⅓ cup raw honey

½ cup apple cider vinegar, preferably Bragg

TIP: To make a nonalcoholic cocktail with any of the shrubs in this book, add 1½ parts shrub mixture to 2 parts tonic water. More or less tonic water can be added depending on your taste preference. If you want a little alcohol in your cocktail, add 1 part shrub, 1½ parts alcohol of choice, and 1 part tonic water.

Elderberry Shrub

This drinking vinegar not only looks pretty but also has immune-boosting and rejuvenating qualities. The elderberry has been linked to improving heart health, treating the flu, and supporting our immune systems. I usually do not heat my drinking vinegars, but in this recipe, I like to heat the elderberries to bring out their unique and fruitful flavor. The end result is a slightly sweet berry flavor with a hint of tartness.

1 cup fresh elderberries (or ½ cup dried elderberries)

1 cup apple cider vinegar, preferably Bragg

1½ cups sugar

1. If using dried elderberries, steep them in ½ cup warm water for 5 minutes.
2. Combine the elderberries and vinegar in a 1-quart jar with a tight-fitting lid. Use the back of a wooden spoon or a muddler to smash the fruit a bit.
3. Close with the lid and let the jar sit on the counter for 5 days. Give the mixture a good stir daily.
4. Next, strain out the fruit with a fine-mesh sieve set over a small saucepan and combine this elderberry-infused vinegar with the sugar. Bring to a boil over medium-low heat, stirring constantly to dissolve the sugar. Boil for 5 minutes and then remove from the heat.
5. Let cool, transfer to a jar with a tight-fitting lid, and keep in the fridge for 3 to 4 weeks.

Elderberry Country Wine

I can't resist making this quick country wine whenever elderberries are in season. Any berry will do if you don't have access to elderberries—blackberries, raspberries, or even blueberries. There are so many possibilities.

1. Put the elderberries in a half-gallon jar. Use the back of a wooden spoon or a muddler to smash the fruit.
2. In a separate large jar or bowl, dissolve the sugar in the water and add the lemon juice. Transfer to the jar with the smashed elderberries. Stir vigorously with a spoon in a circular motion. Loosely cover with a lid or cheesecloth secured with a rubber band around the rim of the jar.
3. During the first 2 days, vigorously stir the mixture four times a day. Tiny bubbles will appear at the top of the liquid. This is a sign that fermentation is taking place.
4. The bubbling will settle in about 3 days. At this point, strain out the fruit and consume the wine immediately or continue the fermentation by placing the wine in a jar with a tight-fitting lid or airlock and releasing the pressure every other day.

2 pounds ripe elderberries, rinsed, well drained, and stems removed

1 pound sugar

8 cups filtered water

Juice of 1 lemon

Jun

I was given a Jun scoby to ferment years after I started making my own kombucha. (The word *scoby* is actually an acronym: Symbiotic Culture of Bacteria and Yeast. A scoby is the living home for the bacteria and yeast that transform sweet tea into tangy, fizzy Jun.) Jun is similar to kombucha, but it is brewed with green tea and honey instead of black tea and sugar. For this reason, there is a lower caffeine content by the time it is fully fermented. Also, I've found the flavor profile of Jun is lighter and fresher than kombucha, and it takes less time to ferment. It is said to have a higher lactobacillus content, which is a win for the gut. The one downside is that it is definitely more expensive to make due to the cost of honey versus sugar. Still, I think the health benefits and taste make it worth trying.

8 cups filtered water

2 teaspoons green tea or 2 green tea bags

½ cup raw honey

1 Jun scoby (you can purchase this online from places such as Kombucha Kamp)

1 cup previously cultured Jun tea (from the purchased scoby or a previous batch)

1. Boil the water, and then remove from the heat and let it cool to 165°F.
2. Steep the tea for 2 minutes. The longer the tea steeps, the stronger the "green tea" flavor your Jun tea will have.
3. Remove the tea and set aside to cool to between 96 and 104°F.
4. Add the honey and stir to dissolve. (You can skip the previous step and dissolve the honey right away in the hot tea, but the health benefits are greater when the honey is not heated at the higher temperature.)
5. Pour this mixture into a half-gallon jar or container. Add the scoby and previously cultured Jun tea. Cover the container with a kitchen towel and secure with a rubber band.
6. Let it rest at room temperature for 3 days to culture. (You can culture longer, but the taste might become too acidic.)
7. Once pleasantly sour and still a little sweet, drink your tea immediately, or try a second fermentation for added bubbles. Think kombucha champagne!
8. Save 1 cup of your Jun tea, and then repeat this process to make more.

TIP: To do a second fermentation, decant the Jun into bottles, cap them, and store in a warm, dark place. Allow them to sit for 2 to 3 days. This will create a really fizzy and flavorful Jun.

The Apiary

RACHNA HAILEY

I first met Rachna Hailey, herbalist and cofounder of The Apiary (which makes cider, mead, and hard kombucha), a couple of years ago at an event where she was serving some herbal cocktail creations. They were divine. With my interest in food and cooking with herbs, I was immediately inspired by her ways of combining ingredients for flavor and well-being.

Rachna was raised in Santa Barbara, California. She left Santa Barbara for Bauman College of Holistic Nutrition and Culinary Arts in Berkeley, and when she later returned to her hometown, she started hosting private herbal cocktail pop-ups while also working at the farmers market.

In her most creative endeavor yet, Rachna and her life partner dreamed up The Apiary. They sought to find a way to incorporate holistic ingredients into fermented alcohol and developed a deep love for honey. Jun was the spark of many recipes upon which The Apiary was founded. They experimented with low-alcohol meads made from local, single-origin honey. The naturalist in Rachna wanted to bring the beverages full circle by adding local herbs and flowers pollinated by the bees that made their honey. Rachna's craft continues to evolve as she shares the mighty capabilities of medicinal herbs with the changing seasons.

TULSI- AND ROSE-INFUSED HONEY

Honey is an extremely "thirsty" ingredient, so this infused honey will end up being slightly more watery and pourable than before the infusion. This texture is better when mixing the preferred acidic ingredients for cocktails. Honey draws in whatever medicinal qualities are incorporated from the infused herbs in an extremely harmonious way.

In a medium-sized jar of local honey, pack in a small handful of dried or fresh tulsi leaves and rose petals and tighten the lid. The infusion time depends on how much honey is used, and your desired potency of flavor. A good place to start is 2 weeks. Stir the honey mixture every other day throughout the infusion time. After the infusion, strain the leaves. (Another option for those who like a strong flavor is to leave the herbs in the honey indefinitely.)

TULSI-INFUSED GIN AND JUN

Makes 1 (16-ounce) cocktail

This is an herbal approach to your classic gin and tonic. Jun has very herbal qualities from the tea and subtly sweet notes from the honey, which makes it a perfect match for gin. The tulsi lends itself to basil-scented adaptogenic properties, and the rose has a floral and delicate aroma. This cocktail can also be adapted with any other kind of infused honey you may be experimenting with. Feel free to get creative with your infusions and garnishes. Rachna likes to serve this drink in a pint-size mason jar.

1 tablespoon tulsi- and rose-infused honey

Juice of 1 large Meyer lemon

1½ ounces gin

Jun, for topping off (see page 88)

Thin slice of lemon, rose petals, and sprig of tulsi, for garnish

1. Mix the honey and lemon juice together vigorously at the bottom of your cocktail glass until the honey dissolves.
2. Fill the glass to the very top with ice, and immediately pour the gin on top. Stir well. The glass should be about three-quarters full with liquid.
3. Top off the rest of the cocktail with Jun, stir again gently, and then garnish with a lemon slice, rose petals, and fresh tulsi.

Lavender-Cherry Wildcrafted Soda

MAKES 1 HALF-GALLON

For this recipe, you can use your favorite fruit and herbs to create a delicious, bubbly probiotic beverage. I used cherries and lavender, but any combination of fresh seasonal fruit and herbs—such as mint, thyme, chamomile, or lemon balm—will do. (My second favorite combination is raspberries with chamomile and mint.) Although you can buy champagne yeast or make your own ginger bug to aid in the process of fermentation, I never do. I simply allow the wild yeast that is present on the fruits and herbs to work its magic. Try it—the experiment is worth the wait.

½ gallon spring water

2 cups fresh lavender

½ pint fresh cherries, pitted and halved

1 cup raw wildflower honey

1 organic lemon, sliced

Pinch of champagne yeast or ¼ cup ginger bug (optional)

1. Add all the ingredients to a half-gallon jar. Stir vigorously with a spoon in a circular motion. Loosely cover with a lid or cheesecloth with a rubber band around the rim.
2. Over the next 1 to 2 days, vigorously stir the mixture four times a day. Tiny bubbles should appear at the top of the liquid. This is a sign fermentation is taking place.
3. Taste each time you stir. When it has reached your desired level of fermentation, pour the wildcrafted soda through a fine-mesh sieve set over a vessel large enough to contain it.
4. Pour the beverage into bottles. I use flip-top glass bottles, but plastic bottles can be used in a pinch. Cap tightly, and allow fermentation to continue at room temperature for another 12 to 24 hours.
5. Test for desired fizziness by carefully opening the bottles. Because you are creating natural carbonation through fermentation, the contents of the bottle may be extra bubbly, expand, or possibly even explode upon opening, so use caution. Refrigerate when you are happy with the flavor and fizziness.

LACTO-FERMENTATION

Lacto-fermentation is a microbial process using beneficial bacteria such as lactobacillus, bifidobacterium, and other lactic acid bacteria (LAB)—commonly known as probiotics—which thrive in an anaerobic fermenting environment. This simple fermentation process requires nothing more than salt, vegetables, and water. No canning or fancy equipment is necessary.

Lactobacillus bacteria converts sugars naturally present in fruit or vegetables into lactic acid. Lactic acid is a natural preservative that helps fight bad bacteria. It preserves not only the flavor and texture of food, but also its nutrients. Simply put, the lacto-fermentation process works because of the lucky fact that potentially harmful bacteria can't tolerate too much salt while healthy bacteria can. Beyond preservation advantages, lacto-fermentation increases the digestibility of the fermented food and, most important, enhances the flavor. I have found this process to be a simple and nutritious way to preserve your in-season abundance without too much fuss.

Lacto-Fermentation Tips

❦ Before fermenting, it is important to ensure your jars are nice and clean in order to avoid contamination. It is not vital that they are sterilized, but if you'd like to do so, add your jars to a large stockpot and cover with water by at least 1 inch. Bring to a low, rolling boil and let simmer for 5 minutes. Remove the jars carefully using tongs, and then place them on towels (cold countertops can shock the jars and break them). Let the jars cool slightly to room temperature, and then proceed with the recipe.

❦ Washing fruits and veggies before fermenting isn't necessary because the lactobacillus bacteria will take over and multiply. Harmful bacteria won't survive. That said, it won't hurt either. If you're concerned about germs and pesticides on your produce, you can wash it or soak it with diluted vinegar (4 parts water to 1 part vinegar).

This will also remove the wax coatings. Washing or scrubbing won't kill or wash off all the good bacteria. There will still be enough present for fermentation.

❦ Picking high-quality produce can make a difference in how your ferment turns out. Homegrown produce is the best, followed by organic, but it's OK to use conventional produce too.

❦ Make sure your vegetables are submerged. Being below the brine provides the environment necessary for anaerobic fermentation to take place. It helps keep any mold atop your brine and not in your vegetables. For this reason, a cabbage leaf or fermentation weight can come in handy.

❦ Create the right salinity for your brine. I generally use a ratio of 1 quart of water to 1 to 2 tablespoons of salt. Salt slows down the fermentation process and heat speeds it up. So when fermenting while it's warmer outside, consider adding 3 tablespoons of salt instead of 2 tablespoons.

❦ Fermentation takes time. There are several fermentative bacteria involved in the process of fully fermenting your vegetables. These bacteria all have specific needs and occur at specific times in the process. For that reason, you must allow your ferment time to process before moving to cold storage. Instead of following a strict time frame, taste the ferments along the way to determine when it's time to refrigerate them.

❦ Temperature is a big factor when it comes to fermentation. A rise in temperature can relate directly to the speed at which the vegetables ferment—meaning, the hotter the day, the faster the fermentation. Hot temperatures can also affect the flavor and texture of vegetables; it can make the taste seem off or the texture too squishy. Do your best to keep the temperature below 85°F.

Red Kraut

This is by far one of my favorite ferments to have on hand. For a little extra flavor and probiotic kick, I love adding it as a topping to tacos, eggs, salads, and soups. One of my favorite variations on this classic red kraut is adding a shredded apple, half a thinly sliced red onion, and one or two shredded red beets. Oh, and a sprinkling of dried blueberries is also a fun addition.

1 head red cabbage (about 3 pounds), cored and finely shredded

1½ tablespoons sea salt

1. Place the shredded cabbage in a large bowl. Sprinkle the salt over the cabbage and massage by squeezing handfuls between your palms and fingers for about 5 minutes. (The purpose of the massage is to help release the juice from the cabbage. The longer you massage, the more cabbage juice will be released.)

2. Pack the mixture into a 1-quart jar with a tight-fitting lid, pressing down on the cabbage until the natural brine rises to cover it. Leave at least 1 inch headspace, and seal the jar with the lid. (As a rule of thumb, red cabbage produces less juice than green cabbage. If necessary to add more brine, dissolve 1 teaspoon of sea salt in 1 cup of filtered water and add to cover the vegetables by 1 inch.)

3. Let your kraut sit on the counter at room temperature (away from direct sunlight) for 1 to 2 weeks. You may see bubbles inside the jar, and brine may seep out of the lid. This is a good sign; it means fermentation is happening. Put a plate under the jar to catch any overflow.

4. Transfer the jar to the fridge when the kraut has reached your desired level of sourness. You may eat it immediately, but it's best after another 1 to 2 weeks.

Kimchi

This kimchi recipe uses green cabbage and green onions as a base. The result is a recipe that really holds on to its flavor profile of saltiness, sourness, and—of course—spiciness. Enjoy it on its own, or add it to various dishes as a side. One of my favorite meals is a small bowl of kimchi topped with a soft-boiled egg, diced avocado, and a sprinkle of sesame seeds or gomasio (a dry condiment used in Japanese cooking that is made from unhulled sesame seeds and salt).

1. Place the cabbage in a large mixing bowl, sprinkle on the salt, and toss well. Add enough water to cover the cabbage. Let the cabbage, salt, and water mixture sit for 2 hours, turning once or twice.
2. Rinse the cabbage once, drain well, and set aside.
3. In a blender, combine the garlic, ginger, fish sauce, cooked rice, and water. Purée until a paste is formed.
4. In a separate mixing bowl, combine the Korean red chili flakes and sugar (if using). Add the rice purée and mix well. Add the cabbage and green onion. Toss well to coat, so the seasoning is dispersed throughout.
5. Pack the kimchi into a large jar with a tight-fitting lid, pressing down on the mixture until the natural brine rises to cover the vegetables. Leave at least 1 inch headspace, and tighten the lid.
6. Let your kimchi sit on the counter at room temperature (away from direct sunlight) for 1 to 2 weeks, or up to 3 weeks, depending on your flavor and texture preference. You may see bubbles inside the jar, and brine may seep out of the lid. This is a good sign; it means fermentation is happening. Put a plate under the jar to catch any overflow.
7. Transfer the jar to the fridge when the kimchi has reached your desired level of sourness. You can eat it immediately, but it's best after another 1 to 2 weeks.

1 large head green cabbage (about 3 pounds), cored and cut into 1½-inch chunks

3 tablespoons coarse sea salt

3 garlic cloves, peeled

½-inch piece fresh organic ginger

3 tablespoons fish sauce, preferably Red Boat

2 tablespoons cooked white rice

6 tablespoons filtered water

1 to 5 tablespoons Korean red chili flakes (depending on desired taste)

1 tablespoon sugar (optional)

1 bunch green onions or scallions, sliced

Kimchi Fried Rice

One of the questions I am asked when teaching others how to make kimchi is how to eat it and use it with other foods. One of my favorite ways is kimchi fried rice, which is a good way to spice up lunch or dinner. It also makes for a quick meal given that most of the ingredients can be prepped ahead of time. You will not be disappointed.

3 tablespoons unsalted butter

½ small onion, peeled and diced

1 cup roughly chopped kimchi (see page 101)

2 tablespoons kimchi juice

3 slices bacon, cooked and chopped

2 cups cooked, cooled rice (preferably short-grain)

2 teaspoons soy sauce

2 teaspoons sesame oil

2 teaspoons vegetable oil

2 eggs

Sea salt

Fresh cilantro, chopped green onions or scallions, and sesame seeds, for garnish

1. In a nonstick sauté pan or a well-seasoned cast-iron skillet, melt the butter over medium-low heat.
2. Add the onion and stir for about 5 minutes, until it is starting to soften.
3. Turn up the heat to medium-high, add the kimchi and kimchi juice, and stir until it comes to a simmer.
4. Add the bacon, and then add the rice, stirring to incorporate.
5. Turn the heat back down to medium. Stir until the rice has absorbed the sauce and is very hot, about 5 minutes. Stir in the soy sauce and sesame oil. Taste, and adjust with more soy sauce, sesame oil, or kimchi juice if desired. Turn the heat to medium-low.
6. While the rice mixture continues to cook, heat a nonstick sauté pan over medium heat and add the vegetable oil. When it's hot, add the eggs, season with salt, and scramble the eggs.
7. Serve the rice topped with the scrambled eggs and garnish with cilantro, green onions, and a sprinkle of sesame seeds.

Sourdough Kimchi Pancakes

SERVES 3 TO 4

Another favorite way to use kimchi is to make these savory pancakes. They're full of flavor and slightly tart, and can be customized in countless ways—with leftover rice, noodles, or veggies.

1. Combine the sourdough starter and eggs in a large bowl and mix thoroughly.
2. Add the kimchi, cheese, garlic powder, paprika, salt, and any leftovers (if using).
3. Heat the oil in a large skillet over medium-high heat.
4. Ladle the batter into the skillet, making small pancakes between 2 and 3 inches in diameter.
5. Let cook until browned, 2 to 3 minutes per side.

3 cups sourdough starter (see page 146)

3 eggs

1 to 1½ cups kimchi (see page 101), drained

½ cup grated cheddar cheese

1 teaspoon garlic powder

1 teaspoon paprika

Pinch of sea salt

Leftover rice, noodles, or veggies (optional)

2 to 3 tablespoons oil, for frying

Stone-Fruit Kimchi

This fruit dish is a twist on the classic kimchi. I created this recipe so my kids would eat kimchi too. It is sweet and slightly savory, with a hint of spiciness. Use habaneros in place of jalapeños if you want more of a kick.

3½ pounds napa cabbage

½ onion, peeled

2 pounds stone fruit, pits removed

1 to 2 jalapeños, seeded

3-inch piece fresh organic ginger, peeled

2 garlic cloves, peeled

3½ tablespoons sea salt

Juice of 1 lemon

1 teaspoon sugar (optional)

1. Thinly slice the cabbage, onion, stone fruit, and jalapeños. Grate the ginger and garlic.
2. Place everything in a large bowl and massage with the salt and lemon juice. (Add sugar if using.) Let the bowl sit on the counter for 1 to 2 hours, mixing occasionally, until the cabbage has wilted and released a little water.
3. Pack the kimchi into a large jar with a tight-fitting lid, pressing down on the mixture until the natural brine rises and covers the vegetables and fruits. Leave at least 1 inch headspace, and tighten the lid.
4. Let your kimchi sit on the counter at room temperature (out of direct sunlight) for 3 to 5 days or up to 1 week depending on your desired taste. You may see bubbles inside the jar, and brine may seep out of the lid. This is a good sign; it means fermentation is happening. Put a plate under the jar to catch any overflow.
5. Transfer the jar to the fridge when the kimchi has reached your desired level of sourness. You may eat it immediately, but it's best after another 1 to 2 weeks.

Lacto-Fermented Radishes

I love having a variety of fermented veggies on hand, and these lacto-fermented radishes are the perfect snack. You can also add them to meals as an addition to a salad, sandwich, or rice dish.

1. Trim the radishes, and then thinly slice or cut them in half.
2. To a 1-quart jar with a tight-fitting lid, add the radishes, desired herbs and spices, and garlic, making sure to leave about 1 inch headspace at the top.
3. In a large measuring cup, combine the water and salt. Stir until the salt dissolves.
4. Pour the salt water over the radishes until it reaches just below the top of the jar. There should be about ½ inch headspace left.
5. Close the lid and let the veggies sit at room temperature (out of direct sunlight) for at least 3 days and up to 2 weeks, until they are as tart as you'd like. The brine will turn cloudy and bubbly, but this is normal. Open the lid once a day to let out the built-up air.

Radishes to fill a 1-quart jar

1 bay leaf (optional)

Pinch of red pepper flakes (optional)

1 teaspoon coriander seeds (optional)

1 garlic clove, peeled and smashed (optional)

3 cups filtered water

1 tablespoon sea salt

Lacto-Fermented Carrots

My kids just can't get enough of these carrots. They are tangy with just the right amount of dill and are the perfect gut-healthy snack or side dish.

Carrots to fill a 1-quart jar

Dill sprig (optional)

Pinch of red pepper flakes (optional)

1 tablespoon pickling spices (optional)

1 garlic clove, peeled and smashed (optional)

3 cups filtered water

1 tablespoon sea salt

1. Cut off the tops and bottoms of the carrots, and then peel them if desired.
2. To a 1-quart jar with a tight-fitting lid, add the carrots, desired herbs and spices, and garlic, making sure to leave about 1 inch headspace at the top.
3. In a large measuring cup, combine the water and salt. Stir until the salt dissolves.
4. Pour the salt water over the carrots until it reaches just below the top of the jar. There should be about ½ inch headspace left.
5. Close the lid and let the carrots sit at room temperature (out of direct sunlight) for at least 3 days and up to 2 weeks, until they are as tart as you'd like. The brine will turn cloudy and bubbly, but this is normal. Open the lid once a day to let out the built-up air.

TIP: The lacto-fermented veggie recipes included in this book are just the beginning. You can substitute almost any vegetable. Think green beans, cauliflower, fennel—even a watermelon rind would work.

Lacto-Fermented Dill Pickles

MAKES 1 HALF-GALLON

This is the essential summertime ferment; it is crunchy, dilly, and juicy. And don't forget to save the brine. Try adding it to a Bloody Mary, whiskey sour, or margarita for an amazing cocktail.

Cucumbers to fill a half-gallon jar, ends trimmed off

3 dill sprigs

4 garlic cloves, peeled and smashed

½ white onion, peeled and sliced

1 bay leaf

6 cups filtered water

5 tablespoons sea salt

6 tablespoons mustard seeds

Pinch of red pepper flakes

2 tablespoons black peppercorns

1. To a half-gallon jar with a tight-fitting lid, add the cucumbers, dill sprigs, garlic, onion, and bay leaf, making sure to leave about 1 inch headspace at the top.

2. In a large measuring cup, combine the water, salt, and other spices. Stir until the salt dissolves.

3. Pour the salt water over the cucumbers until it reaches just below the top of the jar. There should be about ½ inch headspace left.

4. Close the lid and let the cucumbers sit at room temperature (out of direct sunlight) for at least 3 days and up to 2 weeks, until they are as tart as you'd like. The brine will turn cloudy and bubbly, but this is normal. Open the lid once a day to let out the built-up air.

Lacto-Fermented Hot Sauce

MAKES 1 HALF-GALLON

This just might be my favorite ferment. It takes time, but it's worth every minute. I started the process toward the end of summer when I harvested my peppers, and by December I had the most amazing hot sauce. That said, a week or two of fermentation works as well. I sometimes like to add sweet peppers to the mix.

1. To a half-gallon jar with a tight-fitting lid, add the peppers, onion, and garlic, making sure to leave about 1 inch headspace at the top.
2. In a large measuring cup, combine the water and salt and stir until the salt dissolves. Pour over the peppers.
3. Secure the peppers beneath the brine with a fermentation weight. If you don't have a weight, you can use the core of a cabbage (cut to fit your jar size) to weigh the peppers down.
4. Close the lid securely and let sit at room temperature (out of direct sunlight) for at least 2 weeks and up to 4 months depending on your desired flavor.
5. Once fermented to your liking, strain the pepper mixture over a bowl and reserve the brine.
6. Place the peppers in a blender. Blend until smooth, adding either the brine or apple cider vinegar (if preferred) to thin.
7. Funnel the hot sauce into airtight bottles and refrigerate. The flavors will continue to develop and get more complex over time.

1½ pounds hot peppers, such as jalapeño, serrano, habanero, or cayenne, sliced lengthwise

1 pound sweet bell peppers, sliced lengthwise

½ yellow onion, peeled

6 garlic cloves, peeled

4 cups cool filtered water

¼ cup sea salt

¼ cup apple cider vinegar (optional)

Lacto-Fermented Eggs

MAKES 1 QUART

My small flock of backyard chickens often provides me with an overabundance of eggs. This recipe preserves the eggs and makes an easy and delicious snack, or a great addition to salads and sandwiches. You can eat fermented eggs as is, make deviled eggs, or add them to your favorite salad or avocado toast. A meal idea is a lettuce cup with some diced eggs, sprouts, fried chorizo or bacon, and sliced radishes.

6 hard-boiled eggs, peeled

2 garlic cloves, peeled and smashed

Sprig of dill

1 small shallot, peeled and sliced

2 cups filtered water

1½ teaspoons sea salt

1 bay leaf

¼ teaspoon black peppercorns

¼ teaspoon mustard seeds

2 tablespoons sauerkraut juice (optional)

Pinch of red pepper flakes

1. To a 1-quart jar with a tight-fitting lid, add the eggs, garlic, dill, and shallot, making sure to leave about 1 inch headspace at the top.
2. In a large measuring cup, combine the water, salt, and other spices. Stir until the salt dissolves.
3. Pour the salt water over the eggs until it reaches just below the top of the jar. There should be about ½ inch headspace left.
4. Close the lid securely and let the eggs sit at room temperature (out of direct sunlight) for 2 to 3 days depending on your desired flavor. The brine will turn cloudy and bubbly, but this is normal. Open the lid once a day to let out the built-up air.
5. Transfer the jar to the fridge, where it can be stored for up to 2 weeks.

TIP: Hard-boiled eggs take about 10 to 12 minutes to cook. Add the eggs to a pot with water to cover, bring the water to a boil over medium-high heat, and don't start timing until the water starts to boil. Place the eggs in ice-cold water after draining, and let them sit for 5 minutes before peeling.

Lacto-Fermented Ketchup

Ketchup is a preferred condiment in most households, and this recipe does not disappoint. It is slightly sweet and spicy, with just the right amount of tang from the fermentation process. I use honey as the sweetener, but you could also use maple syrup or whole unrefined cane sugar. This recipe has become one of my family's favorites. Use it on anything you would put traditional ketchup on. Our favorites are roasted sweet potato wedges and eggs.

1. In a large mixing bowl, combine the tomato paste and honey (or sweetener of choice).
2. Whisk the fresh whey into the sweetened tomato paste along with the apple cider vinegar, salt, allspice, cinnamon, and cloves. Continue whisking these ingredients together until the paste is smooth and thoroughly combined.
3. Spoon the homemade ketchup into a jar, and cover with a cloth secured with a rubber band or close with a lid.
4. Allow the jar to sit at room temperature (out of direct sunlight) undisturbed for 3 to 5 days depending on your desired flavor.
5. Uncover the homemade ketchup and give it a thorough stir before transferring it to the fridge. Naturally fermented ketchup will keep for several months in the fridge.

2 (6-ounce) cans tomato paste or 12 ounces homemade tomato paste

¼ cup raw honey

2 tablespoons fresh whey or sauerkraut juice

2 tablespoons raw apple cider vinegar, preferably Bragg

1 teaspoon unrefined sea salt

1 teaspoon allspice

1 teaspoon ground cinnamon

½ teaspoon ground cloves

Quick Pickled Veggies

As much as I love lacto-fermenting and canning, it does take time. Here's a quick and flavorful pickle recipe to have on standby when there's no time for the other options.

6 Kirby cucumbers, quartered lengthwise

6 young spring carrots, trimmed, peeled, and cut in half lengthwise

1 handful large green onion or scallion pieces, or green beans

A few cauliflower florets

Several sprigs fresh dill

½ teaspoon celery seeds

½ teaspoon coriander seeds

½ teaspoon mustard seeds

¼ teaspoon black peppercorns

1 bay leaf

Pinch of red pepper flakes (optional)

15 garlic cloves, peeled

2 cups filtered water

1 cup white vinegar

1 tablespoon sea salt

1. To a 1-quart jar with a tight-fitting lid, add your desired veggies, herbs and spices, and garlic, making sure to leave about 1 inch headspace at the top.
2. In a medium saucepan, bring the water, vinegar, and salt to a simmer over medium-high heat. Stir until the salt dissolves, and then remove from the heat.
3. Pour the hot brine over the vegetables to cover them completely, and then let cool. Cover and refrigerate.
4. The pickles will taste good in just a few hours, and even better after a couple of days. They'll keep for about 3 months.

PICKLING SPICE, THREE WAYS

These are some of my favorite combinations of spices when lacto-fermenting or pickling. These ingredients make enough pickling spice to add to 4 cups of brine.

TRADITIONAL

½ teaspoon celery seeds
½ teaspoon coriander seeds
½ teaspoon mustard seeds
½ teaspoon black peppercorns
¼ teaspoon allspice
1 bay leaf
4 garlic cloves, peeled and smashed
½ teaspoon red pepper flakes (optional)

SPICY

1 teaspoon black peppercorns
1 teaspoon mustard seeds
½ teaspoon coriander seeds
½ teaspoon red pepper flakes

CURRY

½ teaspoon mustard seeds
½ teaspoon peppercorns
¼ teaspoon coriander seeds
¼ teaspoon cumin seeds
1 bay leaf
2 to 3 slices fresh peeled ginger
2 to 3 slices fresh peeled turmeric
½ teaspoon red pepper flakes (optional)
2 tablespoons brown sugar (optional)
2 cardamom pods (optional)

Miso

You can buy store-bought miso, but making it from scratch is easier than you might think. You mostly need patience since the aging time is usually 4 to 6 months or longer. The shorter the ferment, the milder the color and taste (white miso); the longer the ferment, the deeper the color and taste (red miso). You can buy the rice koji online or at your local Asian market, and chickpeas are a great substitute for the soybeans. For this recipe, make sure to use a kitchen scale so the measurements are precise.

1 pound soybeans or legume of choice (chickpeas work great)

1 pound rice koji (you can buy it online or at your local Asian market)

7 ounces sea salt

1. Soak the soybeans overnight.
2. Rinse the beans and then add to a saucepan with water. Bring to a simmer over medium heat and cook until they are very soft, about 45 minutes. Drain them, but reserve some liquid for later use.
3. Mash the cooked soybeans and place them in a large mixing bowl. Once the beans are mashed thoroughly, they should be cooled enough to add the rice koji.
4. Mix the rice koji with 5.6 ounces of the salt, and then mix the rice koji with the mashed soybeans. The leftover water from cooking the soybeans can now be slowly added to the mixture to achieve a consistency like cookie dough. Roll the mashed soybeans into baseball-sized balls.
5. Wash the container you will be using to ferment the miso (a large fermentation crock works best, but you can use any large container with a lid) and sanitize it by wiping with a paper towel soaked in white vinegar.
6. Stuff the miso balls into the clean container from the bottom, packing it tightly. It is very important to not leave any air pockets. Push to level the top.
7. Smooth the surface and wipe off any soybean mash from the container. Sprinkle the remaining 1.4 ounces of the salt to cover the surface, and then cover with a muslin cloth.
8. Weigh down the miso by placing a plate or fermentation weight on top of the cloth-covered miso. (You can also make your own weight by putting 8 ounces of salt in a plastic bag.)
9. Seal the top lightly with a lid. Place another muslin cloth over the top and secure with twine or a rubber band. Store the container in a cool, dark place for 3 months. Write the date prepared on the lid.
10. After 3 months, open the lid, remove the weight, and stir the mixture with a wooden spatula. Smooth the surface again and place a weight

and clean muslin cloth on top. Place the container back in a cool,
dark place for another 2 to 3 months depending on the desired flavor.

11. After 2 to 3 months, taste the miso. If it's to your liking, transfer the
container to the fridge. If you want to ferment longer, stir, cover, and
let sit again. Repeat the process once a month until it's to your liking.

MEAT AND FISH

For me, it is critical to purchase organically grown local produce, and it's just as important to know what goes into the meat I purchase. That is why I shop at my local farmers market and fish market—I can purchase directly from the farmer and they can tell me how the animal was raised and what it was fed. This gives my family an appreciation for the time and energy it took to get to our plate. Because high-quality meat can be more expensive, we tend to eat less of it at home and save it for a special night each week. I like to experiment with the lesser-known cuts of meat, like sweetbreads and tongue, because I believe in eating more of the animal than is typical in our American diet. When we eat a variety of cuts of meat, we are approaching meat consumption in a more sustainable way. It is my hope that you too will try to support your local farmers and ranchers and ask them about other cuts of meat and ways of preparing them.

Grilled Sweetbreads with Rosemary Chimichurri

Sweetbreads are considered somewhat of a gourmet food in many cultures around the world, but I have found they often get a bad rap in the United States. In honor of eating more than just tri-tip and ground beef, I invite you to consider serving this delicacy for dinner. This recipe makes delicious grilled sweetbreads that are topped with a robust rosemary chimichurri sauce. You can eat them as is, or place them on top of grilled bread or steamed rice.

1 pound sweetbreads

1 gallon cold filtered water

1 cup distilled white vinegar

2 teaspoons sea salt

2 tablespoons extra virgin olive oil, plus more for brushing grill

Sea salt and freshly ground black pepper

Rosemary chimichurri (see page 177)

Rosemary petals (optional)

1. Rinse the sweetbreads. Transfer them to a large pot and add the water, vinegar, and salt. Bring to a boil over high heat.
2. Reduce the heat and simmer gently for 10 minutes.
3. Drain the sweetbreads in a colander. Transfer to a bowl of ice-cold water to cool.
4. While the sweetbreads are cooling, prepare the grill for cooking by lightly oiling the rack and turning the heat to medium.
5. Drain the sweetbreads, pat dry gently, and separate into roughly 1½-inch pieces.
6. Toss the sweetbread pieces with the oil in a bowl, and then thread onto skewers (about three to five pieces on each). Season with salt and pepper.
7. Grill the sweetbreads, turning occasionally, until golden brown, about 5 to 7 minutes.
8. Transfer the sweetbreads to a platter and let stand, loosely covered with foil, for 5 minutes.
9. Top with rosemary chimichurri and rosemary flower petals (if using).

Bone Broth

The benefits of bone broth are plentiful. This nutritious beverage is said to have anti-inflammatory properties, is healthy for our gut, and may help protect our joints and ward off osteoporosis. It also happens to be super-tasty and is my go-to beverage of choice during the winter months. Another reason I like to cook bone broth is I am using more parts of the animal that might otherwise go to waste.

1. Preheat the oven to 400°F.
2. Place the bones, garlic, and onion in a roasting pan or on a large rimmed baking sheet. Drizzle with the olive oil, tossing to coat. Roast until browned, about 30 minutes.
3. Scrape the roasted bones, garlic, and onion into a large stockpot or Dutch oven. Add the celery, bay leaves, peppercorns, salt, parsley, and vinegar.
4. Add enough filtered water to cover the bones and vegetables, about 12 cups.
5. Cover the pot, bring the broth to a boil, and then reduce the heat to a low simmer, with the lid slightly ajar, for at least 8 to 12 hours. During the first few hours of simmering, a frothy and foamy layer will form. Skim it off with a shallow spoon and discard.
6. Remove the pot from the heat and let the contents cool. Strain out the bones and vegetables using a fine-mesh sieve set over a bowl.
7. When cooled, transfer to a glass jar and store in the fridge for up to 5 days, or freeze for later use.

TIP: Cooking food from scratch often increases the amount of vegetable food scraps you create. Little bits of celery, the ends of onions, tomato cores, bell pepper bits, or the ends of carrots can be saved and added to your bone broth. I sometimes freeze my veggie scraps, and when it's time to make broth I take them out and add them directly to the pot.

3 pounds bones (if using beef, a combination of marrow and short ribs; if using chicken, backs and necks)

1 garlic head, halved crosswise

1 onion, peeled and quartered

1 tablespoon extra virgin olive oil

2 celery stalks, roughly chopped

2 bay leaves

2 tablespoons black peppercorns

1 tablespoon sea salt

1 bunch parsley (or herb of choice)

1 tablespoon apple cider vinegar, preferably Bragg

12 cups filtered water

Winter Vegetable Bone Broth Stew

SERVES 4 TO 6

This stew recipe is a family favorite when winter comes around. Cooking with bone broth gives the soup a richer flavor with added nutritional value. We tend to add lots of vegetables, but add stew meat, ground beef, or organ meat if you prefer.

1 tablespoon extra virgin olive oil

2 onions, peeled and finely chopped into 1-inch pieces

3 teaspoons dried marjoram

3 teaspoons dried thyme

1 bay leaf

1 pound winter squash (kabocha, butternut, or pumpkin) peeled, seeded, and diced into 1-inch pieces

2 carrots, peeled and chopped into 1-inch pieces

1 fennel bulb, chopped into 1-inch pieces

1 cup canned tomatoes, with juice

5 to 6 garlic cloves, peeled and minced

6 to 8 cups homemade bone broth (see page 129)

Handful of winter greens (kale, spinach, or Swiss chard), finely chopped

Sea salt and freshly ground black pepper

1. Heat a large Dutch oven or pot over medium-high heat. Add the olive oil and onions and sauté until the onions are translucent, about 5 to 6 minutes.
2. Add the marjoram, thyme, and bay leaf and sauté for 30 seconds. Add the squash, carrots, fennel, tomatoes, garlic, and bone broth.
3. Simmer the soup for 15 to 20 minutes, until the veggies are cooked.
4. Add the fresh winter greens and season with salt and pepper. Cook for 1 more minute.
5. Remove the bay leaf. Serve the stew on its own or with a slice of fresh sourdough bread (see page 150).

Rosemary-Garlic Pot Roast

SERVES 4 TO 6

Pot roast can sometimes get a bad rap for being dry and bland, but not this one. This pot roast is juicy, full of flavor, and fall-apart-in-your-mouth tender. I eat more veggies than meat, so this is the perfect main dish for me, as it's also loaded with mushrooms. Make sure to have some crusty bread on hand for dipping—the sauce with rosemary, garlic, and mushroom is so good.

1. Preheat the oven to 250°F.
2. Wash the roast and pat dry with a towel. Season with salt and pepper.
3. Heat the olive oil in a Dutch oven over medium-high heat. Sear the roast on all sides until brown. Add the bone broth.
4. In a small bowl, mix the garlic, rosemary, and garlic sauce together. Spread the paste over the roast. Cover the Dutch oven and cook in the oven for 4 to 5 hours, until the meat is tender.
5. Take the roast out of the oven and let it sit for 10 to 15 minutes in the uncovered Dutch oven. While the meat is resting, melt the butter in a frying pan and sauté the mushrooms and vermouth over medium-high heat until the mushrooms are soft. Season with salt and pepper. Set aside.
6. Transfer the roast from the Dutch oven to a cutting board. Place the Dutch oven with the drippings on the stovetop. Bring to a simmer over medium heat until the juices are reduced by half, about 10 minutes.
7. Add the mushrooms to the sauce, and then slice the roast and place on a serving platter. Spoon some of the sauce over the roast, and garnish the serving platter with fresh rosemary. Spoon the remaining sauce into a gravy boat or bowl and serve alongside.

1 (3-pound) grass-fed chuck roast

Sea salt and freshly ground black pepper

2 tablespoons extra virgin olive oil

1 cup homemade bone broth (see page 129)

¼ cup peeled and chopped garlic

¼ cup chopped fresh rosemary leaves, plus more for garnish

2 tablespoons raw garlic sauce (see page 180)

2 tablespoons unsalted butter

3 cups cremini mushrooms, sliced

1 tablespoon vermouth

Rooster Coq Au Vin

SERVES 4 TO 6

I recently learned how to process chickens, and the first bird I processed was a rooster. With Julia Child as an inspiration, this dish came to mind. This recipe creates a tender and flavorful chicken dish that is perfect on its own or served with fresh crusty bread for dipping.

1 (3-pound) whole rooster (or chicken), cut into 8 pieces (or 7 to 9 bone-in, skin-on thighs and legs)

3 cups red wine

1 bay leaf

2 garlic cloves, peeled

2 teaspoons sea salt, plus more for seasoning

½ teaspoon freshly ground black pepper, plus more for seasoning

1 tablespoon extra virgin olive oil

4 ounces slab bacon, cubed

2 carrots, peeled and thickly sliced

1 large onion, peeled and thickly sliced

¼ cup brandy

1 cup chicken bone broth

1 large bunch thyme (8 to 10 sprigs)

1 tablespoon unsalted butter, melted

1½ tablespoons flour

8 ounces cremini mushrooms, thickly sliced

1. Place the rooster or chicken in a large, deep casserole dish.
2. In a small bowl, mix together the red wine, bay leaf, garlic, 2 teaspoons salt, and ½ teaspoon pepper.
3. Pour the red wine mixture over the chicken. Cover and marinate in the fridge for 8 to 12 hours.
4. Preheat the oven to 250°F.
5. Heat the oil in a large Dutch oven over medium heat. Fry the bacon for 8 to 10 minutes until browned, and then remove it to a large, paper towel–lined plate to drain.
6. Transfer the chicken pieces to the Dutch oven, in batches if necessary to avoid overcrowding; reserve the marinade. Once the chicken is browned on all sides, transfer to the plate with the bacon.
7. Add the carrots and onion to the pot, and season with a little more salt and pepper. Cook over medium heat until the carrots are soft and the onion is translucent, about 10 minutes.
8. Add the brandy and scrape all sides of the pot to incorporate any extra bits into the sauce. Return the chicken and bacon to the Dutch oven, and then add the wine marinade, broth, and thyme sprigs. Bring to a boil over high heat.
9. Once boiling, cover with a lid and put it in the oven for 55 minutes, until the chicken is no longer pink.
10. Remove from the oven (keep the oven on) and mix the melted butter with the flour and then stir into the sauce. Add the mushrooms to the pot. Taste and adjust the seasoning if needed. Put the pot back in the oven with the lid off for 10 to 15 minutes to allow the sauce to thicken.

Chicken Pâté

In honor of cooking the parts of the animal that might be overlooked, I invite you to try this chicken liver pâté. This recipe combines the sweetness of port and the unique taste of preserved lemon to create a pâté that is slightly sweet, light, and big on flavor.

1. Preheat the oven to 350°F. In a small saucepan over medium-high heat, sauté the shallots with the olive oil and 2 tablespoons of the butter for 5 to 6 minutes.
2. Add the port, garlic, and fresh herbs. Simmer until the liquid is reduced by half. Transfer to a food processor and add the preserved lemon, liver, eggs, the remaining 4 tablespoons of butter (melted), cream, salt, and pepper.
3. Blend just to combine. Strain through a fine-mesh sieve set over a bowl and then transfer the mixture to a 9-by-5-inch loaf pan greased with butter.
4. Place the loaf pan in a larger baking dish, and then fill the larger dish with tap water halfway up the side of the loaf pan. Bake for 55 minutes, until set. Use immediately, or refrigerate for up to 3 days. Serve with toasted bread.

2 large shallots, peeled and diced

1 tablespoon extra virgin olive oil

6 tablespoons unsalted butter, plus more for greasing

5 tablespoons port

2 garlic cloves, peeled

1 to 2 teaspoons minced fresh herbs (sage, thyme, or rosemary leaves)

1 strip preserved lemon (see page 71)

½ pound chicken livers

2 eggs

½ cup heavy cream, preferably organic

½ teaspoon sea salt

¼ teaspoon freshly ground black pepper

Slow-Cooked Garlic and Herb Tongue

If you make just one recipe from this book, choose this one. In most cultures, it is common to cook and eat most, if not all, parts of the animal. Nothing is wasted. However, in America we have grown accustomed to eating only one or two parts of the animal, and at times we're even unaware of the lesser-known parts. This recipe creates a tender piece of meat from the tongue that is flavorful on its own but can also be eaten in tacos, in a sandwich, or added to soups.

1 beef tongue
(about 3 pounds)

6 to 8 garlic cloves, peeled
and cut into ¼-inch slices

1 onion, peeled and
quartered

2 bay leaves

1½ teaspoons black
peppercorns

2½ teaspoons sea salt

1 bunch fresh herbs, tied into
a bundle (such as thyme,
rosemary, and parsley)

1. Clean the tongue thoroughly with water and pat dry with a towel. Cut small slits all around the tongue and slide in the slices of garlic. Place the tongue in a large pot with enough water to generously cover.
2. Add the onion, bay leaves, peppercorns, salt, and fresh herb bundle.
3. Bring to a simmer over medium-high heat, and then lower the temperature to medium-low.
4. Cook the tongue, covered, for approximately 3 to 4 hours, until tender.
5. Remove the tongue from the pot, and let it cool a little before attempting to remove the skin. The tongue needs to be skinned while it is still warm, as it will be difficult to peel if it cools for too long. When the cooked tongue is still very warm, but not hot, the skin will almost fall from the meat.
6. Once it is peeled, slice the tongue diagonally against the grain into ½-inch-thick slices.
7. Serve on sourdough toast, in tacos, or as the protein component in a rice bowl.

TIP: Reserve some of the tongue cooking liquid to store any meat that isn't eaten immediately. The cooking liquid will help keep it moist.

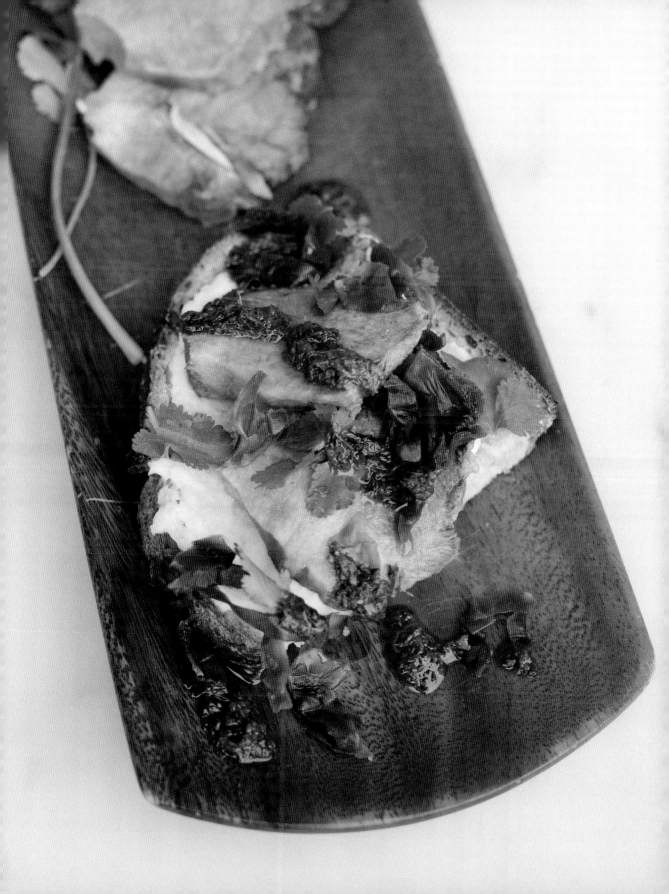

Fermented Honey Garlic Miso Pork Chops

Pork chops can be difficult to cook, but not if you take a simple approach and let the marinade do most of the work. These Japanese-inspired pork chops are tender and juicy.

1. Place the honey garlic syrup and cloves, thyme, miso, 3 tablespoons of the olive oil, and sake in a small bowl and mix until combined.
2. Spread the marinade over the pork chops and then place them in a plastic bag or a dish with a tight-fitting lid. Let sit in the fridge for 8 to 12 hours.
3. When ready to cook, heat a 12-inch cast-iron skillet or frying pan to medium-high heat, and coat with the remaining tablespoon of olive oil.
4. Sear the pork chops for 1 minute on each side, and then turn the heat to medium and cook for an additional 4 minutes on each side.
5. Remove from the heat. Garnish with more thyme.

2 tablespoons fermented honey garlic syrup (see page 74)

6 fermented honey garlic cloves, strained from syrup and finely chopped (see page 74)

1 tablespoon chopped fresh thyme leaves, plus more for garnish

3 tablespoons white miso (see page 122)

4 tablespoons extra virgin olive oil

2 tablespoons sake or rice vinegar

4 (1-inch-thick) pork chops

Braised Local Halibut with Preserved Lemon and Herbs

One of the benefits of buying directly from a local fisherman or fish market is knowing what's in season and learning about different parts of a fish that you might not have tried before. This also means you're supporting well-managed fisheries by not buying only one type of fish, which helps sustainability. For this recipe, I used local halibut, but I have also used rockfish and cod with great results.

1½ pounds fresh wild halibut

2 tablespoons extra virgin olive oil

Freshly ground sea salt and black pepper

1 cup white wine

8 tablespoons (1 stick) unsalted butter

8 quarters preserved lemon (see page 71)

1. Wash and gently pat dry the halibut. Season with 1 tablespoon of the olive oil, salt, and pepper.
2. Place the remaining tablespoon of olive oil in a large frying pan over medium heat. Lay the fish in the pan. Flip once the fish turns golden.
3. Pour the wine over the fish, and then add the butter and preserved lemon. Cover and let simmer over low heat for 10 to 15 minutes, or until done (use a paring knife to peek between two bits of flesh in the center of the fillet; the middle should look translucent, which means it's almost cooked through). Plate with some of the sauce.

TIP: Save any remaining sauce to use for your next soup stock or as a dip for bread.

SOURDOUGH

I have always been health-conscious. I am the person who meticulously reads food labels, and I care about what I put into my body. This interest expanded when I had a family, and I started paying attention to ingredients for them too. I remember going to buy a loaf of bread at the store, turning over the package, and seeing a long, paragraph-like list of ingredients. It was an eye-opener. How could this be right? Isn't bread simple? It really shouldn't need more than flour, water, and salt, maybe some *levain* or yeast. That's when I journeyed into the art of sourdough bread baking. As a self-taught home cook, I learned how to make a starter using just flour and water, and then started making a simple no-knead bread. I've learned a variety of techniques over the years, but I find the no-knead method is a great place to start. The recipes that follow are my all-time favorites. I hope you enjoy them as much as I do.

Bread Baking

SOURDOUGH STARTER

Makes 1 starter

Making a sourdough starter is a process of natural fermentation that includes a simple mixture of flour and filtered water. Some sourdough starters are family heirlooms passed down through generations, which means a little piece of the starter can be used in the process of making a new starter. This allows for the precious gift of time and fermentation to be passed along. Other starters are made from scratch, and if it goes badly, it's OK; it's easy to make again.

2 tablespoons sourdough starter (optional)
¼ cup bread flour, plus more each day
3 tablespoons filtered water, plus more each day

1. In a small bowl, whisk together the sourdough starter (if using), and the flour and water.
2. Pour into a 1-quart mason jar, put the lid on with a half turn (not tight), and let it sit for 12 hours.
3. Discard ¼ cup of the starter. Whisk in ½ cup flour with ½ cup water and cover again with the lid (not tight). This is called feeding your starter.
4. Continue discarding ¼ cup of the starter, feeding it by whisking in ½ cup flour and ½ cup water, and loosely covering with the lid every 12 hours for 1 week, until the starter is pillowy and bubbling.
5. As you feed your starter, make sure to whisk the flour and water. Aerating the starter will help yield the best and most reliable results.
6. Make sure your jar is only half full after each feeding to accommodate the sourdough's expansion. If you've made too much sourdough starter for the capacity of your jar, pour some off.

Flour Choices and Water

I really didn't consider the type of flour I was using when I first started making sourdough. I used all-purpose flour, but not all flour is created equal, and I quickly learned that the type of flour makes a big difference. For this reason, I recommend using a good-quality flour when starting out, which means unbleached and without added chemicals. If you are new to baking, I recommend using bread flour. Bread flour has a higher protein and gluten content, which means it's easier to work with and can produce a better rise. You can use all-purpose flour, but because it's lower in protein, it can create a wetter dough, making it more difficult to work with. Whole-grain flours are great too, but they can be tricky, as they are higher in minerals, which can speed up the fermentation time and create a wetter dough. My personal preference is organic, stone-ground flour, which I use whenever possible.

When baking in general, I find filtered, unchlorinated water to be best for consistent results. Sourdough culture does not like chlorine. Using quality ingredients helps create the ultimate sourdough success.

Helpful Tools

PARCHMENT PAPER: Always line your pan or Dutch oven with parchment paper. This is key, especially if you don't want your perfect loaf of bread to come out looking half eaten. Parchment paper allows you to easily slide the loaf of bread from the pan.

DOUGH WHISK: This tool helps incorporate the flour and water together.

DOUGH SCRAPER: A scraper helps handle the dough when shaping.

PASTRY BLENDER: Usually made of narrow metal strips or wires attached to a handle, this cooking

utensil is used to mix a fat into a flour in order to make pastries.

STAND MIXER: This kitchen appliance comes equipped with attachments to help automate the tasks of stirring, whisking, beating, or kneading.

MIXING BOWL: Make sure your bowl is large enough to mix all of your ingredients.

KITCHEN SCALE: A scale is an important piece of equipment in getting a more consistent loaf. It measures ingredients, allowing for more precision, and measuring in grams makes baking even more precise and consistent.

DUTCH OVEN: This one isn't totally necessary, but it works wonders and helps get a better rise.

PATIENCE, LOVE, AND KINDNESS: The art of bread baking, or any ferment really, requires patience and self-kindness. Even if it doesn't turn out exactly as planned, remember that sourdough is wild and adds an unpredictable layer, which helps make the reward feel more satisfying.

Maintaining the Sourdough

After a week, your sourdough should be sturdy enough to withstand storage. If you bake infrequently, meaning less than once a week, store the sourdough starter in the fridge. Before you plan to bake, bring it to room temperature and discard all of the starter except 2 to 3 tablespoons. Feed the starter ½ cup flour and ½ cup of water, let sit for 6 to 8 hours, and then discard all of the starter again except 2 to 3 tablespoons. Then feed the starter with ½ cup flour and ½ cup water 6 to 8 hours before you plan to bake.

If you bake more frequently, meaning every day or a few times a week, you can store your sourdough at room temperature. This requires feeding the starter daily by first discarding all but 2 to 3 tablespoons, adding ½ cup flour and ½ cup water, and then stirring vigorously. Discard more starter if needed to accommodate for expansion, and use the discarded starter for things like sourdough biscuits, sourdough waffles, flatbread, and crepes.

If a brown liquid appears floating on top of your sourdough starter, simply pour it off. This often means the starter was fed too much water in relation to the flour, or the starter has gone too long without a feeding.

Tips

- Good sourdough bread can only be made with a sourdough starter culture that's alive and bubbling.

- Your starter should smell fresh and fruity. If the smell changes to something resembling nail polish, you might be starving it, so consider feeding it more frequently.

- Create a rhythm with your sourdough. As a general rule of thumb, you want to feed your starter once a day if it's left out on the counter or once a week if it's in the fridge. You also want to time the feeding so the starter has time to bubble up and be ready for the next creation.

- When you do not wish to use your starter for a few days, you can store it in the fridge for up to 3 weeks before it needs refreshing again.

- Try the float test before baking sourdough bread. If the starter floats on top of water, it's ready to use in baking.

- Always use a kitchen scale to measure ingredients when baking bread. Precision is important.

- When proofing sourdough bread, I like to use a bread basket lined with cheesecloth. That way I don't have to dust the loaf with as much flour, and there's less chance it will stick to the basket.

- Keep a bread-baking journal and track your process. Write down when you feed the starter, the temperature both inside your kitchen and outside, if the starter floated, etc. All of these variables influence the bread-baking process, and keeping a record allows you to make adjustments based on your results.

- Be patient. Every time you bake, you will learn more about what works and what doesn't, no matter what recipe you follow. Take time to experience the process and enjoy each loaf.

No-Knead Sourdough Bread

This recipe is great if the thought of baking bread is overwhelming, or if you want to ease your way into the art of bread baking. It's simple and does not require massive amounts of kneading. Play around, adding herbs, garlic, nuts, dried fruits, or seeds to change up the flavor. This bread has a crackly crust with a soft and tangy, dense, and nutty interior. Beware: it usually gets eaten pretty fast. When making bread, it is important to use a kitchen scale to precisely measure ingredients.

About 6 to 8 hours before starting the bread-making process, discard all of your starter except 2 to 3 tablespoons. Add 1 cup of bread flour and 1 cup of water. Whisk vigorously, cover, and let sit. This will give the starter a 100 percent hydration rate. If after 6 to 8 hours the starter is not extra bubbly, check in another 2 to 3 hours. If you're still having trouble getting the starter to be vigorous and bubbly, then start the process all over again.

350 grams filtered water (80 to 85°F)

100 grams starter

450 grams bread flour

50 grams whole wheat or rye flour

10 grams fine-grained sea salt

Rice flour for dusting (optional)

1. In a large bowl, combine the water and the starter. (Since you are only using 100 grams of the starter, make sure to reserve a portion of the starter and feed it again in order to keep the sourdough going.)
2. Next, add the flours and salt to the bowl with the water and starter, and mix until a soft, spongy dough forms.
3. Cover with beeswax wrap or plastic wrap and let it sit for at least 8 to 10 hours in the bowl, or until the dough has tripled in size. This can sometimes take longer due to ambient room temperatures.
4. Form your loaf. Lightly dust flour or rice flour on your kitchen counter. Scoop the dough out onto the floured surface, and then sprinkle lightly with more flour or rice flour.
5. Gently create a rectangle. Fold into thirds, and then into thirds again to create a ball.
6. Place more flour or rice flour on a clean tea towel. Invert the loaf with the rough edge facing up, and place it back in the bowl.
7. Cover and let it sit on the counter for at least 60 minutes or up to 3 hours, or up to 12 hours in the fridge.
8. When ready to bake, place a Dutch oven (or other large ovenproof dish with a lid) in the oven. Preheat the oven to 500°F with the dish inside and lid on. Keep the dish in the oven for at least 30 minutes and up to 1 hour.
9. Carefully remove the hot pot from the oven. Remove the lid. Gently place the loaf in the pan inverted so the rougher surface is now on the bottom. Score the loaf if you desire.

10. Put the lid back on, turn the oven down to 450°F, and bake for 20 minutes.
11. Remove the lid, and bake for another 20 minutes, until the loaf is deep golden brown.
12. Cool on a wire rack, uncovered, for at least 1 hour.

TIP: I prefer to refrigerate my dough for 12 hours. A long proofing stage allows the acid-producing bacteria in the *levain* to create a more developed, tangy flavor than you would get if the bread proofed for just a few hours at room temperature. Slowing down the fermentation in the fridge gives you much more flexibility as to when you can bake your bread.

Sourdough Waffles

Maintaining a healthy sourdough starter means accumulating excess amounts that can either be discarded or used. I choose to use. These waffles are delicious, easy, and nutritious, but they do need to be started 8 to 12 hours in advance. I serve them topped with homemade yogurt or kefir, fresh fruit, and a slight drizzle of maple syrup. They are also great plain or toasted as a midmorning snack or treat, or, on occasion, a yummy sandwich bread. The waffles keep in the fridge for a week and freeze beautifully. Just pop them in the toaster and then top with your favorite goodies.

1. In a large bowl, combine the starter, flour, kefir, lemon juice or vinegar, and honey (if using). Cover and let it sit on the counter overnight, 8 to 12 hours.
2. Plug in your waffle iron. It should be hot and ready to go by the time you have finished making your batter.
3. To the sourdough mixture, add the melted butter, eggs, vanilla, almond flour, flax, and cinnamon and whisk until the batter is combined.
4. Add the baking soda, baking powder, and salt. Whisk more, until the batter rises and gets puffy.
5. Open the hot waffle maker and pour in enough batter to fill the mold. Cook until golden brown. Enjoy with your favorite toppings.

1 cup sourdough starter

1 cup flour

1 cup kefir (see page 16), or milk of choice

1 tablespoon lemon juice or apple cider vinegar

1 tablespoon raw honey (optional)

¼ cup melted unsalted butter (or desired fat or oil)

2 eggs, whisked

1 to 2 teaspoons vanilla extract (according to taste preference)

2 tablespoons almond flour

2 tablespoons ground flax

Pinch of ground cinnamon

1 teaspoon baking soda

1 teaspoon baking powder

½ teaspoon sea salt

Sourdough Pastry Crust

I use this sourdough pastry crust recipe to make pie crusts, hand pies, and even empanadas. The tang of the sourdough gives the crust extra flavor and flakiness.

1 cup all-purpose flour, plus more for dusting

¾ cup whole wheat flour (or desired flour)

1 teaspoon sea salt

1 tablespoon sugar

1 cup (2 sticks) butter, cut into ½-inch cubes and chilled

1 cup sourdough starter

1. In a large bowl, blend together the flours, salt, and sugar with two pastry blenders.
2. Cut in the butter until it resembles a course meal, with some chunks of butter remaining.
3. Gradually stir in the starter. Fold it in with a spatula until it starts to come together. Turn the dough out onto a lightly floured surface.
4. Gently fold the dough into thirds, press the dough, and repeat three or four more times until the dough comes together and is no longer crumbly.
5. Gather the dough into two equal balls, wrap with plastic wrap, and allow to chill in the fridge for 7 hours.

Stone Fruit Pie

This is the pie to make when stone fruit is in season. The taste of stone fruit baked into a pastry crust is nostalgic to me. It reminds me of the delicious cobbler I made as a kid with peaches from our family's tree. This recipe is great because it can be used with any stone fruit you want.

1. Take the pastry crust dough out of the fridge and bring to room temperature, about 20 to 25 minutes. Slice the stone fruit while waiting and then set aside.
2. In a medium bowl, mix together the sugar, cornstarch, cinnamon, nutmeg, and salt.
3. Add the stone fruit and gently toss. Let it sit at room temperature for 15 minutes or so, until some juices are released.
4. Roll out one ball of the dough to about an ⅛-inch thickness to make the bottom crust. Place in a pie dish. Roll out the other ball of dough to the same thickness and cut into strips.
5. Pour the filling into the pie dish. Top with traditional lattice pieces, alternating one, and then the other, going both directions across the pie. Another option is to use one sheet of pie dough and decorate as you wish, making slits in the dough to create a decorative top.
6. In a small bowl, whisk the egg and then brush the crust liberally with the egg wash. Return to the fridge to chill for 30 minutes.
7. While the pie is chilling, preheat the oven to 375°F. When ready to bake, place the pie on a baking sheet to catch any drips, and then place the baking sheet in the preheated oven. Bake for 55 to 60 minutes, until golden brown. When the pie is done, let it cool for 1 to 2 hours before slicing and serving.

TIP: Peaches need their skins peeled off before using, but plums, apricots, and nectarines don't.

Sourdough pastry crust (see page 154)

3 pounds (about 8 cups) mixed stone fruit (plums, apricots, and nectarines), pitted

⅓ cup coconut or brown sugar

⅓ cup cornstarch (or 3 tablespoons quick-cooking tapioca)

1 heaping teaspoon ground cinnamon

¼ teaspoon grated nutmeg

½ teaspoon sea salt

1 egg, for wash

Rosemary Sourdough Crackers

MAKES 2 TO 3 DOZEN

This recipe is a perfect way to use leftover sourdough starter, which I often keep in the fridge. Don't let the simplicity fool you. Although there are only a few ingredients, the result is a savory cracker. It is perfect to pair on a cheese platter, with your favorite seasonal preserve, or eat on its own.

1 cup unfed sourdough starter from the fridge

¼ cup coconut oil, at room temperature

½ teaspoon sea salt

1 to 2 tablespoons finely chopped fresh rosemary leaves

1 cup all-purpose, spelt, or whole wheat flour

Extra virgin olive oil, for brushing

Coarse sea salt, for topping

1. In a large bowl, combine the starter and coconut oil. Mix thoroughly.
2. In a small bowl, mix the salt and rosemary with ¼ cup of the flour and add to the sourdough mixture.
3. Knead it in the bowl, adding the remaining flour, ¼ cup at a time, to make a dough ball that comes together.
4. Place the dough in a bowl and close with a tight-fitting lid or cover with plastic wrap. Let it rest at room temperature for at least 8 hours.
5. After about 8 hours of fermentation, place the dough in the fridge for at least 2 and up to 4 hours.
6. When ready to bake, preheat the oven to 350°F.
7. Take a small portion of the dough (about ¼ cup), and roll it into a rectangle between two pieces of parchment paper to a thickness of ⅛ inch.
8. Brush some olive oil on the rolled-out dough and spread it to the edges. Sprinkle liberally with the coarse sea salt.
9. Cut the dough vertically and horizontally into quarters with a pizza cutter or sharp knife.
10. Transfer the cut-out dough, still on the parchment paper, onto a baking sheet and bake for 15 to 20 minutes or until almost golden brown. Repeat with the remaining dough.

Sourdough Chocolate Cake with Chocolate Honey Buttercream Frosting

One of my preferred places to eat in Santa Barbara is Savoy Café, and one of my family's favorite desserts is its chocolate cake with buttercream frosting. This sourdough creation is my ode to our favorite dessert.

TO MAKE THE CAKE:

1. The night before you want to bake your cake, combine the starter, buttermilk, flour, maple syrup, and coconut oil in a large mixing bowl. Cover with a kitchen towel, beeswax wrap, or plastic wrap and let it sit on the counter at least 7 hours and up to 24 hours.
2. When ready to bake the cake, preheat the oven to 350°F.
3. Using an electric mixer, combine the eggs, cocoa powder, baking soda, salt, nutmeg, cinnamon, and vanilla with the sourdough batter.
4. Spoon the batter into an 11-by-7-inch cake pan greased with butter.
5. Bake for 20 to 22 minutes, or until a toothpick inserted in the center comes out clean.
6. Let the cake cool completely before frosting.

TO MAKE THE FROSTING:

1. To make the frosting, combine the butter, maple syrup, honey, cocoa, vanilla, and salt in a stand mixer fitted with a paddle attachment.
2. Mix on low speed until combined. Increase the speed and whip until creamed.
3. Store the frosting in the fridge. If you're making it ahead of time, allow it to come to room temperature before spreading it on the cake. It's very buttery and creamy, so if you plan on serving it outside on a hot day, consider refrigerating until serving.

FOR THE CAKE:

½ cup sourdough starter

1 cup buttermilk, preferably organic

1¾ cups all-purpose flour

¾ cup maple syrup

⅔ cup coconut oil, melted

2 eggs, whisked

⅔ cup cocoa powder

2 teaspoons baking soda

½ teaspoon sea salt

Pinch of grated nutmeg

1 heaping teaspoon ground cinnamon

1 teaspoon vanilla extract

Unsalted butter, for greasing

FOR THE FROSTING:

1½ cups (3 sticks) unsalted butter, softened

2½ tablespoons maple syrup

2½ tablespoons raw honey

½ cup unsweetened cocoa

1 teaspoon vanilla extract

½ teaspoon sea salt

Gluten-Free Sourdough

The art of sourdough bread baking has been around for centuries. However, it wasn't until relatively recently that bakers started playing with the idea of gluten-free bread as a healthy and delicious alternative to glutinous breads. As a rule of thumb, sourdough is prized for its health benefits because it's easier to digest. It contains the healthy gut bacteria lactobacillus, which means most of the phytic acid is broken down in the process of fermentation, preventing the spike in blood sugar that traditional bread usually causes.

The challenge with gluten-free sourdough is understanding how gluten-free flours work together to create a bread worthy of eating. I've found a superb texture and taste by combining the right gluten-free flours with the souring process. With my passion for healthy eating and living, I have created the following gluten-free recipe (see page 164) so everyone can enjoy the benefits and taste of gluten-free sourdough bread.

Gluten-Free Flours

ARROWROOT: This white flour from the root of the West Indian plant of the same name can be exchanged in equal quantities for cornstarch in recipes.

BEAN FLOURS: Including garbanzo bean flour and fava bean flour, these flours are typically high in protein and have a distinct flavor. They are better suited for heartier recipes, such as bread.

BUCKWHEAT FLOUR: Even though this flour has wheat in its name, it is actually related to rhubarb, not wheat. Its distinct taste is best when combined with other, more bland flours, like rice or millet. A little goes a long way with this flour, and it can be exchanged for equal parts oat or sorghum.

CORN FLOUR: Made from ground corn, this flour is too coarse for cakes, but it's nice for pancakes, cornbread, and tortillas. (Don't confuse it with cornmeal, also gluten-free, which is coarser.) The texture, if not the flavor, might make it a good substitute for recipes that call for semolina.

MILLET FLOUR: This nutrient-rich flour is ground from the grain of the same name. It has a subtle flavor and can be used for sweet or savory baking. In particular, it is prized for imparting a delicate crumb, so it's suitable for baked goods like muffins or quick breads like banana and zucchini. It can be exchanged for sorghum, oat, or quinoa.

NUT FLOURS: Nut flours are flours made out of nuts. They cannot be substituted in equal quantities for flour, because they are dense and too high in protein. They are used more frequently to replace a portion of flour in a recipe. Some common nut flours used for baking are almond and hazelnut.

POTATO STARCH FLOUR: Made from ground potatoes, this is a fine, white powder of a flour. It is popular for cakes and more delicate baked goods.

POTATO FLOUR: It sounds like potato starch flour, but potato flour is very different. It is a thick, dense flour. When used for bread recipes, it can lend a soft, moist texture, but it is too dense for delicate cakes.

QUINOA FLOUR: The coating on the seeds of this grain, from which the flour is milled, can be bitter. So try to look for flour that is "debittered." This flour adds a pleasant density and nuttiness to baked goods and is well suited for scones, biscuits, and pancakes. You can substitute millet flour for quinoa.

RICE FLOURS: Rice flours are a key ingredient in most gluten-free baking. White rice flour is a bland

flour, which works well with just about any flavor, and its light texture makes it well suited for baking cakes and delicate baked goods. Variations include brown rice flour, which is ground from unhulled rice kernels, and sweet rice flour, which is used as a thickener and made from sticky rice. Don't substitute it for white rice flour.

SORGHUM FLOUR: Made from sorghum, which is a relative of sugarcane, this flour is tender and adds a mild sweetness, but is rarely used alone. You can substitute oat or millet flour if needed.

TAPIOCA FLOUR: Made from the root of the cassava plant, this is a light, starchy flour that adds a superior texture and "chew" to baked goods. It is frequently used in gluten-free baking, along with other flours.

TEFF FLOUR: Made from an African cereal grass, teff is highly nutritious and high in fiber, protein, iron, amino acids, and calcium. Used with a combination of other gluten-free flours in recipes, it can add an appealing, nutty flavor and a ton of nutrition to your baked goods.

GLUTEN-FREE STARTER

Makes 1 starter

Making a gluten-free sourdough starter isn't any different than making a regular sourdough starter. All you need is flour, water, air, and time. The only difference is that gluten-free sourdough requires playing with a variety of flours that are free of gluten. A gluten-free sourdough starter can be made in as little as 7 days. Although this recipe is for creating a brown rice flour starter, I have also successfully made gluten-free sourdough starters with white rice, teff, sorghum, and oat flour.

½ cup organic brown rice flour, plus more each day
¼ cup filtered water, plus more each day

1. Combine the flour and water in a 1-quart mason jar with a lid.
2. Whisk until smooth. If too crumbly and not wet enough, add 1 tablespoon of water at a time until you reach a thick consistency (it should not be runny). Cover loosely with the lid, and let it sit at room temperature.
3. After 12 hours, discard ¼ cup of the starter and add ½ cup flour and ⅓ cup water. Mix until smooth and cover loosely with the lid again. Repeat this process every 12 hours (twice a day) for the next 6 to 7 days. The starter will start to develop air pockets and become more bubbly each day.
4. If the jar gets too full of starter, simply discard some of it, but keep adding water and flour at regular intervals.
5. When your gluten-free sourdough starter is very bubbly, and rises about a third of the way up the jar after 4 to 6 hours of feeding, you are ready to use it to make bread.

Maintaining Your Starter

Once established, your gluten-free sourdough starter needs to be fed daily (if left on the counter) or once a week (if placed in the fridge), with the same ratio you used when creating it. The sourdough starter should have the consistency of a thick frosting when it's fed the flour and water and then mixed well.

If you bake frequently (every day or a few times a week), you can store your starter at room temperature. Discard ¼ cup of the starter (or use it to bake with), and then feed it with ½ cup gluten-free flour and ⅓ cup filtered water once a day. Discard extra starter when necessary to accommodate for expansion. If you bake infrequently (once a week or less), store the starter in the fridge, up to a week, until ready to use. When you want to bake bread, take what you need from the fridge until it runs low, and then feed it to replenish your supply.

GLUTEN-FREE SOURDOUGH BOULE

Makes 1 loaf

Gluten-free sourdough bread baking can be tricky. It's not easy to find moist bread that also rises and tastes delicious. I've played with variations and ingredients, and have come up with a very tasty gluten-free sourdough that is also gum-free and vegan.

100 grams brown rice flour

100 grams gluten-free sourdough starter

100 grams filtered water

10 grams organic cane sugar (or desired sweetener)

350 grams room-temperature water

25 grams psyllium husk

75 grams oat flour

75 grams sorghum flour

75 grams millet flour

75 grams tapioca flour

10 grams sea salt

1. The night before baking the bread, mix the brown rice flour, starter, filtered water, and cane sugar in a small jar. Cover loosely with the lid. Let it sit for 8 to 12 hours in a warm, dry place.
2. When you're ready to bake the bread, combine the room-temperature water and psyllium husk in a medium bowl and mix well. Let it sit for 5 to 10 minutes until a thick gel forms.
3. Add the starter that you made the night before and mix.
4. In a separate bowl, whisk the remaining flours and salt together.
5. In the bowl of a stand mixer fitted with a dough hook or paddle attachment, add the wet and dry ingredients. Beat the dough until well combined, about 2 to 5 minutes on medium speed.
6. Shape the loaf and place it in a well-floured proofing basket or a deep bowl. Cover with a kitchen towel or plastic wrap.
7. Allow it to rise in a warm, dry place for 4 to 6 hours.
8. Preheat the oven to 425°F with a Dutch oven (or other large ovenproof dish with a lid) inside.
9. Flip the dough upside-down on a piece of parchment paper, score, and transfer to the hot Dutch oven.
10. Bake, covered, for 30 minutes. Then carefully remove the hot lid, turn the oven down to 400°F, and continue baking until the bread is a deep, golden brown, about 15 to 20 minutes more. Remove from the oven.
11. With oven mitts, carefully lift the bread out of the Dutch oven, and place it on a rack to cool completely, about 2 hours.

RAW

Get your nutrients from the raw source—no cooking necessary! I love growing herbs and lettuce in my garden, and one of my favorite booths at my local farmers market is one that is always overflowing with seasonal fresh herbs. Not only can herbs be easy to grow—you can grow them in pots, garden beds, or simply in the ground—they can really make a dish come alive with flavor. Some of my favorites to grow are basil, mint, cilantro, parsley, rosemary, thyme, oregano, and chives. You really can't beat the flavor boost homegrown herbs and greens bring to home-cooked meals.

Herb Salad with Edible Flowers

Adding herbs to a salad enhances the flavor and takes everyday greens to a whole new level. This herb salad is the perfect combination of greens, herbs, and flowers. Get creative and pick your favorite combination of all three. This recipe is also great when substituting 1 cup shaved fennel for the lettuce. Always gently wash and dry fresh herbs, salad greens, and edible flowers.

3 cups hand-torn fresh garden herbs, such as parsley, cilantro, tarragon, mint, dill, and chives

1 small handful whole edible flowers, such as violas, marigolds, or calendula, plus more for garnish

1 cup hand-torn butter or gem lettuce

1 shallot, peeled and thinly sliced

Zest and juice from ½ organic lemon

Extra virgin olive oil

Sea salt and freshly ground black pepper

1. Toss together the herbs, flowers, lettuce, and shallot in a large bowl.
2. Finely grate the zest from the lemon half over the salad. Then, squeeze the lemon juice over the salad and drizzle with the olive oil.
3. Season with salt and pepper, and toss again to coat.
4. Arrange more edible flowers on top as a garnish.

Garden Pesto with Mint and Basil

Pesto is a staple in my house. I have it on hand to spread on bread, over roasted veggies, or drizzled on top of grain bowls and soup. You won't want to buy store-bought pesto once you start making your own. To make it vegan, I simply add more nuts. In addition to the pine nuts, I add ¼ cup roasted and lightly salted almonds, plus 2 tablespoons of nutritional yeast. In the winter, I substitute cilantro for basil. If cilantro isn't available, I use kale or spinach.

¼ cup freshly grated parmesan cheese

¼ cup pine nuts

1 tablespoon freshly squeezed lemon juice

2 garlic cloves, peeled

1½ cups chopped fresh basil leaves

½ cup chopped fresh mint leaves

½ cup extra virgin olive oil

Sea salt and freshly ground black pepper

1. In a food processor fitted with the metal blade, pulse the cheese and nuts until a coarse mixture forms.
2. Add the lemon juice, garlic, basil, and mint and pulse again until well combined.
3. With the food processor running, slowly add the olive oil through the feed tube in a steady stream.
4. Transfer the pesto to a bowl and season with salt and pepper.
5. Serve immediately or store in an airtight container in the fridge for up to 3 weeks.

Creamy Polenta with Roasted Broccoli, Poached Eggs, and Garden Pesto

This recipe is great for breakfast, brunch, or dinner. If corncobs aren't on hand to make the broth, you can always substitute vegetable broth or water. But I invite you to try the corncob broth. It's sweet, golden, and adds just the right touch to the creamy polenta.

1. To make the corncob broth, put the corncobs, peppercorns, parsley, and bay leaf in a large stockpot and add enough water to cover, about 14 cups. Bring the mixture to a boil over high heat. Reduce the heat to medium-low, and simmer for 45 minutes to an hour. Strain into a bowl and season with salt. Use immediately, or refrigerate until ready to use. You should have about 6 cups; reserve 4 cups for the polenta.

2. To make the broccoli, preheat the oven to 400°F. On a large sheet pan, arrange the broccoli florets in a single layer. Drizzle with the olive oil, season with salt and pepper, and toss together. Roast for 15 to 20 minutes, until cooked and slightly browned. Remove from the oven.

3. To make the polenta, bring the reserved corncob broth to a boil over medium-high heat. Add the salt. While whisking gently, pour the polenta into the boiling broth in a steady stream. Whisk constantly until the mixture is smooth and begins to thicken. Reduce the heat to medium-low and simmer, whisking often, until thickened but still creamy, about 30 minutes. Stir in the olive oil.

4. To finish, crack the eggs into a small plate or bowl, and bring a saucepan of water filled at least 2 to 3 inches deep to a simmer. Tip the eggs into the pan. The yolks should follow the whites. Cook for 2 minutes, and then turn off the heat. Leave the pan for 8 to 10 minutes. Lift each egg out with a slotted spoon and drain.

5. To serve, spoon some of the creamy polenta into bowls, and then add some of the roasted broccoli, a poached egg, and some pesto. Top with fresh herbs and parmesan (if using). For a little added kick, add some lacto-fermented hot sauce.

TIP: The sweet corncob broth can be used to add flavor to soups, polenta, or any recipe calling for vegetable broth. During the summer months, when my family eats a lot of corn, I freeze the cobs. When I have enough, I make a big batch of this broth and freeze it for later use.

FOR THE CORNCOB BROTH:

12 corncobs (kernels removed)

¼ teaspoon black peppercorns

Handful of fresh parsley

1 bay leaf

Freshly ground sea salt

FOR THE BROCCOLI:

1½ pounds broccoli, cut into florets

2 tablespoons extra virgin olive oil

Freshly ground sea salt and black pepper

FOR THE POLENTA:

4 cups corncob broth

1 teaspoon freshly ground sea salt

1 cup polenta

3 tablespoons extra virgin olive oil

4 eggs

Garden pesto (see page 172), for serving

Chopped herbs, for serving (optional)

Freshly grated parmesan, for serving (optional)

Lacto-fermented hot sauce (see page 115)

Garden Chimichurri

This garden-fresh chimichurri is the perfect accompaniment to anything grilled or roasted. Chimichurri isn't limited to its traditional use as a marinade or sauce to top grilled meats. I also use it for vegetables, fish, or even as a dipping sauce for fresh-baked bread.

¼ cup extra virgin olive oil

1 tablespoon chopped fresh oregano leaves

¾ cup chopped fresh cilantro leaves

2 garlic cloves, peeled

1 tablespoon balsamic vinegar

⅛ teaspoon red pepper flakes

Sea salt and freshly ground black pepper

1. In a food processor fitted with the metal blade, combine the oil, oregano, cilantro, garlic, vinegar, and red pepper flakes until the herbs and oil form a thin paste-like dressing similar to a vinaigrette. Transfer to a bowl and season with salt and black pepper.
2. Serve immediately, or store in an airtight container in the fridge for up to 2 weeks.

Rosemary Chimichurri

Rosemary grows like a weed in my garden, even during the winter months, so that's why I decided to create this condiment. It's delicious on meats, vegetables, and fish. You can substitute arugula for the parsley for a little extra peppery flavor.

1. In a food processor fitted with the metal blade, combine the oil, rosemary, parsley, cilantro, garlic, lemon juice, vinegar, and red pepper flakes until the herbs and oil form a thin paste-like dressing similar to a vinaigrette. Transfer to a bowl and season with salt and black pepper.
2. Serve immediately, or store in an airtight container in the fridge for up to 2 weeks.

¼ cup extra virgin olive oil

1 tablespoon chopped fresh rosemary leaves

½ cup chopped fresh parsley leaves

¼ cup chopped fresh cilantro leaves

2 garlic cloves, peeled

1 tablespoon freshly squeezed lemon juice

2 tablespoons white wine vinegar

⅛ teaspoon crushed red pepper flakes

Sea salt and freshly ground black pepper

Farm Cart Organics

KATHERINE LESH

Katherine Lesh has known organic farming all her life. Her father, Tom Shepherd, was one of the pioneers of organic farming in Carpinteria, California. As an adult with a family of her own now, Katherine and her husband Jason run a farm cart and sell CSA-inspired farm boxes that include 75 percent locally grown organic produce. They work hard to stand behind the words "organic" and "local" as much as possible. They've already helped more than five farmers become certified organic so they can sell their produce at the farm cart and in the farm boxes, which is not an easy task. It is Katherine's passion and continuing support for organic, seasonal, and local produce that inspires us.

Besides being a master at roasting vegetables, Katherine's true craft is connecting people with their food sources—inspiring people to buy real food that comes from the ground and not a package. She has an "anyone can cook, just get in the kitchen and try" kind of attitude, and makes cooking accessible and carefree. Her favorite part of cooking is tasting as you go. Her best advice: don't be scared to use salt and fresh herbs.

MASSAGED KALE SALAD WITH STRAWBERRIES

Serves 4

2 bunches lacinato kale
½ cup extra virgin olive oil
3 tablespoons balsamic vinegar
2 tablespoons mayonnaise
2 garlic cloves, peeled and minced
Pinch of sea salt
¼ cup shredded Parmesan cheese, for topping
Slivered almonds, for topping
Sliced strawberries, for topping

1. Remove the ribs from the kale and cut the leaves into super-thin slices. Use ¼ cup of the olive oil and massage it into the leaves for about 5 minutes, until they become soft and tender.
2. In a bowl, whisk together the remaining olive oil, balsamic vinegar, mayonnaise, garlic, and salt until combined.
3. Add the dressing mixture to the massaged kale and toss until completely coated.
4. Top with the cheese, almonds, and strawberries.

Raw Garlic Sauce

This Middle Eastern garlic sauce is light, creamy, and full of flavor. I use it as a dip with fresh vegetables like cucumbers, carrots, or sweet peppers, in place of mayonnaise on sandwiches, or on the side to accompany fish or meat dishes.

1 cup peeled garlic cloves

2 teaspoons sea salt

4 cups grapeseed oil

8 teaspoons freshly squeezed lemon juice

1. Place the garlic and salt in a food processor fitted with the metal blade. Pulse in short bursts, occasionally removing the lid to scrape down the sides of the bowl with a spatula, until finely minced.
2. With the food processor running, slowly drizzle in ½ cup of the oil through the feed tube. After the first ½ cup has been added, pour in a teaspoon of the lemon juice.
3. Continue alternating between ½ cup of the oil and a teaspoon of the lemon juice until you've added all of the oil and lemon juice. (Alternating between the two is the key to proper emulsification, which creates a light and fluffy garlic sauce.)
4. Continue processing until the sauce is white and thick with a consistency similar to mayonnaise, about 10 to 15 minutes.

Sprouting

I had a close relationship with our home garden on the dairy farm. My mom would take me to the garden store to buy seeds and plants galore. My memories are filled with creating a flower garden of pansies, marigolds, and snapdragons around my family's patio every spring, as well as a vibrant vegetable plot full of summer's bounty of cucumbers, zucchini, and tomatoes.

Garden space became limited as I got older and moved away from the farm, so I dabbled in growing sprouts on my kitchen counter. Even now, with outside garden beds and an urban backyard to grow a small cornucopia of fruits, vegetables, and herbs, I still enjoy sprouting indoors because it offers separate pleasures and benefits than outdoor gardening.

Sprouting increases the nutrient content of seeds and legumes and makes them easier to digest.

It takes just a few days to sprout most foods, which makes it an inexpensive way to grow food all year long. And it's low maintenance! If you have room for a mason jar on your counter, you're good to go.

What Seeds to Use

Alfalfa seeds are the most popular, but there are a lot of other options, like mung bean, lentil, radish, sunflower, pumpkin, wheat, chickpea, and broccoli, to name just a few. You can pretty much sprout any legume, seed, or nut.

Sprouts vs. Microgreens

Sprouts and microgreens are often lumped into one food category. However, the differences between the two are determined by whether or not the seed is planted in soil and exactly how much of the plant is being consumed. Microgreens are grown in soil, and the stems (usually 1 to 3 inches in length) are cut off and eaten. Sprouts are essentially germinated in water, and nothing is cut off. The whole thing is eaten.

Basic Sprouting Instructions

Gather sprouting seeds, a mason jar with a rubber band and cheesecloth or a special screw-top sprouting lid, and filtered water. Put 1 to 4 tablespoons of seeds in the jar. Add the water, swirl, and then drain the water. Add 1 cup of cool water, and secure the cheesecloth and rubber band or lid. Soak for 4 to 8 hours. After the initial soak is complete, drain the jar, refill it with cool water, swirl, and drain again. Invert the jar and prop it at an angle into a bowl. Repeat the rinsing and draining process twice a day. In 3 to 6 days, when the sprouts are about 1 to 2 inches long, they are ready to be eaten. Eat your sprouts, or cover the jar with the original lid and store in the fridge for 5 to 7 days.

AVOCADO TOAST WITH SPROUTS AND PICKLED KUMQUATS

Serves 1

Take avocado toast to the next level with this super-simple and nourishing version with sprouted greens and pickled kumquats.

1 tablespoon extra virgin olive oil
1 slice sourdough bread (or bread of choice), toasted
½ ripe avocado, halved, pitted, peeled, and mashed
A handful of sprouts
Pickled kumquats (see page 68)
Sea salt and freshly ground black pepper

1. Drizzle the olive oil in an even layer on the freshly toasted bread.
2. Spread the mashed avocado on the bread, and then top with the sprouts and kumquats.
3. Season with salt and pepper and serve immediately.

TIP: In addition to avocado toast, sprouts can be added to soups, rice dishes, savory porridge, sandwiches, and salads. They even make a great snack on their own.

COOKING WITH CHILDREN

I've found that our children have become more interested in preparing and eating the foods we're growing in our garden. When our daughter was about a year old, she would sit in our backyard, pick kale from our edible garden, and simply munch away.

When we pick up our CSA box, or shop at the farmers market, we also get a sense of what's fresh and seasonally available in our area. We talk about the food choices we make as a family, and why we eat what we eat. For example, just recently I purchased hard white wheat berries at the farmers market. After I told my daughter why I bought them, she was thrilled with the idea of turning the wheat berries into flour to make sourdough bread. So we did it together, and along the way we talked about the farmer who sold us the wheat berries, the process for making sourdough bread, and so on. I hope these moments teach our children how to connect back to the earth and provide knowledge about nourishment for their own bodies no matter how old they are.

Dinner seems to be a great time for everyone to pitch in and help prepare. Kids can chop veggies, but also stir, add spices, and even help you taste along the way. This gives your child the skills to know how to prepare food for themselves as they age, but it also gives them confidence that you trust them in the kitchen and that their input matters.

Spring Rolls with White Miso Ginger Dressing

Think of this as a make-your-own-spring-roll bar. Your kids can help chop the veggies and herbs while you cook the rice and make the dressing. Lay out all of the ingredients, and everyone can come up with their own spring roll creation.

FOR THE DRESSING:

3 tablespoons white miso (see page 122)

2 tablespoons rice vinegar

2 tablespoons tahini

2 tablespoons neutral oil, like safflower oil

1 tablespoon coconut aminos

1 teaspoon peeled and finely grated fresh organic ginger

1 garlic clove, peeled and minced

FOR THE SPRING ROLLS:

8 (6-inch) Vietnamese rice spring roll wrappers

¼ cup chopped fresh cilantro leaves

¼ cup chopped basil leaves

¼ cup chopped mint leaves

¼ cup peeled and grated carrots

½ cup thinly sliced cucumber

1 avocado, thinly sliced

½ cup thinly sliced bell pepper

½ cup cooked chickpeas

½ cup thinly sliced green onions or scallions, both white and green parts

TO MAKE THE DRESSING:

1. Place the miso, vinegar, and tahini in a jar with a lid and shake well.
2. Add the oil, coconut aminos, ginger, and garlic, and shake until combined. If too thick, add a little bit of water.

TO MAKE THE SPRING ROLLS:

1. Dip the wrappers in water. Remove them quickly and spread them flat on a plate.
2. Place a sprinkling of the herbs and a small handful of your desired ingredients—carrots, cucumbers, avocado, bell peppers, chickpeas, and green onions—in the middle of the wrapper.
3. Drizzle with the dressing.
4. Tightly roll the wrapper. First, fold the sides inward, and then fold the bottom over the sides and middle, and keep rolling to the top of the wrapper. Serve with the white miso ginger dressing.

TEACHING KIDS TO USE A KNIFE

I taught my children at a very early age how to hold a knife (granted, it was a butter knife to start with) and gave them easy foods to cut, such as hard-boiled eggs, cooked veggies, and bananas. As they gained confidence, I graduated them to sharper knives and harder foods to cut, such as broccoli and cauliflower, and then even harder foods, such as carrots and potatoes. I always make sure that when we cook together they are at the right height to help with meal prep. Kitchen counters are built to be just the right height for most adults. You want your kids to stand on a stool or chair that puts the counter at about waist height. They should be able to clearly see what they are cutting, stirring, or preparing.

Cucumber Salad

This is my daughter's creation and our favorite family recipe to make together. She loves cucumbers with lemon juice and sea salt as a snack. One day we had feta on hand, and just like that, this salad was born. Kids usually have fun chopping the cucumber and squeezing the lemon. You can help add the drizzle of olive oil and salt and pepper, or be adventurous and let them try that too.

2 cups diced cucumbers

½ cup cubed feta

Juice of 1 lemon

Extra virgin olive oil, for drizzling

Freshly ground sea salt and black pepper

1 to 2 tablespoons roughly chopped fresh herbs, such as a combination of mint, cilantro, parsley, and dill

1. Combine the cucumbers and feta in a small salad bowl. Squeeze the lemon juice over the cucumbers, drizzle with the oil, and then season with salt and pepper.
2. Sprinkle your herb of choice onto the salad and lightly toss.

Mini Herb and Cheese Frittatas

Our hens give us plenty of eggs, so we naturally find ourselves eating a lot of protein-packed egg dishes throughout the week. My kids always have a fun time whisking the eggs together with the herbs and cheese. They especially like transferring the batter into muffin cups so everyone has individual egg frittatas.

1. Preheat the oven to 350°F and grease a muffin tin with oil.
2. Whisk the eggs, milk, salt, and pepper until well blended. Add the cheese, chives, parsley, red pepper, bacon or ham, and kale and mix.
3. Pour the egg mixture into the prepared muffin cups about three-quarters full.
4. Cook for 8 to 10 minutes or until set.

8 eggs

¼ cup whole milk, preferably organic

¼ teaspoon sea salt

½ teaspoon freshly ground black pepper

½ cup freshly grated parmesan cheese

1 tablespoon chopped fresh chives

1 tablespoon chopped fresh parsley leaves

2 tablespoons chopped red bell pepper

2 tablespoons cooked and chopped bacon or ham

2 tablespoons chopped kale

Coconut Curry Veggie Stew

SERVES 4

Monday evening is soup night at my house, and this is the soup my kids ask for the most. This nutritious soup features a variety of vegetables, coconut milk, and some mellow curry spices. Your little ones will have fun chopping veggies, stirring the soup together, adding spices, and tasting to see if it's ready for the dinner table.

1 tablespoon coconut oil or ghee

1 large onion, peeled and finely chopped

1 tablespoon ground coriander

1 tablespoon ground cumin

1 teaspoon ground turmeric

2 carrots, peeled and chopped

2 ribs celery, chopped

½ head cauliflower or broccoli, chopped (about 1½ cups)

3 small sweet potatoes, cut into 1-inch cubes (about 1 cup)

1 large tomato, diced

2 tablespoons peeled and finely grated fresh organic ginger

2 garlic cloves, peeled and minced

½ cup coconut milk

1 teaspoon sea salt

½ teaspoon freshly ground black pepper

¼ to ½ cup chopped fresh cilantro leaves

1. Heat a large Dutch oven or pot over medium-high heat. Warm the coconut oil and sauté the onion until translucent, 5 to 6 minutes.
2. Add the coriander, cumin, and turmeric and sauté for 30 seconds.
3. Add the carrots, celery, cauliflower, sweet potatoes, tomato, ginger, and garlic. Add water to cover.
4. Simmer the soup for 15 to 20 minutes until the veggies are tender.
5. Add the coconut milk, salt, and pepper. Cook for 1 more minute.
6. Stir in the cilantro and serve.

Sourdough Flatbread Pizza

MAKES 4 (5-INCH) PIZZAS

This flatbread recipe creates a soft yet crispy sourdough pizza. I feed my sourdough starter in the early morning, and it is ready by early evening. Let your kids choose their favorite toppings. The possibilities are endless.

½ cup fresh sourdough starter

1 teaspoon sea salt

1 cup filtered water

2⅓ cups bread flour

1 tablespoon extra virgin olive oil

Corn flour, cornmeal, sprouted flour, or arrowroot powder, for dusting

Mozzarella cheese

Desired pizza toppings, such fresh vegetables, prosciutto, olives, or mushrooms

1. In a large bowl, stir the starter, salt, and water until it just comes together. Add the flour. Stir until it is well mixed and forms a rough, sticky dough, about 1 minute.
2. Cover the bowl loosely with a lid, beeswax wrap, or plastic wrap and set aside at room temperature.
3. After resting the dough for 30 minutes, add the olive oil and mix by gently squeezing the dough. Cover the bowl loosely and set aside again at room temperature.
4. After 30 minutes, use wet hands to scoop the dough up from one side of the bowl, stretching it up and folding it over the dough that remains in the bowl. Rotate the bowl and repeat this process for six to eight folds.
5. Cover the bowl loosely and set aside. Continue resting the dough and folding it in this manner every 30 minutes for a total resting time of 3 hours. When ready, the dough will be glossy and very smooth. At this stage, the dough can be refrigerated overnight or divided in four and gently stretched into thin rounds for pizza.
6. Preheat the oven to 450°F.
7. Roll the dough out into a circle, about 5 inches or so in diameter, using a minimal amount of corn flour to prevent sticking. Repeat with the remaining pieces of dough.
8. Bake the crusts on a baking sheet for about 6 minutes, until golden brown.
9. Remove the crusts from the oven and add cheese and other desired toppings. Bake until the crusts are brown and the cheese is melted, 6 to 8 minutes.

TIP: These freeze well too! Just parbake the crust for 6 minutes, cool, and then freeze.

Creating a Seasonal Food Menu

Eating with the seasons is one of the best ways to add variety, excitement, and nutrition to the dinner table. Seasonal meal planning is the simple act of taking some time to plan any number of your meals for the week or month ahead to incorporate what's growing now. There are a variety of reasons meal planning can be beneficial. When you plan and cook your own meals, you are most likely saving money when compared to purchasing the same type of meal in a restaurant or buying premade items at the grocery store. It's also healthier to create a seasonal meal plan. When you eat from what's in season, you

are adding a wider range of nutrients to your body by mixing it up a bit and eating foods that you might not otherwise. Also, when you make an effort to choose from what's in season and plan ahead, there is often less waste and you save time in the process because you have a plan.

My favorite part about eating with the seasons is the taste. Fresh carrots taste nothing like the ones from the store. They are sweet and bursting with flavor. When it comes to tomatoes, there really is nothing like a ripe summer tomato fresh from the garden. And the juiciest and most deliciously sweet strawberries come directly from home gardens or the farmers market.

One of the things I love about belonging to a CSA is that it often shares recipes for what's in season. And when you shop locally at the farmers market and get to know your farmers, they might give you extra tips on how to prepare what they are growing. Doing so has introduced my family to a variety of fruits and vegetables we might not otherwise have tried.

As the seasons change and fall and winter bring cooler days and nights, we naturally crave warmth and comfort. Winter squash and root vegetables are what Mother Nature brings as nourishment. (Winter is also a time to rely on your canned summer vegetables!) Spring emerges and brings light, bright produce, such as lettuce, greens, and peas. When we are at the height of heat in the summer months, juicy, water-rich produce is abundant to hydrate our bodies and provide antioxidants to protect us from the sun. There is a rhythm and purpose to seasonal foods, and because of this there is a greater sense of appreciation when we eat with the seasons.

On the opposite page, you will find some basic seasonal produce and ideas of what you might create with nature's bounty.

WINTER

IN-SEASON PRODUCE: winter squash, beets, parsnips, rutabagas, sweet potatoes, cabbage, carrots, onions, Brussels sprouts

BREAKFAST DISHES: oatmeal with apples or other preserved fruit; eggs and sauerkraut; sourdough waffles with preserved fruit

MAIN DISHES: vegetable stew with winter squash; cabbage stir fry; parsnip and carrot fritters; grain bowls or creamy polenta with roasted winter squash, onions, beets, and carrots

SIDE DISHES: roasted winter squash; warm beet salad; parsnip and sweet potato fries; mashed parsnips and rutabagas; sautéed cabbage; sauerkraut; preserved honey garlic–glazed carrots

SPRING

IN-SEASON PRODUCE: Swiss chard, kale, dandelion greens, collard greens, spinach, lettuce, arugula, fava beans, snap peas, strawberries, broccoli, asparagus, radishes, carrots, garden-fresh herbs

BREAKFAST DISHES: scrambled eggs with spinach or other greens; fried eggs with asparagus; granola with fresh strawberries and milk or milk kefir

MAIN DISHES: dandelion greens topped with chicken or other proteins, such as legumes or quinoa; beef and broccoli or chicken and snap pea stir fry; grain bowls or creamy polenta with spring greens, roasted asparagus, and carrots; mashed fava bean tartine; coconut curry veggie stew; mini herb and cheese frittatas; spring greens quiche

SIDE DISHES: roasted broccoli; Swiss chard with bacon and onions; kale chips; spinach and strawberry salad; sautéed fava beans; roasted asparagus; lacto-fermented radishes

SUMMER

IN-SEASON PRODUCE: tomatoes, peppers, green beans, berries, melons, cucumbers, eggplant, peaches, yellow squash, zucchini, new potatoes, corn, stone fruit

BREAKFAST DISHES: zucchini bread; yogurt with fresh seasonal fruit; eggs with fresh salsa; seasonal fruit smoothies

MAIN DISHES: pasta or pizza with tomatoes, garlic, and herbs; fajitas with peppers; roasted eggplant on pasta or pizza; stuffed peppers or zucchini; veggie kabobs; sandwiches topped with tomatoes, cucumbers, and avocado; grain bowls or creamy polenta with roasted zucchini, yellow squash, and tomatoes; zucchini and corn galette; summer veggie quiche

SIDE DISHES: cucumber and tomato salad; stir-fried green beans; steamed green beans; steamed or roasted potatoes; fruit salads; zucchini ribbons; pickled green beans; lacto-fermented dill pickles

FALL

IN-SEASON PRODUCE: apples, pumpkins, kabocha squash, sweet potatoes, potatoes, butternut squash, carrots, collard greens, kale, beets

BREAKFAST DISHES: pumpkin muffins; baked apples; apple cinnamon rolls; pumpkin oatmeal

MAIN DISHES: pumpkin chili; potato soup; butternut squash soup; white bean stew with seasonal greens; roasted root vegetables with sausage over creamy polenta; sweet potato, kale, and sausage hash; sweet potato curry; grain bowls or creamy polenta with roasted butternut squash and collard greens

SIDE DISHES: roasted sweet potato and apples; sautéed collard greens; roasted carrots with carrot-top pesto; pickled winter squash; roasted beets

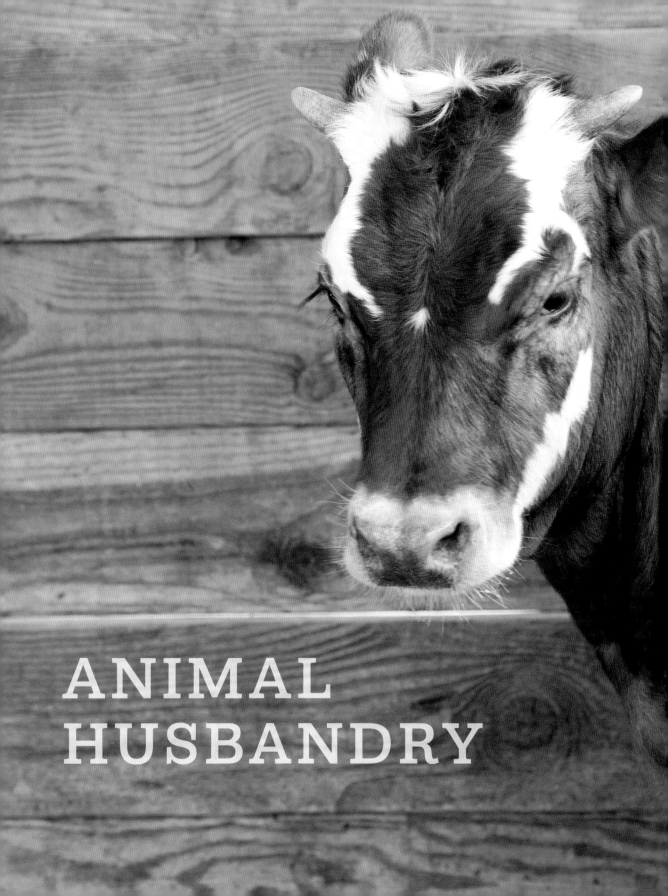

ANIMAL
HUSBANDRY

Fresh Nutrients and
Beautiful Experiences

LAUREN

ANIMALS HAVE ALWAYS BEEN AN INTEGRAL PART OF MY LIFE. MY PROFOUND fascination and connection with them have been there since I can remember. Growing up, we had everything from cats and dogs to chickens, sheep, horses, and even a few cows. At 10 years old, I shadowed a persnickety dairy farmer of very few words and I learned so much from him. I eventually became the morning milker at the farm, milking his 60 cows on my own. This small Vermont dairy farm was my heaven. There was always something exciting to experience: births, deaths, calves to bottle feed, ill cows to doctor. I'd come home covered in manure and reeking so strongly that my mother made me take my overalls off outside the door and run to the shower, but I always had a big smile on my face.

I studied animal science at the University of Vermont, with a minor in conservation biology. I learned the ins and outs of raising and managing domestic animals with a healthy dose of wildlife conservation. I was also lucky enough to do a 6-month stint working in Africa with cheetahs and black rhinos, and then with some top biologists in China studying the Przewalski's horse.

After college, I moved to California and was drawn to the California Wildlife Center, where I worked rescuing and rehabilitating native, injured wildlife. There, I saw firsthand the harm inflicted on animals when humans encroached upon their habitat, both land and sea, and it was incredibly difficult. However, there was a great reward in being able to see a rehabilitated owl, pelican, or seal be released.

I met my husband, Keith, in California, and together we moved to a rural, four-acre ranch in Gaviota, where we started a family and a small hobby farm. Over the past decade, we have raised horses, milk cows and calves, beef cattle, chickens, turkeys, ducks, rabbits, bees, cats, dogs, and pigs. Our children, Milly and June, are part of the farm's daily rhythms, joys, and woes. There are a lot of mouths to feed each morning, including ours first. Then we make the rounds to check on the animals. We milk the cow if needed, muck the pens, check waters, administer any medications, and collect eggs. And in the evening, we do it all over again.

I'm excited to share my knowledge and adventures of a life spent surrounded by and loving animals. The pages ahead are filled with lessons learned through trial and error, common sense and observation, and from family, friends, and mentors. I wish you a journey surrounded by animals that will touch your heart and teach you many inspiring life lessons. The relationship between humans and animals goes well beyond eggs, milk, meat, and honey, although those are some of the incredibly delightful perks.

THE BASICS

The definition of animal husbandry is the science of raising, breeding, and caring for domesticated animals. The animals I'll discuss in the coming pages can provide food, such as milk, meat, eggs, and honey. Regardless of the animal, you are in charge of making sure it is raised thoughtfully and naturally, with a healthy diet and caring environment.

We humans have an ancient and naturally deep connection with animals, and our well-being and quality of life improves when these relationships are nurtured. Not only do we have an ancient symbiotic relationship with many species, but owning animals today has also been shown to boost our immune systems, improve our moods, and even help with depression and PTSD. Raising children with animals can actually help fight allergies, as well as teach compassion and responsibility.

More than anything, bringing animals into our lives invites the slow pace, the simple back-to-nature lifestyle. Animals allow us to relate to universal experiences like births and deaths. The degree in which animals are a part of our lives is completely unique and individual. Caring for animals requires a shift in priorities, attention, forethought, and constant care. In return, we get nourishment, resources, and irreplaceable relationships.

Preparation

Trust me, it is very easy to see an animal, especially a baby one, and take it home without much forethought or planning. From personal experience, things go much smoother if you put extensive thought into the species and breed of animal you want. There are many things to consider when deciding whether to bring an animal home. First, how much time do you have to take proper care of the animal, whether it's a cat, dog, or larger farm animal? Seriously consider the potential costs and time associated with having that animal, such as feeding, housing, and vet care.

I have broken the process of getting a new animal for your animal husbandry project into three phases: research, planning, and bringing your animal home. Hopefully, these sections will help you better understand the big picture and prepare for success on the journey ahead.

Research

Picking the right livestock or pet is the very first step in approaching animal husbandry. Weigh out your needs with your expectations of the animal's needs. Do you want an animal for dairy, meat, eggs, honey, fiber, or companionship? Then consider the emotional attachment to your animal. Do you want an animal that is responsive, more like a pet, or do you want an animal that is in the field and more detached? To do this, you must know which species you are interested in. Then, based on that, you can determine which specific breeds will be the most useful for you, and which will most likely match your expectations. It's important to base your decisions on your personal level of interest and intentions for owning and raising the animal, along with the amount of space, time, and money the animal requires. Ultimately, it must work well for you, or it certainly will not work well for the animal.

Once you choose the type of animal, it's time to consider the breeds. The definition of a breed is "a stock of animals or plants within a species having a distinctive appearance and typically having been developed by deliberate genetic selection." The animal's look, size, and behavior can generally be predicted by knowing about specific breeds. Unless you are getting an animal of mixed breeds, you should be able to understand and closely predict not only what the animal will look like, but also what their behavior might be like—as well as characteristics like milk or egg production or body development for meat. Because breeds have been developed for certain purposes, it helps to look back at a breed's history to fully understand it.

Once your species and breed are decided, it can help to write down your goals for your animals and keep referring to your notes while looking for your specific animal. The research phase of choosing your project and animal should be slow and deliberate. Consult helpful online resources, look for books on the subject, and consider finding mentors and taking local classes in order to understand the big picture of what having a specific type of animal entails. Also, I would highly encourage you to find someone who actually owns the animals you are considering; they could be an invaluable help in answering questions and showing you what a day in the life looks like. There are folks I have met in this process that I call up often for advice. I have found that most animal folks love talking about their animals and helping a newbie out.

Planning

Once you've decided on the right animal, it's time to start planning the area where it will live. This stage is fun and has many pertinent and complicated questions to answer: Where is the best location to house and pasture the animal? What type and size of shelter is required for the animal? What type of containment is

needed to keep the animal safe and happy in the designated areas? How will you deal with manure disposal? What other needs may your animal require?

Water and feed management are two very important decisions to consider. Your animal always needs easy access to clean, fresh water, so consider the location of its shelter in relation to its water and food source. Plan to have a food-storage area that is convenient, dry, and safe from rodents. When making all of these decisions, be practical. Decide on convenience, simplicity, and what is optimal for the safety and comfort of your animal.

Bringing Your Animal Home

Now is the moment you've long awaited. Be calm and thoughtful when first introducing your animal to its new home. Give yourself and the animal time to assimilate. If you already have animals of the same or different species, it's a good idea to introduce them through fence lines for the first 24 to 48 hours. At first, it may be overwhelming, but you'll establish a routine within a few days and begin to see what a wonderful experience lays ahead. And hopefully, you will realize how much difference your preplanning and research has made in creating a seamless transition for both you and your animals.

CHICKENS

Laying chickens are a great place to start your animal husbandry adventure. They are entertaining, relatively easy to keep, and flexible with space. I enjoy starting my day by saying good morning to my clutch of ladies and being gifted with an egg to scramble fresh. I am not an avian science expert, but the information in this section is based on more than 10 years of experience having chickens. My hope is to spark your interest in having your own backyard flock, and this information can help get you started.

There are many different ways to keep chickens, and there are so many resources out there that can support you. (Make sure to check the list of my favorite resources in the back of the book.) Chickens can live in small city backyards or free range in a large area. After the coop and run are set up, the cost of daily upkeep is relatively low. For me, the joy and food source our chickens provide are priceless.

POULTRY: Domestic fowl such as chickens, turkeys, ducks, and geese

BROOD: A group of baby chicks

FLOCK: A group of juvenile to adult chickens

PULLET: A young female chicken less than one year old

COCKEREL: A young male chicken less than one year old

HEN: A female chicken

ROOSTER: A male domestic chicken

LAYERS: Female chickens that are laying eggs

FERTILIZED EGG: An egg that has been laid after a rooster and hen have mated

COOP: A shelter for your chickens providing protection from predators and the elements

RUN: A corralled area where your chickens have access to the outdoors

ROOSTING BAR OR PERCH: A bar off the ground that chickens can rest and sleep on

ROOSTING: When chickens are resting on their perches

NESTING BOX: A box provided for the chickens to lay their eggs

BROODY: The instinctive behavior chickens have to stay on their eggs for incubation

CULLING: Reduction of the animal population, usually for health reasons

MOLTING: The process of shedding old feathers

PREENING: The process of a bird cleaning and waterproofing its feathers

PREEN GLAND: A gland at the base of a bird's tail that produces oil to aid in preening and waterproofing

DUST BATH: A process where the chicken covers itself in dirt and dust in order to remove excess oil and parasites like lice and mites, while also helping with water resistance of the outer feathers

Fresh Eggs

Fresh eggs taste so much better to me than store-bought eggs; their color is bright and their nutrition is rich. Scientists have found that fresh eggs have double the amount of folic acid and vitamin B12. Eggs from chickens raised on pasture are exponentially higher in fatty acids, omega-3s, and vitamin E, but at the same time are lower in cholesterol. Results show that the healthier and happier the chickens, the better and more nutritious the eggs.

In contrast, most store-bought eggs are produced in large-scale, industrial laying facilities where thousands of chickens are cramped so tight they can hardly move. They are overfed low-grade, cheap by-product food and are kept under artificial light. Caged or not, these conditions are horrendous. These unnaturally overcrowded conditions breed widespread sickness, and, to counter that, the hens are regularly fed low-dose antibiotics. It is emotionally intense to hear about these inhumane conditions, but awareness is important. Having backyard chickens is a step toward breaking away from industrial chicken farming and an amazing step toward connecting back to the animals that provide us with healthy food.

If chicken keeping is not an option for you, consider supporting local farmers who treat their birds humanely. Labels in the store with words like "organic," "cage free," and "free range" can be misleading because they can mean the birds still have little or no access to the outdoors. On the other hand, pasture-raised birds are required to have at least 108 square feet each and are outdoors all day. So for the healthiest, most humane option, look for organic and pasture-raised eggs. Purchasing these eggs directly from a local farmer, at the farmers market, or at a local health food store is truly your best option for fresh, healthy eggs from happy chickens. Another perk—you'll be supporting small farms!

A Day in the Life of a Chicken

We start our day by saying good morning to our ladies, check and make sure they look healthy, check their water and feed level and refill if necessary, feed them any food scraps we have, and collect their eggs. At this point, there's the option of letting the chickens out into the yard to free range, but there's also the constant risk of dogs and predators like raccoons. When evening comes around, we check to see if their feed or water needs refilling. We also check for any eggs that were laid since the morning, and then make sure everyone is in and close the coop for the night.

Once a month, we clean the coop. We clean the nesting boxes, add new straw, and shovel out from underneath. We clean out the waterer, rake the run, and then sprinkle a coop deodorizer all over the coop and run. All of these chores together take about an hour. The daily routine is sometimes thrown off if there's a sick chicken or if something breaks and needs repair, which is inevitable. But for the most part, backyard chicken keeping is a quick and easy daily routine.

Chicken Breeds

There are hundreds of different breeds of chickens that can look and act different, have different egg-laying productivity, and even lay different colored eggs. It's a good idea to learn about the different breeds before getting chickens, as some will be a better fit for your situation than others. Here are some of my favorite backyard breeds, most of which can be found at your local feedstore.

Rhode Island Red

Like their name suggests, Rhode Island Reds have beautiful red plumage. They are known for their hardiness and great egg production. They lay about five to six brown eggs a week at peak laying season. They're known to be curious, friendly, and, in my experience, great with children. They're not aggressive; they're easy to handle, mostly friendly, and overall a great breed choice for beginners.

Buff Orpington

This heavier-built breed has light orange feathering. I have found Orpingtons to be incredibly laid back, friendly, and easy to handle. Their thick feathering makes them cold-hardy, and for me, they've been low-maintenance birds. They are good layers, laying about four to five light brown eggs per week. They do have a tendency to be a bit broody, but overall they are a great breed for backyard chickens.

Barred Plymouth Rock

This heavy-bodied, beautiful black-and-white-feathered breed has been my family's favorite because of the birds' personalities. I have found they are extremely social and like human interaction. Dusty, my daughters' favorite chicken, will follow them around wherever they go. She even lets my four-year-old pick her up and carry her around. They lay about four to five brown eggs a week and have a striking plumage.

ESSENTIALS FOR SETTING UP YOUR OWN FLOCK

- Secure coop
- Perches in the coop
- Nesting boxes and coop floor
- Straw or pine shavings for nesting box
- A run
- Chicken feed
- Feeder
- Waterer
- Grit
- Crushed oyster shells

Silkie

Known for their big, exotic plumage, Silkie chicks can sometimes look more like cotton balls than chicks. They're sweet, curious, and have docile temperaments, but are known to be a bit broody. They have great mothering skills and can be great if you want them to hatch chicks. Their eggs are light tan. They aren't the most productive layers, but they make up for it in their personality and cuteness.

Preparing for Chickens

You will want to prepare and set everything up for your chickens before going out and getting them. The following information will cover general housing and maintenance.

The Coop

Coops come in many different shapes and sizes, and are made from various materials. You can look around for scrap materials and build your own coop, buy one from a local feedstore, order a kit online and put it together yourself, or hire a carpenter for a custom build. The choice is up to you. It's better for your birds to have more square footage inside the coop than less, but the rule of thumb is 4 square feet per bird. I'm not going to cover coop plans here, but several of the chicken-keeping resources listed in the back of this book give great details on coop layouts. Below are the factors to consider and must-have features.

LOCATION, LOCATION, LOCATION

The coop's location should be considered before any building begins. Check out local rules and regulations to see how they will influence the location of the coop. Then, proximity to neighbors should be considered, as any neighborly conflicts can take the joy out of backyard chicken keeping. Even the cleanest of coops can smell, so you may want to put it somewhere where the smell won't bother you or your neighbors—think downwind.

Pick a location that creates ease and convenience when collecting your eggs, checking on your ladies twice daily, and carrying the feed to fill their feeder. It helps to be close to a hose so you can install an automatic waterer, which saves you time and stress in the long run. Last, think about environmental factors like drainage and sun exposure. Work with what you have, and make a pro and con list for the location options before you start building.

PROTECTION

During the day, the doors are open and the chickens can enjoy being outdoors, but every night they must be locked and secured in the coop for protection. This means the coop needs to be predator proof and secure from environmental conditions like rain, wind, and sun. With all of this protection, keep in mind the need for ventilation to provide fresh air and circulation. I have found a 2-by-12-inch vent just below the roofline and a 2-by-12-inch vent at the base of the coop seems to create enough airflow without exposing the birds to too much draft.

No matter what type of coop you have, make sure there's a wire underneath or wire dug and backfilled deep into the perimeter (12 to 18 inches down) so nothing can tunnel in. Reinforce the sides of the coop to make sure nothing can push in the wire on the sides. Any doors should be secured with latches that only a human can open. Every coop must have a roof, which can be made of any solid, waterproof material. I prefer corrugated metal to plastic or wood.

FEEDERS

The coop must have a feeder. Feeders come in different sizes, and are either plastic or metal. I prefer the larger metal hanging feeders because they can hold plenty of feed, which saves me time. Ideally, your feeder should hang down and be a few inches off the ground, not only so the feed stays cleaner, but also for easy pecking access.

NATURAL COOP CLEANER AND ODOR CONTROL

Food-grade diatomaceous earth is a natural cleaner that can be used to kill parasites and bugs, keep your coop dry, and remove odors. It can even provide health benefits for your chickens because it is packed with minerals. Sprinkle around the coop, especially covering any wet areas; sprinkle on your chickens while they are roosting; and sprinkle in their food and mix in. Make sure to wear a mask when handling diatomaceous earth, as it is bad for your lungs if inhaled.

Using herbs in your coop can also help with odor control, and using it in your chickens' feed can help support their immune system. Here's a list of herbs that can be sprinkled throughout the coop:

- Chamomile
- Dandelion
- Garlic
- Lavender
- Mint
- Oregano
- Parsley
- Rosemary

It needs to be in a sheltered area to stay out of the sun and rain, either in the run or in the coop. Make sure it's not under your perches or it will get covered in chicken poop.

Feed

A chicken's day revolves around food. Once they start laying, your ladies need a wide range of food and a lot of it. They need to be healthy and filled with nutrients in order to provide you with nutritious eggs. Manufactured feed should be readily available to your flock. I use organic laying pellets, like Modesto Milling organic poultry layer pellets. For a healthy, happy chicken, you can also supplement their feed with oat hay, garden weeds, bugs from roaming outside, and some kitchen scraps.

Laying hens also need a large amount of calcium in order to form the eggshells. There should be enough calcium in your feed if you're buying high-quality laying chicken feed. But if necessary, you can supplement calcium. Most feedstores offer a crushed oyster shell product that can be scattered on the ground, mixed into the chickens' feed, or offered separately in order to ensure their mineral intake.

In addition to the described diet, your ladies also need to eat rocks—yes, rocks!—otherwise known as grit. Chickens do not have teeth, so they swallow tiny stones that find their way to the birds' gizzards, where they help grind the incoming food to aid digestion. If your birds are let out every day to roam, they should be able to find enough grit on their own. If your birds are

not let out to free range every day, you'll need to purchase grit at the feedstore and scatter it around their run.

But how do chickens eat their food without teeth? The food is taken in through their beak, and it moves from their mouth down to their esophagus and into a holding area called the gizzard. The gizzard is a strong muscular sac that uses small hard particles of sand and rock to grind and process their food, which is why they need grit in their diet. This process, combined with digestive enzymes, is how their food is broken down without having teeth. The food then moves to the small intestine. Nutrients are absorbed, and what's left passes through the cecum, a small sac where bacteria helps further break down undigested food. What is left then passes through the large intestine, where water is absorbed and the remaining waste is dried out. The waste passes through the cloaca and out the vent. Urine is mixed with the waste, so it is one dropping. Pretty cool, huh?

Waterer

There are many different kinds of waterer options for your chickens, from gravity waterers to nipple waterers. It's worth researching the different kinds to see what makes sense for you and your flock. I've always used an automatic waterer that hooks up to a hose bib and automatically refills as the chicken drinks. The downfall is you have to clean and scrub the waterer monthly, and it's not a pretty job, but to me it's better than refilling water daily. Even though the water is automatic, I still do a visual check to make sure it's full. Your chickens need to have access to clean water at all times, whether in the coop run or out free ranging.

Apple cider vinegar can be added to your chickens' water to boost their health. It is thought that the vinegar helps boost chickens' digestive and immune system while helping with calcium absorption and maintaining healthy pH levels. Using apple cider vinegar can also help keep your waterer free of harmful bacteria. Add 1 teaspoon of vinegar for every gallon of water once a week. Only use vinegar in plastic waterers, as it can corrode metal ones.

Nesting Boxes

Nesting boxes are little cubicles that encourage your chickens to lay in a nice, clean, private place. The amount of nesting boxes you will need depends on the size of your flock. I make one nesting box out of wood for every three to four birds. The boxes are 1 foot deep by 1 foot tall by 1 foot across—this size should be suitable for the average chicken. It's important to fill the boxes with a soft substrate for the hens to lay their eggs on. I like to use straw in my nesting boxes, but some people prefer pine shavings. I clean out the boxes about every 4 weeks, or on an as-needed basis. Make sure you have a door behind your nesting box that you can open from outside the coop for incredibly easy egg gathering. Just open it up and collect your prize eggs.

Perch

Chickens prefer to sleep off the ground. A roosting perch or bar is a smooth, wooden bar about 1½ to 3 feet off the ground and about 2 to 4 inches wide where the chickens can wrap their feet around the bar and roost. In natural environments, they would roost in trees to avoid predators. Sleeping elevated also helps chickens avoid the pathogens, bacteria, lice, and mites that can live on the coop floor. Chickens will roost from dusk until dawn and get nice and cozy in their sleep trance together. The chickens at the top of the pecking order will get the higher (safer) perches. Make sure you have enough perches so all of your flock can roost.

Run

A run is an area where your chickens can access the outdoors daily, but also be somewhat corralled and protected. A run for your chickens does not need to be nearly as sheltered or solidly built as your coop. The run can be a continuation of your predator-proof coop, or it can be as simple as a chicken-wire fenced area. Chickens can fly a few feet off the ground, so take their flying into consideration when deciding fence height. Another option if you have a fenced area for a run could be clipping their wings every few months to reduce flight. A run is great to have even if you let your chickens out to free range. I recommend researching run options and learning what makes sense for you, your budget and time, and your flock.

To Free Range or Not to Free Range?

Chickens love to be let out to wander. It is not only great for their health and diet, but also stimulating to their brains. I find it helps overall well-being. The chickens will explore, look for bugs and grubs, scratch, and take dust baths, and it looks to me like they are truly loving their freedom. The downside I have found is it can make for a messy yard, they can get into your garden, they can poop wherever, and the chances of being attacked by a predator increase.

A good compromise and trick I've learned is to let my flock out a couple hours before dusk. This way, they've most likely already laid their eggs in the nesting box, they don't have too much time to make a big mess or get into trouble, and at dusk they'll head back to their coop to roost for the night. As the head of your flock, the decision to let your chickens out is up to you, and you will find out what works by trial and error.

I strongly recommend letting your chickens out several times a week. However, if their run is big enough and you decide not to let them out, make sure you supplement their store-bought feed with grit, greens, and crushed oyster shells for the chicken's health and stimulation.

Ready for Chicks

Finally, after all the research, planning, and building, you are ready to start your own flock! You can buy juvenile or even adult chickens, but they are usually more expensive and harder to find. Chicks are a great way for a beginning chicken keeper to get started. There is nothing like fluffy little cheeping chicks to start your journey. In this section, I will cover what you should know and prepare before bringing your sweet chicks home.

Brooder Box

The brooder box will need to be ready for the chicks before bringing them home. Think of a brooder like a chick nursery. It's a secure area where chicks spend their first 6 to 8 weeks of life. A brooder box can be anything from a wooden box to a plastic bin or even a cardboard box. Make sure the box is big enough for the chicks to run, move freely, and grow. The chicks will triple in size in just a few weeks. If the box

isn't big enough, you can always move them into a bigger brooder box as they grow. Add litter—a soft, absorbent substrate like pine shavings or straw—to the bottom of the box. Chicks are little pooping machines, and it's important for their health to keep the brooder box clean. It's also necessary for the brooder box to have a heat lamp, a feeder full of chick feed, and access to clean water at all times.

Heat Lamp

It's critical for chicks to have a heat lamp. Newly hatched chicks do not have feathering to insulate them like an adult chicken. A 250-watt heat lamp is ideal and should be available at your local feedstore. The heat lamp should be placed above the chicks, with the ability to adjust it by raising or lowering as needed. Be safe with the location of the heat lamp; make sure it's not touching anything that could start a fire. The heat source should be around 95°F to start. I don't use a thermometer; instead, I observe the chicks closely. If they don't go under the heat lamp, it's too hot and I raise it. If they are constantly huddled together under the lamp, it means they are too cold, and I lower it. I know the temperature is just right when my chicks are moving freely around the brooder, in and out from under the lamp. As their feathers grow, I raise the heat lamp higher each week, observing their behavior and adjusting accordingly.

Feeder and Waterer

I highly recommend buying a 1-quart chick feeder and a 1-quart waterer for a small flock. Any open container full of food or water will quickly become messy. The chicks will jump in, poop in it, and knock it over. They must have water and feed available at all times in order for them to thrive and grow. I prefer organic chick crumble by Modesto Milling, and sprinkling ground oatmeal in your new chicks' feed can prevent digestive issues. I also like to offer my chicks cut-up greens, like kale and beet greens, to start promoting foraging and scrap eating early.

Getting Chicks

Your brooder is all set up and ready to go, so now you need some chicks. There are a few options for where and how to purchase your chicks. Chicks can be purchased at a local feedstore or from a local, reputable breeder. Chicks can also be purchased and sent to you directly in the mail. In this method, the chicks are shipped just after they hatch, and they can survive without food or water for 2 days because their bodies absorb the last of the yolk nutrients just before hatching. Although this process works, I don't recommend it because it's very stressful for the chicks and some die during transport.

In my experience, purchasing chicks through a local feedstore is the easiest option. The folks working at the feedstore are also often extremely knowledgeable and can help with all of your chicken care needs. There may be limited breed options at your feedstore, but they're usually great for backyard chicken keeping. Feedstores usually carry chicks only in the spring and summer, which are the best times of year to raise them.

ESSENTIALS FOR CHICKS

- Brooder box
- Pine shavings or straw for brooder box
- Heat lamp and bulb
- Chick feeder
- Chick waterer
- Chick feed
- Ground oatmeal

Bringing the Chicks Home

Make sure the carrier you are bringing your chicks home in has enough airflow and is a good temperature for the chicks in between the store and your home. Put them directly into the brooder once they're home. Make sure your chicks have found their food, water, and heat lamp. I like to give my chicks at least a day of rest before I start handling them (which is so hard when you have anxious little ones!). This allows them time to adjust and recover from the travel. Handle the chicks with great care once you start picking them up. Overhandling or rough handling can cause injury and even death, so try not to handle them too much. Baby chicks should not be away from access to the heat lamp for more than a couple minutes. They can spend more time away from their brooder, bonding with you, as they grow bigger and stronger. I've learned to hold our chicks by having one hand below and one hand above the chick, so its head is sticking out, but my hands have a gentle grasp on its body. Handling your chicks is sweet and fun, but just watching them run around, interact with each other, and sometimes fall asleep on one another is incredibly entertaining as well.

PULLETS AND COCKERELS

Many breeds of chicks are sexed, which means experts separate the sexes when they first hatch. Female chicks are called pullets and males are called cockerels. Some breeds are easier to sex than others. A straight run of chicks means they have not been sexed, and chances of a pullet or cockerel are 50/50. Though sexing chicks is not 100 percent accurate, it's pretty close; it has about a 95 percent accuracy rate. Your untrained eyes will not be able to see a rooster in the sexed brood of pullets until about 8 to 12 weeks of age, when you may begin hearing a cock-a-doodle-do. If you accidentally get a rooster, you can keep it, find a home for it, or butcher it.

ROOSTER OR NO ROOSTER?

Hens will produce eggs whether you have a rooster or not. The rooster's job is to fertilize the eggs in order for more chicks to develop. Eggs need to be fertilized under the right conditions in order to hatch, and some people prefer to eat fertilized eggs. A rooster might be for you if you want to hatch your own chicks, or like the sound of a rooster crowing at first light—and throughout the day. Another reason to have a rooster is for the flock's protection, especially if you intend on letting your chickens free range. A rooster will protect his hens until the death. Beware, however, that roosters can be aggressive toward anyone they see as a threat to their flock, including you. I really thought my rooster and I were buddies, and then one day I turned my back and—bam!—he was attacking me. Having a rooster is a personal choice. Some people really love it, and others don't.

No Pasty Butts

All your chicks should stay healthy with a clean and spacious brooder and enough warmth, feed, and water. Still, things happen, which is why it's good to keep a close eye on them. The best way to ensure your chicks' health is to observe them a few times a day. That's the fun part of the job! The hope is to know what normal chick behavior is in case a chick gets sick and starts to show abnormal behavior, which you will then be able to identify. It's a cause for concern if at any time a chick seems lethargic, isn't eating or drinking, is cheeping in a loud, stressed way, or isn't cheeping at all. Any of these symptoms can be a sign of "pasting up" or "pasty butt," which is perhaps one of the most common and deadliest health issues a chick can face.

Pasty butt is essentially when a chick's excretion vent gets clogged by feces sticking to its butt, making the chick unable to poop. If you see this, immediately wet the affected area with a warm, wet cloth and start pulling off the dried fecal matter. You will most likely be pulling off some down feather too, but that's OK. After cleaning the affected area, you can also gently probe the chick's vent with mineral oil and a Q-tip to help ease the situation. After the acute vent closure is handled, feed the chick finely ground oatmeal mixed in with its feed to help resolve and prevent pasting up.

If a chick seems sick and doesn't have pasty butt or any obvious injuries, it is a good idea to separate that chick with its own food, water, and heat lamp. Unfortunately, chicks are tiny and fragile. Sometimes they get injured or have health issues, and sometimes they just die. It's simply nature's way.

From the Brooder to the Coop

Your chicks are ready to graduate from the brooder to the coop once they've lost their soft down feathers and their adult feathers have grown in. This means their adult feathers can now regulate their temperature. I usually start to leave the heat lamp off during the day around 4 weeks old, putting it on only at night until the chicks are about 6 weeks of age. All of this of course depends on the weather. If you are not introducing your started chicks to a new flock at 6 weeks, and if all their down has been replaced with feathers, you can go ahead and put them in their new coop.

If you're introducing your chicks to a new flock, it is better to wait until they're bigger and stronger. I usually wait until they are about 8 to 10 weeks old. In this case, make sure they have enough room in the brooder, as they get increasingly larger and more active. There is a social hierarchy within normal chicken behavior, and the new starter chickens will be at the bottom of the pecking order (yes, that is where that saying comes from). This behavior can seem intense, as the older chickens boss around, chase, and peck the teenager chickens. As long as there is ample room, food, and water in the coop,

the youngsters learn to steer clear of the bosses and everyone should assimilate rather quickly.

I like introducing new chickens at night while both parties are roosting. I'll put the starters in around dusk and by the morning, though the pecking order is still in place, everyone is usually acting like nothing is really new. Still, I always keep an extra eye on them the first few days after introducing to make sure everyone is getting along.

Health Management

There is still so much to learn about your flock, and focusing on a healthy diet and environment are the best ways to prevent future issues. But inevitably, chickens get sick, injured, and die young for even the most diligent chicken keeper. Because health management is such a large topic, I'm going to answer a few common beginner questions, but I implore you to find resources for specific problems and questions as they arise. Your local feedstore should be able to help you with basic chicken ailments and questions, and hopefully you can find a chicken mentor to rely on in addition to the enormous number of books and online resources available to help you manage your flock's health.

Something Seems Wrong with My Chicken

Chickens are usually very good at letting you know when something is wrong. If you know your chicken's normal behavior, spotting a sick or injured chicken should be pretty easy. Usually they will be away from the rest of the flock and not scratching or pecking. Their feathers will be fluffed up, and they will just seem off. If you notice something is wrong with one of your chickens, whether it seems lethargic or injured or is being attacked by the flock, immediately remove that chicken and put it somewhere quiet and safe. Then mash up some chicken feed with milk,

make sure the bird also has water, and observe it. If the bird has a wound, it should be cleaned with hydrogen peroxide and smeared with an antibacterial salve. The chicken must be kept separate until the wound is completely healed. If the bird appears ill and is not improving after a few days of isolation, it could be time to cull that bird from the flock or call a vet if you choose.

My Hen Won't Get Off Her Eggs

Some hens get broody after laying an egg, which is the natural instinct to want to lay on and incubate their egg. An extremely broody hen will fluff herself up and even peck at you to stay away. She may barely leave to get food and water throughout the day. This can be handled by removing her from her nest, which may have to happen over and over throughout the day (wearing gloves is a good idea to protect yourself). If broodiness continues, you may even have to completely cut off her access to the nesting box.

My Chicken Is Losing Feathers

Once a year, usually in the fall, chickens lose their feathers in order to grow new ones. This is called molting. With some birds, you will barely notice their molting, while others can look almost bare. Make sure they have adequate nutrition during this period; I like to give my birds extra protein. Feather loss can also indicate other health issues. If the feathers do not seem to be growing back or if the bird seems to have nonstop itching, something else—like mites—is probably wrong.

My Flock Is Attacking One Chicken

Chickens that are bored or live in overcrowded conditions can resort to cannibalism. Nutritional deficiencies or lack of water can also be a contributing factor for this instinctive behavior. If another bird is weak or injured, it is not uncommon to see the flock pecking and pulling out the feathers of the weakling (this can happen in your brooder too). Having healthy conditions and removing and isolating any injured or weak chickens from the flock should help prevent any cannibalism.

Your Own Flock

I hope this section on chickens has given you a glimpse into what backyard chicken keeping can look and feel like. Having your own flock is a continuous cycle throughout the year, connecting you to nature's rhythm. When you have your own flock and are collecting and eating fresh eggs, there is a feeling of satisfaction, respect, and gratitude for an age-old tradition that is hard to get when you buy a carton of eggs at the store. The process of having chickens is all about learning through trial and error and developing your own connection to these avian beings. It doesn't mean chicken keeping is easy or always perfect, but it is your experience. The door is wide open for you to keep learning. I wish you happy chicken keeping and a journey filled with deep experiences, joy, and lots of eggs!

Meat Birds

It can be incredibly rewarding to raise, butcher, and consume your own bird meat, but this section is certainly not for everyone. If raising and butchering your own chickens is not for you, try to find chicken meat at your local farmers market or look for labels that say "organic" and "certified humane raised and handled" in your grocery stores. Conscious shopping or raising your own meat are the healthiest options for both humans and birds.

The broiler industry is where chickens are raised for meat, and like so many other farming industries, it has become factory farming to ensure massive output and profits. Broiler birds are packed into houses where they don't see sunshine, can barely stretch their wings, and are debeaked around 10 days old. They're unable to participate in normal chicken behavior like pecking because of their extreme lack of space.

Factories create artificial environments, and the birds are fed low-dose antibiotics throughout their short life in order to fight bacterial infections, which flourish in these unnatural and unhealthy conditions. The birds are bred to produce the maximum amount of meat in a short amount of time. Some side effects of this process are heart failure and broken legs due to such rapid growth rates. This is the quality of the chicken meat from any average store. There's so much more to know about the harsh conditions of factory farming, and why raising your own meat or conscious shopping is important on so many levels. I encourage you to continue to learn.

My family has chosen to eat meat, and therefore we feel it is important to understand and be a part of the entire process of the animal's life. We feel like this gives us more of an appreciation for our food. My husband and I always work together when butchering, and we are by no means experts. We are constantly learning more every time we butcher.

There are many different approaches to and theories on butchering animals, but for the sake of keeping it simple, I'll explain what has worked best for us so far. If this is your first time slaughtering, I highly recommend taking a butchering class or learning from someone with experience until you get the hang of it. This section is intended to inspire beginner backyard butchers and offer a bigger picture of the process of raising your bird from start to finish.

We are deeply satisfied knowing our meat came from our birds, where we know exactly how they lived, what they ate, and how humanely they were butchered. There is a beautiful connection to the animal that builds an immense appreciation. I hope this section inspires and helps you reconnect to the source of meat on your table, whether that means raising your bird from start to finish or taking more care and pride in your shopping.

Getting the Right Broiler

There are several different breeds of broiler chickens you can choose from, including the Cornish Cross, Freedom Ranger, Bresse, Jersey Giant, and many more. Each of these breeds has different growth rates and ideal butcher weights. On average, it takes about 3 to 4 months (12 to 16 weeks) for broilers to reach the ideal weight for slaughter.

Breeds that are bred for a fast growth rate and meat production can have health problems, which I want to stay clear of and therefore do not use. I prefer Freedom Rangers because they have a slower growth rate and their builds seem healthier. Ultimately, the breed choice is up to you, so it's a good idea to research options or talk with someone who has raised different breeds of broilers.

KEY TERMS

BROILER CHICKEN: A young chicken that will be used for meat

SLAUGHTER: To kill an animal for food

BUTCHER: To cut up an animal for food

HARVEST: To kill an animal

CHOANAL SLIT: The slit in the roof or top beak of the chicken's mouth

SCALDING: To use extremely hot water in order to help defeather the chicken

BRAIN SCRAMBLE: Stabbing the brain in order to cut off its communication system

EVISCERATION: To remove the entrails from a creature, or disembowel

CROP: The area behind the bird's neck where it stores food for preprocessing

VENT: The area where urine and fecal matter are excreted

You can order your batch of broiler chicks from a hatchery online, or, if possible, find a local breeding source. Raising broiler chicks follows the same process as raising laying chicks. You want them to have the best life possible. Happy, healthy chickens mean tasty, healthy meat. I choose to feed my broiler chicks food that is specifically for growing meat birds. I like Modesto Milling organic chick starter and poultry grower crumbles until about 8 to 10 weeks of age, and then switch to Modesto Milling organic poultry broiler finisher pellets until it's time to butcher.

The Harvest

I always have a pit in my stomach on butchering day, and I always have compassion for the animal I'm butchering. This feeling hasn't decreased even after years of doing it, and the complexity of that feeling is part of the process for me. There's pride for raising the animal, but at the same time sadness for taking its life.

A question my husband and I often get is how we handle butchering animals with our children. We tell them from the moment the animal is born, hatched, or arrives that it is for our food. We

SUPPLIES

← A large, sanitized table (stainless steel or plastic folding tables work great)

← Sharp knives

← A killing cone, which stabilizes the bird upside down during the butcher

← A clean cutting board

← Latex, disposable gloves

← Large, clean clippers for taking off the legs and neck

← Buckets for blood, entrails, and feathers

← Thermometer for checking scalding water temperature

← Bucket filled with hot water at 145°F

← Access to a fresh hose for rinsing the bird

← A vacuum sealer and bags for storage

← Somewhere to immediately chill meat, like an ice chest or fridge/freezer

THE SLAUGHTER

Make sure your birds have fasted for 24 hours before slaughter, but that they have had access to clean water. First, catch the chicken, carry it upside down by the feet, and place it in the killing cone feet-side up. Pull the head firmly through the bottom of the cone so the bird is upside down. Make sure a bucket to catch the blood is below. You may need an extra pair of hands to keep the bird in place. The bird should be in a stunned state and should be relaxed.

My husband and I believe the quickest and most humane way to butcher is to use the brain-scramble or brain-stabbing method. To do this, you must open the bird's beak. Through the choanal slit in the roof of the bird's mouth, take a sharp knife, pierce it into the brain above the pallet, and twist. Make sure your hand is not behind where you are cutting, as you want to avoid the knife piercing all the way through the bird and injuring you. The bird should shudder and then become limp.

Cut the throat through the jugular vein in the bird's neck. Make sure the head is all the way down in the cone to let it bleed out as quickly as possible. This process can take anywhere from 5 to 10 minutes. Remove the bird from the cone once it has bled out and is unresponsive.

name the animals and take great care of them, but we are honest from the beginning and throughout each animal's life. We tell our children that it is OK to feel sad, thankful, or anywhere in between. It's OK if they partake in any part of our home butchering, and it's OK if they don't feel like having any part in it. We leave it up to them, and keep the conversations open and honest.

The main goal and intention to our approach is to harvest the chicken with the least amount of stress or pain possible. This is not only best for the animal, but also best for the meat. Lactic acid and adrenaline are pumped through an animal's body if it becomes stressed, and this can cause the meat to become tough. We like to do every step by hand, which means no machines, like pluckers, to help. Setup takes 30 minutes to an hour, and then each bird takes about 20 to 30 minutes to slaughter and then butcher. We usually do about 10 to 20 birds a day.

The Butcher

Use your whole chicken! You can use the various parts of the chicken instead of discarding them. It is a good idea to save the giblets—the neck, gizzard, heart, and liver. Traditionally, these parts are used to make stocks, gravy, and—my favorite—liver pâté. But their uses don't stop there. Learn, get creative, and experiment. See Emma's section for some more ideas.

REMOVE THE HEAD AND FEET

Start with removing the head and feet. To remove the head, cut directly through the neck bones just under the jawline of the chicken. To remove the feet, make your cut at the knee joint of the bird. The easiest way to cut or quarter your bird is always cutting through the joints, in between the bones. First, it's the path of least resistance, and second, you'll keep your knife sharper this way by not cutting through bone. When you're cutting the feet off, imagine cutting the joint just below the drumstick or chicken leg. The clippers can help.

REMOVE THE NECK

Make sure the bird is on its back. With a sharp knife, start by cutting a circle through the skin around the base where the neck meets the body cavity. You should then discover the crop, which you will need to remove by separating it from the actual neck bone. You may need to reach two fingers into the right side of the bird just below the neck to find the crop. The crop is a translucent sac where the bird stores its food for preprocessing. The crop should be empty, as the bird should not have been fed for 24 hours prior to slaughter. If it's not, try to remove the crop without leaking the contents. If any contents are spilled, rinse the area thoroughly.

With clippers or a sharp knife, remove any tube structures you find around the neck, including the esophagus, windpipe, and the actual neck bone. When removing the neck bone,

SCALDING AND PLUCKING

Place the bird in a bucket full of scalding hot (145°F) water. Swirl it with a large spoon, making sure it is evenly under the water. Check after 60 seconds to see if the feathers can easily be removed. Once the feathers can be removed, bring the bird back onto the table and pluck the entire bird, discarding the feathers. Don't worry if you need to put the bird back into the scald tank for the tougher feathers; just be aware that it will start to cook the meat if left in too long.

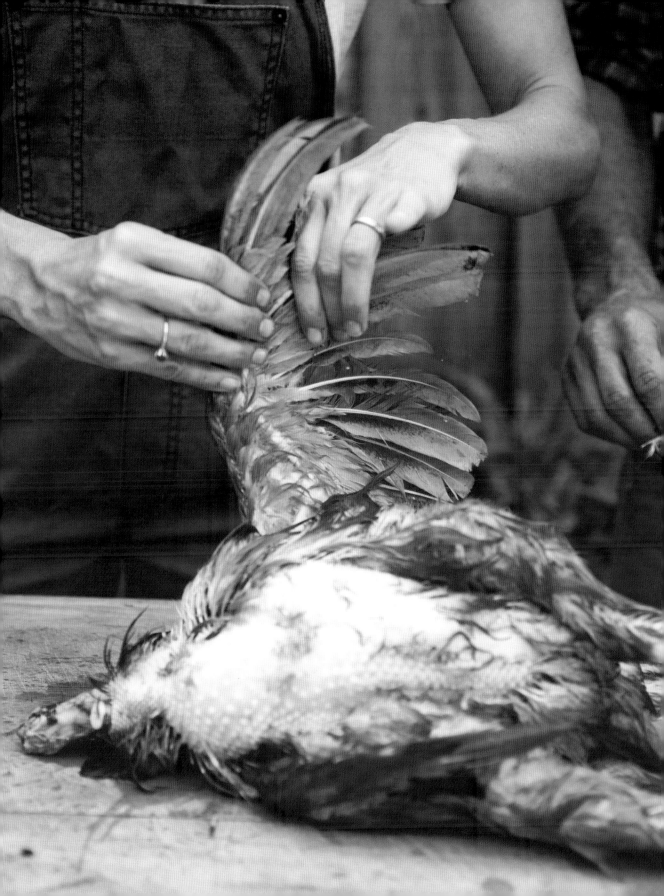

cut as far down and close to the bird's body as you can. Cutting the neck may take a little elbow grease, so don't be afraid to get in there!

GUT THE CHICKEN

With the bird still on its back, you will need to cut a line across the cavity (stomach) a couple inches above the excretion vent. It helps to pinch the skin above where you are making the cut. With a sharp knife, make a 1- to 2-inch slit across the bird, through the skin and fat. Try not to make the slice too deep, as you do not want to pierce the intestines.

Now, with two fingers on either side, reach in and pull hard in opposite directions to open up the back end of the body cavity. Next, cut out the bird's excretion vent. Starting at the bottom of your now-open cavity, cut a V-shape around the bird's vent in order to fully remove it.

With the vent gone, it's time to reach in and pull the insides out. You'll need to loosen everything up, and it might take some more elbow grease to do so.

Reach inside of the bird and loosen the organs. Loosen everything you can feel from the lining of the body before pulling. You will feel a hard, ball-like organ (the gizzard), which is a great hold to grab onto when pulling out the organs. Try to get everything at one time; this makes for a cleaner exit and less likelihood of the bladder popping or intestine breaking. Make sure you scrape against the rib cage to get the lungs out. Make sure to get all the organs out, including the gizzard, entrails/intestines, liver, heart, and lungs. Don't let the organs go to waste! Gizzards, livers, and hearts are a great part of the harvest.

If keeping the liver, be sure to remove the gallbladder, which is the tiny sac connected to the liver that you can distinguish by its green color. Cut into the liver to cut that bit out. If the gallbladder breaks, it can taint the flavor of your meat.

If keeping the gizzard, cut into the mass until you find what's inside—tiny stones! Rinse the gizzard out and remove the waxy yellow lining. It's ready to fry up or add to soup.

RINSE AND PACKAGE

Rinse the bird inside and out several times with cold water and put the bird straight in a cooler full of ice to chill.

Vacuum sealing is an essential part of freezing and storing your birds. Sealing is a relatively easy process where you put the bird in a plastic bag and the vacuum sealer sucks out the surrounding air and seals the bag. It properly freezes your bird so it won't get freezer burn. I usually let the butchered bird chill for about 30 minutes to an hour in the cooler before I vacuum seal it, and then I put the vacuum-sealed bird in the fridge to "age" for 24 hours before freezing it.

You can purchase a vacuum sealer and bags for around $70, and it's well worth it. A vacuum seal is essential in order to store your fresh meat in the freezer.

Have a Dinner Party

Share your hard work and the bounty of your home-raised bird with friends and family! I hope this section has given you some insight into what raising and harvesting your own birds could be like. Whether you have butchered your own bird or not, hopefully this is the beginning of a journey of looking at your meat in a new, critical, and educated way.

Morris Honey Company

NICOLE ULABARRI

Nicole Ulabarri is a ball of energy, always talking about her bees and what hives need to be checked, moved, harvested, need queens, and more. As a budding beekeeper myself, I can't get enough of her. Nicole is a third-generation beekeeper who now runs Morris Honey. She is as hardworking as they come, and her knowledge of bees and their behaviors, needs, and challenges is mind-blowing. She opens a hive and knows exactly what is going on inside—which bees have which jobs, and which is doing what. Bees take a lifetime to master. The more you learn, the less you find out you know, but beginning beekeeping has brought my family joy, humbleness, and, of course, sweet honey. I am so honored to share a slice of Nicole's lifetime expertise.

Honeybees

The honeybee is a crucial player in the production of more than 90 fruits and vegetables grown in the United States. It is a pollinator for so many of the crops each American enjoys on a daily basis. Morris Honey Company bees not only pollinate the almond blooms in the Central Valley of California in February and March, but also provide pollination for Canola plants in North Dakota in the summertime.

Honeybees are a great example of one of the highest-functioning societies that exist. While observing a healthy, happy colony, you will notice that each bee has a specific job and remains focused on it. This includes the nursery, where the nurse bees take care of the eggs; attendant bees that tend to the queen bee's every need; forage bees that gather nectar and pollen, flying up to 3 miles away from the hives; and, of course, the queen bee that keeps the entire colony running efficiently.

Beekeeping Basics

When handling bees, always consider safety first. Always wear the proper equipment and have a smoker. To learn the most about bees, find an experienced beekeeper who can help you set up a hive. As a first-time beekeeper, the basics of understanding the components of a hive and safety gear will take some time, but eventually, you will get more comfortable with these aspects and start to learn about the hive and the bees themselves. Nicole suggests that you sit and observe the bees in flight. You don't even need to open the hive to learn. Just watch their flight patterns, what time and temperature the most flights exist in, and when they are all heading back home to the hive.

Periodically, you should open your hive and start learning about its internal workings. Start on the very outside frame and pull up one frame, working

toward the middle. You should not disturb the bees frequently, as you may damage the queen or cause other harmful disruptions. Nicole also suggests paying a bit extra for a "marked queen" when you go to populate your hive. This will make identification of the queen much easier until your eye is trained to easily spot her. When you start learning about bees, you will catch the buzz. They are fascinating and have so much to teach us!

Backyard Honey Harvesting

Collecting honey in your backyard has to be one of the most rewarding hobbies around. Not only do you get the gift of continually learning about these fascinating creatures and their honey-making process, but you also get your own golden, unbelievably sweet honey at the end of all your hard work and care. There are different ways to collect and harvest honey—and of course more expensive equipment can be used—but here are some basics.

First, you need to know when to harvest the honey. There are a few indicators that tell you it's time. The first is at the end of a good nectar season, after the bees have had their fill collecting nectar and pollen and have capped more than 80 percent of the honey cells on the frame. The season varies depending on

where you live, so make sure you are in tune with your local seasons, bloom dates, and bees. Checking the hive every two weeks leading up to harvest time is a good idea so you can see the progress being made and know you are harvesting at the correct time. Know where your honey is versus where your brood frames are. It is best to wait until the bees have collected *all* the honey they can, so be patient!

Once you know it's the right time and you have all of your equipment on and ready, including your smoker lit, it's time to begin. Using the smoker, approach the beehive from behind and puff the smoke around the hive entrance. Remove the top and smoke the opening to drive the bees lower into the hive. Next, remove the cover and open up your super boxes using your hive tool. Smoke your hive again, and pull out your first capped honey frame. (Double check to confirm these are frames filled with honey and not brood.) Now, use your bee brush to gently brush any bees off of the frame, being careful not to hurt any of the hard workers. Last, put the full frame in an empty box ready for transport to where you will be collecting the liquid gold.

Bees need their honey to survive the winter and in times when there isn't nectar for them. The number of honey-filled frames you'll need to leave for your bees depends on your climate, so it's best to consult with a local, knowledgeable beekeeper who can help you decide how much to leave behind and if you'll need to feed during non-nectar seasons.

Now that you have your honey-filled frames, you are ready to extract the honey! Place your strainer on top of your open bucket. Use your uncapping knife and fork to extract the honey from the frame. If your frame is foundation-less, meaning the bees built the entire comb, cut the complete comb out of the frame. If your frame has a foundation, cut the built comb off the foundation. Either way, the comb and honey should go into the strainer, which will catch all the comb while the honey falls into the bucket below. Use the tap on your honey bucket to bottle your honey. Now you have one of nature's richest gifts in your hand!

Key Terms

SAFETY EQUIPMENT: Bee suit including veil, gloves, and boots

SMOKER: Used to light material and create smoke that is then used to calm the bees; generally burlap is used to fuel the smoker, but other options include wood pellets and dried leaves

HIVE TOOL: A multipurpose tool used to lift the lid and help inspect the hives

BEE BRUSH: A tool used to gently brush bees off the comb or wherever else needed

HONEY-UNCAPPING KNIFE: A very sharp knife designed to cut through the wax capping on the comb (comes in hot or cold versions; the hot knife plugs into the wall and heats up to make cutting the comb easier)

HONEY-UNCAPPING FORK OR CAPPING SCRATCHER: A tool designed to help scratch off the wax capping to release the honey

HONEY STRAINER: A double sieve with two separate mesh screens in order to filter the honey effectively

BOTTLING BUCKET: A bucket with a spigot at the bottom that makes bottling the filtered honey easier

HONEYBEE: Many varieties exist, but the most common are the Italian and Carniolan

BEEHIVE: The box structure that houses the bee colony

BEE COLONY: The group of bees living together in the hive, including the worker bees, the queen, and in the summer the drone bees

SUPER BOXES: Boxes that store the comb

HONEYCOMB: The frames that are in the super boxes; each frame is used for either storage of pollen and nectar or as a place for the queen to lay her eggs

BROOD: Eggs in the colony of developing bees

BEE LID: Lid to place on top of the hive

BOTTOM BOARD: Placed on the bottom of the hive under the boxes to create a floor between the bees and the ground

PACKAGE BEES: Bulk bees sold with a queen that can be ordered online and then installed in your hive (an experienced beekeeper should help you introduce the queen)

DAIRY COWS

The most profound human and animal connection I've had was with a Holstein cow I named Purdy when I was 12 years old. I met her at the dairy farm where I helped. Purdy was premature and had failed to thrive as a calf, and I suggested bringing her home with me so I could give her more attention. She thrived with all of the diligence, patience, and constant care that my family and I were able to give her. She was so attached to me that, like Mary and her lamb, everywhere I went, Purdy was sure to follow. Even after returning her to the dairy farm, she'd come running from the pasture if I called her name. I had the honor of delivering her first calf, which I named Belle.

The dairy farm closed a few years later, when I was in my late teens, as so many small dairies unfortunately do these days. It felt as though a chapter in my life had closed. It wasn't until I met my husband and had a family of my own that I got another cow. I wanted it for me, and to bring the experience of having a cow and its fresh milk to my children. As I write this, my cow Ruby is ready to have her calf any minute. Her belly is huge; her udder is full in preparation. All I can do is love on her and wait. This is truly one of the best and most exciting times of the year for me, so here I am, patiently (or not so patiently) waiting for this year's calf to arrive.

As you can probably tell, this section is particularly heartfelt for me. I love having a dairy cow, but it is a huge commitment and definitely

A Brief History of Milk

It is thought that cows, goats, and sheep were domesticated for their meat and milk a mere 10,000 years ago. Having a dairy animal ensured a constant source of nutrients for our ancestors. Abundant grass and hay ensured the cows would produce the milk necessary for butter, yogurt, and cheese. The cow quickly became the premier dairy animal due to its temperament, its ability to work and carry heavy loads, and the versatility and nutritious content of its milk.

It wasn't until the mid-1800s that crowded urban areas introduced large dairy farms to cities in order to provide fresh milk for the masses. With the rise in excess grain from alcohol distilleries, this new dairy feed seemed too good to be true—and it was. The grain nutrient from this waste was poor. With their extremely unsanitary conditions, these farms soon became home to foodborne illnesses such as tuberculosis and typhoid fever. It wasn't until the late 1800s—when French biologist Louis Pasteur discovered pasteurization, a process in which raw milk is heated to kill infectious microbes—that these diseases began to diminish.

Dairy farms then headed back out into the countryside, where cows could graze on fresh grass, have healthier diets, and enjoy the sunshine—until factory farming came along. (Catching the theme?) The average dairy cow is confined inside, and overcrowding leads to disease. To counteract such exposure, cows are prophylactically injected with antibiotics and rBGH, a hormone that increases milk yield. This not only leads to bovine health issues, but also human ones. Frightening, isn't it?

Having your own dairy cow is not feasible for everyone, of course, so how can you make the best decisions as a dairy consumer? Getting your milk directly from a local dairy farmer, herdshare, or at your farmers market is the most ideal situation. Being able to talk to the folks

not for everyone. In this section, I'll provide an overview and basic information about what owning a dairy cow looks like. It won't answer all your questions, but it's a starting point for a learning journey to begin. I encourage you to read more books on dairy cow care, visit a local dairy or someone with a cow, or take a class if available.

who are caring for the animals providing your dairy and supporting small farms is incredibly impactful and empowering as a consumer.

When heading to the grocery store, there are so many options when buying milk and dairy products that it can feel overwhelming. Most labels do not address the treatment of the animals, but rather what they are fed. For example, "organic" means the cow has been fed organic feed and has not been injected with rBGH (artificial growth hormones) or been on antibiotics, but it doesn't mean they get turned out to pasture. The label "rBST-free" indicates milk produced without hormones or rBST, but this label does not indicate how the animals are treated or what they are fed. A "grass-fed" label means the cows have access to grass during the growing season and have not been fed grain, soy, or by-products, but unless otherwise stated, hormones and antibiotics are allowed. There are animal welfare certifications, but they are difficult to find at your average grocer. It can be so frustrating. The hope is that feed and welfare standards become stricter and labeling becomes clearer. Until then, try to seek out a farmer you can talk to if you can.

Raw vs. Pasteurized Milk

Most of us have been taught that raw milk is dangerous, and it certainly can be if the animal and milk are not handled correctly. In the mainstream media, you rarely hear about the benefits of fresh, raw milk. The main problem is its short shelf life. A solution to this has been pasteurization, which has greatly increased the shelf life of milk, making the global milk industry possible. But in the process of heating the milk to kill bad bacteria, the good vitamins and important enzymes are also lost. The pasteurization process also alters the milk's natural proteins. In California, as well as a few other states, it is legal for retailers to sell raw milk, so you can find it in specialty grocery

stores. Having your own dairy animal gives you the choice to either pasteurize the milk at home or drink it raw.

My family chooses to consume our milk raw. I am comfortable with this choice because I know the health of my cow, and I follow a thorough, sanitary milking and milk-storage routine. We consume our milk within a couple of days to ensure freshness, and if there is excess we make our own yogurt.

The choice is up to you. If you'd like to pasteurize your milk at home, heat it to 145°F for 30 minutes, stirring occasionally. Then pour the milk into a jar and immediately put it on ice for 20 to 30 minutes to reduce the temperature. Store it in the fridge.

A Day in the Life of a Cow

The average day of my family's milk cow starts with feeding her a breakfast of hay. Then we check her water, clean out her manure in the barn area, and milk her. It is a total process of about 30 to 60 minutes. Her day is mostly spent eating, walking around, resting, laying down, swatting at flies, interacting with other cows, mooing (especially when she sees me and knows food is coming), chewing her cud, and being milked (if she's in milk). I try to check on her in the afternoon if I'm home. I'll say hello, scratch behind her ears and under her chin, and give her a treat or two. Sometimes I take her for a walk or let her in the yard to graze, though if unattended she will eat my garden in no time! It's important to spend time with your lady cow, especially if she is by herself. When evening comes around, it's time for her hay dinner. We check the water again, clean the manure out of the barn, and say goodnight.

A Year in the Life of a Cow

A year in the life of a dairy cow is a cycle that will keep on repeating in order for your cow to keep producing milk. This annual cycle takes planning and a good deal of forethought and management on your part. Just like every other mammal, your cow must have a calf in order to produce milk. Most cow owners breed their cow yearly. This yearly cycle looks something like this: She is first bred at 18 months old, either naturally if there is a bull available or by using artificial insemination (AI). She gives birth about 9 months (283 days) later and will then be producing milk. She will be bred again 3 months after giving birth. About 7 months after she is bred, she will be dried off, which means she will get a break from being milked and producing milk, and then 2 months later she will again give birth and the cycle continues. This is the average life of a dairy cow, but of course, once you have your own cow, her management will be up to you.

Dairy Cow Breeds

There are more than a thousand different breeds of cows throughout the world. Breeds have been developed through selective breeding for their ability to live in certain climates, for their looks, and of course for specialized human uses, such as milk and meat production. I grew up in Vermont with large Holstein cows, but for a family cow, I have chosen a smaller breed, the Jersey. I did this for several reasons, the main one being that my daughters were small and I thought a smaller cow would more easily facilitate their helping. However, there are so many great breeds out there, so I encourage you to research and choose the right breed for your needs. It's a critical piece of the picture to ensure success between both you and your bovine. Here are a few different breed options.

Dexter

A great homesteading cow, this gentle, small-sized breed originated in Ireland and is known as a dual-purpose breed supplying both good milk and meat. Full grown they weigh around 700 pounds, and they produce 1½ to 3 gallons of rich milk a day. This milk has a high butterfat content.

Holstein

This classic breed is known for its beautiful black and white markings and is also known for its grand size and mega milk production. Weighing in at around 1,600 pounds, these cows can produce upward of 8 or 9 gallons a day and are primarily used for commercial milk production. I would not recommend this lovely cow for a beginner milker.

Jersey

Standard Jersey cows are known for their docile temperaments and smaller size. Their milk is high in butterfat, and they produce between 3 and 4 gallons of milk per day. They weigh around 900 to 1,000 pounds.

Miniature Jersey

Weighing a few hundred pounds less than a standard Jersey, miniature Jerseys produce about a gallon or less of milk a day. They are relatively easy to handle and are known for being sweet and docile. They are curious by nature and, in my opinion, make wonderful family cows.

Brown Swiss

Perhaps one of the oldest dairy breeds, the Brown Swiss originated in Switzerland. They can be brown, tan, gray, or even whitish. They are known to be docile and easy to handle, yet they are on the bigger side. They weigh around 1,300 pounds and produce around 5 gallons of milk a day. Their milk has a high butterfat content and is often used for making cheese. Someday I want a Brown Swiss.

Milking Shorthorn or Dairy Shorthorn

This breed is a mid-sized cow with red and white markings. They are known for their easy temperaments, grazing efficiency, and fertility. They are hardy cows also known for their longevity. They produce high-quality milk in the mid-production range, around 5 to 6 gallons per day.

Needs

A family dairy cow needs a fenced space, shelter, clean water, hay or grass as feed, grain when in milk, and vitamins and minerals. Your dairy cow should be friendly and docile and love human attention, as you will spend a great deal of time down by her udder and back end. A wild, scared cow can be dangerous and unmanageable. Dairy animals need attention, and it is important to nurture a connection with them. A trusting relationship will ensure that milking and management is a pleasurable experience for both of you. A cow can be solitary but does prefer a buddy, even if it's a different species.

My family's cow lives on about two acres of land, but with the California climate being what it is, the area does not supply nearly enough grass for her primary diet. Her main diet, therefore, is purchased hay, and we grain her when she's in milk. She has access to a sheltered barn area, where fresh water and minerals are always available. The sheltered area is also where we milk her.

Mother and Calf Management

I feel it is important to explain how I manage the mother and her calf. A normal dairy farmer removes the calf from its mother at birth, and the distraught calf is then supplemented with milk replacer, a dried powder mixed with water given by bottle and bucket. Instead, I choose to keep the calf nursing and hand milk the mother once a day, taking only what milk I need. The cow's milk regulates itself naturally, and the calf and my family happily share the bounty together. Keeping the calf on its mother makes sense for us for several reasons. First, there is no stressful separation for mother and calf. Second, the calf receives all the nutrients it needs naturally from its mother. And last, by doing it this way I don't have to stress if I am unable to milk for some reason that day—all will be well. Remember, though, if the calf is not nursing off the mama, you will need to milk twice daily and always at the same time in order to relieve her udder and prevent infections like mastitis from developing. How you manage your cow and calf are up to you.

Finding Your Cow

When considering purchasing your own milk cow, I suggest that you spend time with your prospective cow to make sure she is friendly and cooperative. If this is your first cow, I highly recommend one that has already had a calf and has been or is "in milk." Buying a cow that is already trained to be milked can make the process a lot easier, safer, and more enjoyable. She should be halter trained, since she must be restrained, and lead without worry or stress. This will make life with your cow so much easier. She should relish attention and not be the least bit skittish.

If you are buying a heifer—a cow that has not had a calf and therefore hasn't been milked— make sure she is hand raised and accustomed to human attention. Make sure you are able to walk up to the cow you are considering while she is not in a stanchion and touch and caress her all over. This part of the process is so very crucial; the last thing you want is to have a mean and dangerous cow to handle. A family, hand-raised cow will in the long run be worth its weight in gold.

If possible, bring your bovine vet or a seasoned cow owner with you to meet your potential lady. There are many questions to ask the potential cow's owner, including the breeding and calving history of the cow. Ask if she is papered and about her health history. Make sure the cow is fully vaccinated and ask to see her records to confirm tests for Bang's disease (Brucellosis) and TB (tuberculosis). If transporting the cow across state lines, you'll need to have the appropriate vaccination documentation. If the owner says she is bred, having your vet preg check her is always a good idea. I purchased a cow that I thought was pregnant. Turned out, she not only wasn't pregnant, but was unable to get pregnant. Sadly, I do think the owner knew she had a problem and chose not to disclose it. That cow now lives at a local farmstand as a well-loved mascot, but I spent a lot of money and time on that lesson.

There are many places to start your search for a cow. I have found cows on the internet, on bulletin boards in feedstores, and by word of mouth. A great place to start is to call your local bovine vet or feedstore to ask if they know where you can get a family-raised cow. Wherever you find your prospective cow, make sure it's from a reputable farm.

Emotional Care

Cows can live alone even though they're herd animals by nature, but they do prefer other cows or animals around for company. If alone, they will need even more attention from you. In order to manage and milk your cow daily, it is imperative that your cow enjoys your company and trusts you. You will be spending lots of time squatting down by her back end while milking, and a wild, skittish cow can be incredibly dangerous. Hopefully you have selected a hand-raised, sweet, calm cow, but it's still important to spend time with her. My cow loves getting scratched under her chin or brushed all over. She's big on treats, like sweet feed or carrots. I try to spend at least 20 minutes a day just hanging out with her, time that's separate from milking or feeding.

Vet

You will need to locate a bovine vet near you for vaccinations, breeding, and in case of emergencies. Make sure to ask your vet which vaccinations are required in your area. Cow vets are expensive because they come to your house, which is easier than transporting your cow every time you need the vet. Hopefully vet visits only happen once or twice a year for breeding and yearly vaccinations. However, if your cow is lying down and won't get up, or she's not eating for a day, you should certainly contact your vet. Being aware of your cow's normal behavior is important in understanding and spotting any off behavior, which could mean there is a problem. Observe your cow for 10 minutes a day. It might sound crazy, but it is so important for her overall health to understand her normal behavior.

Parasite Control

Internal parasites such as roundworms, tapeworms, and others are a concern and can cause your cow's health to decline rapidly. Diarrhea, rapid weight loss, and worms in the

stool are the major signs the cow has worms. There are several options to worm your cow, such as commercial wormers that can be fed, injected, or absorbed through your cow's skin. Younger cows need to be wormed every 3 to 4 months, while older cows can just be wormed in the spring if worms are not an issue. I believe apple cider vinegar helps with worms, as does having free-range diatomaceous earth available for my ladies. Preventing worms is much easier than getting rid of worms, so find a routine that works for you and your cow. Ask your vet to recommend wormers to help narrow down all your options.

Fencing, Land, and Shelter

Accommodations for a cow consist of some fenced-in land and a shelter of some sort. Cows are big animals—depending on the breed they can weigh anywhere between 600 and 1,700 pounds—so the fencing will need to safely contain her. The farmer I bought Ruby from had trained his cows to respect two strands of electric fence, which worked well for his herd. I have not used electric—I rely on T-posts and no-climb wire— but there are a variety of different wire and fence post types you can use. Researching materials that fit the criteria for your budget, land, and cow is a good idea.

Cows are somewhat versatile and can live in different-sized properties. I recommend having your cow on at least half an acre of land. Your cow will need a shelter in order to escape the elements. This is so important for her health and well-being. You must consider your climate when researching and deciding on a barn structure. Cows need to be able to escape the sun, wind, and of course the blistering cold. A great place to start your shelter research is considering your space available, climate, and budget.

Another consideration when planning a barn is where you will do the milking. I milk in the barn to avoid wind, rain, and sun. Depending on your climate, this can range from a roof on a two- to four-sided structure to a room reserved just for milking (my dream). Wherever you decide to milk, just make sure it's clean in order to reduce contaminants during the milking process.

A Safe Place

It will be necessary to have a place where your cow can safely be restrained for things like a vet visit. A stanchion works well for this, and can also be a great place to milk. Sweet feed or grain can be used as a good coercion when training your cow to enter her stanchion. Be aware when using this method that most cows will quickly realize there's a treat and come running into the stanchion. Also, put her in it when she isn't having procedures, so she thinks of it as a safe place. This part can often get overlooked, but training is a crucial part to owning a cow.

Feed and Water

The diet of your cow is incredibly important for her fertility, milk production, and overall health. Cows eat fresh grass, dried forage such as alfalfa hay, or a hay mix. I mostly feed my cow good-quality hay because she has limited access to green pasture. The most common types of hay are grass hays like timothy or bermuda, alfalfa hay, and mixed hay, which is a blend of alfalfa, grass, and oat hay. I prefer to vary these forages into her diet by rotating or mixing the types, since each hay has its specific benefits. Get your cow on a routine, and then stick to it. Changing feed can cause life-threatening digestive issues for your lady.

When my cow is in milk, I also feed her Modesto Milling organic dairy and livestock pellets as I am milking. The rule of thumb I go by is about 1 pound of grain for every 3 gallons of milk she is producing. Feeding her while milking adds

extra nutrition and calories to her diet and also keeps her pleasantly distracted.

How much you feed your cow will depend on the breed and size, as well as where she is in her yearly cycle. The rule of thumb is to feed your cow two percent of her body weight daily. You should know the standards for body conditions of your breed and do a monthly evaluation to make sure your cow is an appropriate weight.

You'll also need to consider proper storage of your cow's feed. Make sure hay is stored away from damp conditions, either under a shelter or covered by a tarp. If hay gets wet and stays damp, it will mold, and you cannot feed moldy hay to your girl! I use galvanized metal garbage cans with lids for grain storage. These cans help keep the grain fresh, dry, and rodent free.

COW STOMACHS

The cow is a ruminant animal, which means it has four stomach chambers in order to digest its food. Other ruminant animals include goats, buffalo, camels, sheep, deer, and giraffes. Here is the simple version of a cow's complex digestive tract: A cow eats her grass, hay, and vegetation, but does not fully break it down while chewing (she only has bottom teeth). The vegetation then moves to the rumen, the largest of the four stomach chambers. The food is broken down with microorganisms and turns into cud. Once the cow has had her fill and is resting, the cud is then regurgitated back into the cow's mouth for further chewing. Once the cud is chewed, it is swallowed again and passes through the other three chambers: the reticulum, the omasum, and the abomasum. What waste remains goes into the small intestine, large intestine, and then what has not been absorbed becomes manure.

Clean, accessible water is a must. As a rule of thumb, cows drink 1 gallon of water per 100 pounds of their body weight daily, and up to 2 gallons in extremely warm weather. I use an automatic waterer that I check on every day to make sure it is functioning properly.

VITAMINS AND MINERALS

You will need to provide supplements for your lady. It can be daunting to figure out which supplements and salt licks are right for her. Your cow's needs depend on the location, soil composition, and grass type. Other considerations are where your hay is grown and whether it's the first or second cut. I suggest consulting with your vet and feedstore, as they should be able to help you find the right combination of supplements. In our area, there's a lack of copper in the soil, so I give Ruby a free-choice cattle lick, which contains trace elements of copper, and free-choice organic kelp. She may only take a few licks a day, but it is packed with beneficial trace elements. I also give her organic apple cider vinegar. I think it's good for her overall health, specifically in preventing parasites. I usually have a cup available for her in a small bucket, which she can, and does, sip from throughout the day. Sometimes I add the apple cider vinegar to her water bucket—¼ cup per gallon of water.

Breeding

Using artificial insemination (AI) is the easiest, safest, and most popular method for breeding dairy cows. AI is when semen is collected in "straws" from a bull and then shipped to your vet, where it's stored in a liquid nitrogen tank at very low temperatures until needed. This method requires you to carefully monitor your cow's heat cycle in order to know when she is fertile. I recommend charting her cycle and symptoms of heat. Hopefully you will see a distinct and regular pattern. Cows go into heat, or estrus, generally every 17 to 24 days, with the average being every 21 days. Once your cow is in heat, she needs to be bred 12 to 24 hours after the first signs appear, as this will be her most fertile window. Being aware of your cow's "normal" behavior will help you more easily identify when it changes, indicating that she is coming into heat. These signs include mounting other cows around her, being mounted and standing, not eating normally, vaginal swelling and discharge, excessive mooing, restlessness, and behaving slightly off. Alert your vet and make a plan if you're using AI and see these signs. If your cow does not come back into heat 17 to 24 days after she has been bred, she might be pregnant. I usually have my vet come do an ultrasound 6 weeks after she is bred to confirm.

Labor and Delivery

A cow's gestation period is around 283 days, or roughly 9 months. Most cows give birth effortlessly and without assistance, but it is always a good idea to have your vet on call just in case. It is best to let nature take its course and just observe the miracle of birth, intervening only if necessary. I always try to be present when our cow is giving birth, as it is such a privilege to watch a new baby come into the world. One time I had been diligently watching, saw no signs she was in labor, and returned home a couple hours later to a dry and healthy calf. With cows, you can look for all the signs that birth is near, but you will never truly know when they'll go into labor.

Still, I am constantly checking my cow for any body changes as labor gets closer. Every cow is different, and some cows show more obvious labor signs than others. Usually, the first sign is the swelling of the udder. This can happen months to days before labor. The udder grows big, but starts to actually squirt milk when labor is imminent. Her vulva will begin to

swell—this is called springing—which can happen a few weeks to a few days before labor. There will also be an increase in vaginal discharge, and she will spend more time laying down.

Contractions will start to happen, and then she's officially in early labor. This first stage lasts around 2 to 6 hours. Contractions can look like the cow standing with her back arched and her tail out straight. She may be licking or kicking at her belly, appearing restless and agitated, or continuously laying down and getting back up.

Next, there is active labor, which lasts anywhere from 30 minutes to 2½ hours. She should start to push, and a sac will emerge. The water sac usually breaks as the calf is being pushed out behind it. Soon, the two front hooves will appear, and then the nose. Once the sac and calf are visible and on the way out, labor should be progressing, which means the calf should be on the ground within 30 minutes. Call your vet immediately if the calf is coming out in the wrong position or if your cow is in active labor but not progressing.

The final stage of labor is the delivery of the afterbirth, or placenta, which happens anywhere from 1 to 12 hours after birth. Do not pull on any exposed placenta during the afterbirth. Call your vet if you've been monitoring and haven't seen any afterbirth delivered. If your cow is not eating and drinking or if her discharge is smelling foul, she could have a retained placenta, which can be a life-threatening situation.

Once the calf is on the ground, the cow should turn and lick it dry. Pull any placenta away from the calf's nostrils and mouth if needed. Within the first hour, the calf should be attempting to stand and look for his or her mama's teat. Colostrum is the milk the mother produces for the newborn, which is rich in antibodies. It's essential a calf intakes a good amount as quickly as possible. The calf should get the hang of nursing and nurse several times in the first 24 hours. The rule of thumb is for the calf to

get five percent of its body weight in colostrum within the first 6 hours of life. If your calf is not nursing within the first few hours, milk out the colostrum and try feeding the calf with a bottle or a calf fluid feeder, which is inserted down its throat and directly into the stomach. You may need to call your vet. Getting colostrum into your calf is the difference between life and death.

The Calf

If you have a heifer calf (a female calf), congratulations! You have yourself another family dairy cow. If you have a bull calf (a male calf), your best option is to make him into a steer by getting a procedure done when he is around 3 months old to remove his testicles. When I have male calves, I castrate them and keep them for about 18 months, fattening them up to butcher. Whether the calf is male or female, you have to make the decision to keep mama and calf together or separate them and bottle feed the calf.

Some people decide to separate them to get as much milk as they can. I always choose to keep mama and baby together, and just take the milk my family needs. Depending on how much milk the calf is drinking, the mom and baby may need to be separated for several hours in order to get some milk. This usually starts when the calf is about 3 months old. I usually separate them at night so I can milk in the morning, and then I put them back together for the rest of the day. I don't wean the calves from their mom completely until they are about 10 months old.

Hand Milking

Being sanitary is everything, and the movement is a firm and gentle downward massage—no tugging or yanking. Hand milking is very involved. It requires a clean, calm, and relaxed atmosphere. Everything that comes into contact with the milk and udder must be sanitized—the milk pail, your hands, the cow's teats, and the base of her udder.

To start my routine, I make sure the area where I'm milking is clear of cow manure and as clean as possible. After picking out any cow plops with my pitchfork, I usually brush my cow to get any debris that could fall into the milk pail off her before milking. This is also a wonderful segue into the milking process for both you and your cow. I do believe my cow enjoys the milking process because it begins with this little bit of intimacy between us.

To ensure maximum cleanliness, I spray my cow's teats and the base of her udder with an iodine-based antiseptic solution. I "strip" each of her four teats, which means I take a few squirts of her milk into a separate cup and take a look at the milk, making sure there are no lumps or blood, which can indicate an infection. This step is an important one, not only to make sure the milk looks normal, but also because the first few squirts of milk could possibly be contaminated with bacteria inside the teat.

This is when I give my lady her grain. The milking pail I use has gone through the dishwasher on the sanitize setting. I set my pail under the cow's udder and assume a squatting position. Since I do not have my cow in a stanchion, I prefer to squat instead of sitting on a stool so I am freer to react should she decide to move. Once I am squatting, I begin to milk.

A common misconception about milking is that you just pull down on the teat. The milk is actually in the udder itself. It needs to move from the udder into the teat, and then be pushed out. Like humans, cows need oxytocin in order to "let down" their milk, which in nature is released when the calf suckles. So hopefully by the time you have cleaned and stripped the teats, she is ready to let down her milk. Keeping a calm, quiet atmosphere can also help with letdown. First, I position the teat between my thumb and index finger. Then I clamp the thumb and forefinger at the top of the teat. Pinching here helps prevent backflow, which is when the milk goes from the teat back into the udder. This is an improper milking technique that can cause serious infections such as mastitis.

I squeeze out milk that's trapped in the teat by using my middle and ring fingers to close down over the rest of the teat, and then I release so the teat can fill back up with milk. Then I repeat, repeat, and repeat again. Don't worry; practice makes perfect. There will be lots of practicing, and you will need to build up the muscle memory in your hands. The udder is in quarters, and that is why there are four teats. I start with the back teats because they are the hardest teats on my cow to milk, and then move to the front two. After milking, I spray her teats again with an antiseptic cleanser until a drip forms at the bottom of the teat.

A Pail Full of Milk

A sterilized jar, a sterile milk filter, a funnel, and an ice bath are the supplies needed to transfer milk from your milking pail to storage. Your milk needs to be filtered and chilled as quickly as possible to reduce bacterial contamination. After milking, no dillydallying—head straight to the house to take care of your milk. First, place the disposable filter in the funnel on the mouth of the jar and then pour your milk through a milk filter (you can find these at most feedstores or online). Your milk should be poured into a clean, sterilized jar or container for storage. Then, the milk should be chilled as quickly as possible. I put mine in the freezer or in an ice bath for about 20 minutes, and then transfer it to the fridge. My family consumes our milk fresh and raw. If we have excess, or if we have not finished the milk within a few days of milking, we use it to make cheese, yogurt, or—the kids' favorite—ice cream.

Having a Cow

The information here merely scratches the surface. There are details I didn't dive into and topics I didn't cover, like whether or not to get a trailer, how to handle a cow, or how to lead it on a halter. If you're really interested in getting a dairy cow, then that is marvelous! There's a huge learning curve, but I think it's one of the most rewarding experiences. I am so grateful to my vet and the others who have helped my cow journey along the way, as well as my parents, who always supported my passion for dairy cows. My favorite reference books are listed at the back of this book. I highly recommend all of them if you are interested in this journey.

I truly enjoy being responsible for this sweet bovine that gives our family so much—not only the fresh dairy, but also the moments we share. I can recall my daughters' expressions of complete awe as they witnessed two of Ruby's calves being born, and their sadness at having to say goodbye to a calf the day we sold her. These experiences have helped us all grow. If you have the calling and the desire to explore life with a cow, and you have been thoughtful and realistic in your research, then I say there is no time like the present.

Mobile Butcher

CHLOE ROSE

Chloe Rose is truly a fascinating woman. For a woman in her 20s, she has experienced more than most of us do in a lifetime. She always seems to be on the move, always going off into the world to learn something new and inspiring. I recently ran into her at the farmers market, and she was on her way to Burning Man, then heading up to the Northwest for apple harvest and cider press season, and then going to Spain to learn charcuterie. She has such a strong presence and moves in a way that exudes confidence yet also the humility and desire to truly learn all sorts of trades. She is an old soul, and I look forward to seeing where else she goes and what she learns in hopes that she travels back to share it with me.

Chloe was born in Placerville, California, but moved all around California and Utah as a child. She really found a home at Quail Springs Permaculture in Southern California when she was a teenager.

Quail Springs changed her life, and that's when she started farming and learned how to grow a relationship with where her food came from. That's also where she saw her first chicken harvest, which shook her up and motivated her to learn more about butchering and harvesting animals.

She tried to learn as much as possible, and therefore be a part of as many harvest and kill days as she could. She learned how to lean into the fear and curiosity that comes with taking a life to feed and give life to others.

Chloe believes that using as much of the animal as possible is a sign of respect for taking the animal's life for food. She fell in love with hide tanning, and the story and connection it gave her to continue that animal's life. Today, Chloe works as a mobile butcher for different family farms, teaching butchering and hide-tanning classes. She inspires us to dive in and keep learning!

PIGS

Pigs are perhaps the most entertaining farm animal to have around. I can't help but laugh every time I am around mine. With their curious personalities, wagging tails, hilarious sounds, and funny faces, they bring a lot of joy—and yes, some smell—to our little barnyard. Some people choose to have a pig for a pet, while others have them for meat. I raise my hogs for meat, but enjoy them along the way. I am incredibly thankful for the lard, pork, bacon, ham, and sausage they provide my family.

Unfortunately, similar to all other factory-farmed animals, pigs raised in factories are confined to overcrowded pens where they stand on cement floors or metal grates. Mothers are squeezed into birthing crates where they're unable to walk or turn around. There's only room to stand up, lay down, eat, drink, and nurse their babies. Factory-farmed pigs are usually fed antibiotics to avoid the easily spread diseases in these cramped, unnatural, and unsanitary conditions.

By raising your own pigs, you are able to control their environment, their feed, and how the pigs are treated when butchered. It is important to me to give my pigs the best, most natural life possible before butchering day. If you're not interested in raising a pig, but enjoy eating pork products, I implore you to find meat at a local farmers market or purchase your meat directly from a local farm. If shopping in the grocery store, I recommend buying organic and humanely raised pigs. Look for labels saying not only "organic" and "antibiotic free," but also addressing animal welfare.

Unfortunately, these labels can be harder to find. The hope is that, through consumer demand and voting, these conditions and labels will become tighter and stricter, and, of course, that more people will support their small, local farmers.

I hope this section offers a glimpse of what it's like to care for and raise your own pigs. If the following information sparks your interest in getting a pig, I recommend spending time around them and with a pig owner so you can learn more. You can locate pig owners by simply asking a local butcher, 4-H leader, or feedstore clerk. Pig folks, I have found, are usually ready to help a fellow hog owner.

A Day in the Life of a Pig

In the morning, we let our piggies out from the shelter they sleep in at night, which protects them from predators, and put them in their pen for the day. We clean up any pig poop, feed them, and check their water. Like all our animals, we take a few minutes to watch them and make sure they're behaving normally; besides, their morning antics are quite entertaining. All of this totals about 15 minutes.

Pigs generally don't require too much of your time on a daily basis. They spend their day looking for food, rooting with their snouts, eating,

sleeping, and playfully interacting with each other. Yes, pigs do love wallowing in the mud too! They love to be scratched, and if you get a rake and scratch their backs you will have a best pig friend forever.

Pigs have minimal sweat glands. Rolling in the mud helps regulate their temperature by cooling them down. Pigs also require a sufficient amount of bedding, as they do like to make comfy sleeping nests, which also helps keep them warm in colder climates. Pigs are incredibly social and enjoy the company of other pigs. Pigs kept alone often become bored, sedentary, and even aggressive or destructive. When evening comes, we call the piggies into their house, feed them, and lock them in their shelter for the night. We often check their water again, even though it's automatic. Our nightly chores take about 10 minutes.

Pig Breeds

There is a wide variety of pigs with differing looks, sizes, growth rates, temperaments, and uses. Some breeds are known for their lard, some for their bacon and meat, and some for both (called dual-purpose breeds). I recommend researching breeds to see which one makes the most sense for you and your possible pig setup. Below are a few of my favorite breeds. I have had a few different breeds of pigs, but prefer the kunekune.

Kunekune

The kunekune is a small heritage breed that originated in New Zealand. They are known as hardy, rotund, and docile pigs. They are notoriously easy to manage and keep. They range in color from black and white to brown to ginger. They can be spotted or a solid color. They vary in height and weight from about 24 to 30 inches tall and anywhere between 140 and 200 pounds when full grown. They have short snouts compared to other breeds, which means they root less. They are also known to be great grass grazers. They can have short or long hair and might have wattles or not. They are a great beginner pig. They can make great pets or be used for meat and lard.

Hampshire

The Hampshire pig is a medium to large pig known for its lean meat. They are mainly black pigs with a large stripe of white going across the front legs and on the upper, rear part of their back. They have long noses, long legs, upright ears, and are quite muscular. They can weigh more than 600 pounds! They are known for their easy temperaments and fast growing rate. They are a good pig if raising for meat, but I wouldn't necessarily recommend them as a pet.

Duroc

This pig is also known as the "red hog." These pigs are known for their size and rapid growth rate. They can weigh more than 700 pounds when full grown, but should be harvested around 200 pounds, which is usually when the pig is between 4 and 5 months old. They are dark red in color, well muscled, have long snouts and legs, and partially droopy ears. They are known for their easygoing temperaments when compared to other, larger meat breeds. Like the Hampshire, I would recommend raising them primarily for butchering rather than as a pet simply due to their size.

Mangalitsa

The Mangalitsa is a lesser-known breed recognized by its woolly coat. Their thick coats are red, black, or blonde, and they weigh about 300 pounds when full grown. They have longer snouts and distinctive, floppy ears. They have been surpassed by larger, faster-growing, higher-producing breeds in the pork industry. Fortunately, they are making a comeback due to their lard production and tasty meat. They are a docile pig known for their friendly temperament.

Finding Your Pig

Have your pigpen set up before bringing your pig home. Buying your pig from a reputable family breeder is ideal. Ask at your local feedstore if you have no leads. Piglets are usually farrowed or born starting in the spring through the beginning of fall. Piglets are usually sold as weaners, which means they have been weaned from their mother's milk and are usually about 2 to 3 months old. If you are choosing a piglet, try to choose the largest and most active of the litter, as that indicates the strongest and healthiest. (Runts are so cute, though; they are hard not to take home!)

It is always a good idea to go and see your potential pig to make sure it is coming from clean and healthy conditions and has been cared for properly. If possible, it's helpful to see the parents to know what your little pig will turn into. You will also want to know the breed standards for the breed you have chosen to make sure it is up to those specific standards. If purchasing a male pig and he is not for breeding, make sure he has been castrated!

Pigs are social by nature. Though they can be housed alone, they prefer to be together, so if you think you want to raise pigs consider getting two. If you decide to get two, it works best if they are similar ages and sizes. Pigs can be hard to move. If your piglet is little, you should be able to transport it in a dog crate, but if it's a bigger pig, you may need a trailer with a ramp, sweet feed, and a crew of people to help get it in the trailer.

Vet

It can be hard to find a vet who specializes in pigs, but most small and large animal vets will be willing to help you out. I have found my large animal vet will help me when I need to get vaccinations or any needed medications, though she doesn't do pig house calls. This is when I have relied on my pig mentors. Having a list of folks to help you out will be your lifeline. It is a good idea to talk to your vet and other pig owners about what vaccines are needed in your area.

Worming

Internal and external parasites are one of the most common problems that can affect your pigs' health. If left untreated, parasites can cause a wide range of detrimental health issues. A regular worming program for your pigs is essential. Trust me, I have had a worm infestation, and it is not pretty. I personally haven't had luck with diatomaceous earth preventing worms, so I use over-the-counter wormers now. Your commercial worming options are to inject the wormer, feed it, give it as a paste, or pour it on the pig's back. I usually rotate the types of wormers, but do one monthly. My routine is to rotate Ivermectin, which is a broad-spectrum

wormer that helps with internal as well as external parasites, such as mites and lice, and Fenbendazole, which is a broad-spectrum wormer for internal parasites. Rotating wormers can help fight a wide variety of parasites, as well as preventing wormer resistance. Make sure you keep a log, as it helps you know exactly when you need to worm again and enables you to stay on a tight schedule.

Paddock, Pasture, Fencing, and Housing

Pigs need a nice, open space, a shelter, and a strong fence to hold them in. Pigs are happiest when wandering, so if you have the space, it's ideal to have them in the big pasture. If you don't have the space, it's OK; a shelter and a paddock are usually sufficient. Pigpens should be at the very least about 10 to 15 square feet per pig under 100 pounds, and at least 25 square feet for the larger breeds of pigs.

Fencing needs to be secure, as pigs are incredibly strong and known for getting out of their fencing. Do not underestimate the strength of a pig. Pigs can root under, lean into, and scratch against fencing. I've even heard of pigs barging full force straight through wooden fencing. Consider the size and the breed's tendency to root before installing a fence. There is a wide range of fencing options for pigs, from wood to hog-panel fencing, and I even have a friend who uses electric fencing. You will need to consider your budget and the amount of space you are fencing. Make sure fencing is low and pigs cannot root under it. Some people like to put a concrete bottom or a strand of barbwire a few inches off the ground on the inside of the fence to prevent rooting out.

Your pig needs access to shelter year-round. Housing can vary depending on what makes sense for you and your budget. Shelters need to be at least three-sided since pigs need to be able to escape the elements. Pigs are sensitive to temperature and can easily die if they get too hot or too cold. The shelter should allow the pigs to get warm, but also escape the hot sun when needed.

Shelters can range from a mobile A-frame house to a full barn, and just about anything in between. Pigs can be destructive, especially the larger ones, so your shelter will need to be solid. Ventilation needs to be considered when building your shelter so air can flow, yet drafts directly on the pigs should be avoided. When designing and building my shelters, I put in some ventilation by replacing some wood with wire just below the roofline rather than lower near the floor where the pigs would be in the direct airflow. Your shelter needs to be large enough to accommodate full-grown pigs stretching out and comfortably sleeping. It should also have enough room for the pigs to amble around inside on days when the weather is inclement and the pigs choose to remain inside.

Pigs love water and mud to cool off and roll in, though it is not a requirement as long as they can go in the shade to cool down. Wallowing in mud helps pigs stay cool, and there's nothing like a thick coat of mud to ward off pesky insects. During the hot months, I usually hose the pigs down and have a little mud pit for them. As you will see, there's nothing happier than a pig in mud. If you can't or don't want to have a mud pit, it is imperative that the pigs have a shaded area out of the sun other than their shed. Drainage needs to be considered when planning a pigpen. Though they love mud, they also need dry areas to avoid hoof rot. Their pens, especially if they are on the smaller side, will need to be cleaned out often to avoid parasites and disease. There are several great resources out there to give you ideas and information on how to build a shelter that is right for you and your pigs.

Food

Pigs are omnivores and need a varied diet in order to stay healthy. They have a single stomach and need two to three meals per day. They should eat approximately two percent of their body weight daily. Some people feed their piggies all hog feed, some feed them all scraps, and some feed both. I usually feed one meal of scraps and one meal of hog feed. I use my family's food scraps, and sometimes neighbors are willing to slosh their scrap buckets over. For hog feed, I prefer Modesto Milling hog grower pellets. I also love letting the pigs out so they can forage on grass, acorns, and whatever else they can find. I think having a varied diet is essential for the pigs' health and well-being.

When feeding your pig scraps, avoid feeding them meat, rotten food, bones, or too much

sugar. Also avoid uncooked beans and potatoes. I steer clear of skins, like pineapple and avocado, too. Also, because a friend's pig almost choked to death on broccoli, I now chop up potential string stalks like celery or broccoli. Obviously, no trash or plastic should be included. It's true that pigs are somewhat like a garbage disposal, but they shouldn't actually eat everything they're willing to.

It can be hard to maintain healthy pig weight, as they act hungry all the time. To make sure my pigs aren't too fat or too thin, I use their hips and spine as weight indicators. Simply press on your pig's hips. If it takes a little firm pressure to feel their bones, this is ideal. If you immediately feel their spine and hips, they are too thin. If you can hardly feel the hips or spine, they are too fat. Maintaining a healthy weight is essential for your pig's health and should be closely monitored.

Vitamins and Minerals

Pigs, like every other animal, need vitamins and minerals to maintain their well-being. Pigs need iron, sodium, selenium, copper, vitamin B12, and vitamins A, D, E, and K, just to name a few. Their needs can depend on their diet, age, size, and production. Swine grains are often deficient in most vitamins and minerals, and even pigs on a varied diet should be supplemented. There is a wide variety of supplements out there, and you can usually buy them at your local feedstore or online. I personally like the pigs to have a salt lick at all times, but I also add a vitamin and mineral mix in a small feeder so it is free choice and they seem to get as much or as little as they need.

Water

Pigs need fresh water to drink at all times. Pigs are messy, especially when it comes to their water. If given a large tub of water, they will lay in it, knock it over, and love every minute of playing

with it. There are different types of automatic waterers to consider for your pigs. There are little troughs, waterer cups, and hog-nipple waterers—the choice is up to you. I tried metal and rubber waterers, and the pigs managed to break every one of them by trying to climb into them. I then discovered the hog-nipple waterer, and it's incredible. It's a little lever that they have to press in order to get a drink. It's amazing how quickly the pigs figured it out, and finally there were no more broken water troughs and water everywhere.

How to Handle a Pig

Pigs can be difficult to handle and move when needed. They are incredibly smart and know immediately when the daily routine is off. The bigger they are, of course, the bigger the challenge. Pigs have poor vision, which makes handling and moving them even more challenging. You cannot put a halter on them, and they are usually so heavy after a few months old, it's nearly impossible to pick them up. Pigs can panic if not handled correctly, and can be surprisingly stronger and faster than anticipated. They can be so sweet, but they can also be dangerous when feeling cornered or stressed. They have teeth and can bite if scared. Small children should never be left unsupervised with pigs.

If you need to move them, the simplest way is to give them only one option—moving forward—while at the same time preventing them from turning around. I put up panels to create a little chute directing them where they need to go. People often use aids such as pig boards or flags to help move them forward or turn them. It is important to remember to be patient while moving your pigs. Gentle encouragement is always more effective than pushing them too hard or too fast. Not feeding them the night before and enticing them with sweet feed has been successful for me

as well. My pig mentor puts her trailer in the pigpen days before and feeds the pigs in it so they are comfortable going in and out by moving day. There's a lot more to know about how to properly handle a pig, so I hope this information is the little tip of the iceberg of knowledge you'll independently seek out.

Butchering

The timing of butchering depends on the breed and the growth rate. Talk to your local butcher, who will be able to help you decide what age and weight is best to butcher your pig. Most big farms butcher their pigs around 6 months of age. Because I have kunekunes, which have a slower growth rate, I usually butcher around 9 to 12 months of age. Waiting too long toughens the meat, though I have butchered older pigs and the meat was still tasty. Boars have a certain smell to their fat and meat, so any male pigs you are raising for meat should be castrated when young. My husband butchers our pigs if we are cooking them whole or quartered; otherwise, we take them to a local USDA-certified butcher to do the deed and get the proper cuts. We don't feed them the night before, and then we load them into our trailer and bring them over to the facility. About a month later, we receive our different cuts, ham, bacon, sausage, and lard.

How to Render Lard
Rendering lard is easy, and it is by far my favorite cooking oil because it is incredibly versatile. It can be used for frying, roasting veggies, making flaky pie crust, and everyday cooking. Lard is rich in vitamin D and has a high smoke point. Your lard should barely have a smell. If it smells rancid, do not use it. Lard from a boar has a very distinctive smell and flavor, and I would not recommend it.

To render lard, gather your leaf fat and water. Chop the fat into small pieces. The smaller

What are those things hanging off the pigs' faces?
Those are called wattles. The kunekunes and a few other breeds can have them. Their actual use is still not clear, though they may have something to do with the pigs' sexual scent.

Why does my pig nudge me?
A pig's instinct is to root. They use their snouts to explore their world since their eyesight tends to be very poor. They nudge looking for food or simply to communicate. I think they nudge me to say, "Hi, look at me! Any treats for me?"

Should I bathe my pig?
Pigs don't need to be bathed, but they will love it if you do! I like to give mine a squirt with the hose when it's hot simply to cool them off. Be careful with soaps, as you don't want to dry out their skin.

Should I put sunscreen on my pig?
If you have a light-skinned pig or a pig with spots of lighter skin, sunburn can happen, so certainly put sunscreen on your piggie and give them some protection!

If my pig is not eating, what should I do?
A healthy pig loves to eat. Not eating is a major indication that something is wrong. It is a good idea to call the vet if your pig is off its feed. You can take a rectal temperature; anything higher than 101°F is a fever. Other times to call your vet is if your pig is lethargic, has a major injury, or is coughing repeatedly, throwing up, or straining to urinate or defecate. Knowing your pigs' normal behavior will help you identify when something is wrong.

the pieces, the faster it will render. Put the pieces of lard into a heavy pot on the stove, and add enough water to cover the bottom of the pot to prevent burning. Keep the lid off to let moisture escape. Turn on the burner and bring to a simmer, around 225°F. Stir occasionally. Watch for the usable lard to melt and the cracklings to appear. The time will depend on the amount of lard you have, but it is usually about 30 to 40 minutes.

Strain the lard into a container through several layers of cheesecloth, preventing the cracklings from going through. I use a glass jar for storage, but make sure to heat your jar up first so it doesn't crack when you pour the warm lard into it. Once the lard has hardened and cooled, it should be white. Store it in the fridge or at room temperature. It lasts about 6 months if stored in the fridge.

Having Pigs

I am so happy that my husband brought home our first pig, Luau. We've thoroughly enjoyed having these comical characters in our backyard. We have learned so much about raising happy, healthy pigs and look forward to learning more and getting our breeding program functioning efficiently. I am also thankful to all my pig mentors, who helped me when I needed it. It is so satisfying knowing exactly how the pork we eat has been raised, and for us, the work is worth that reward. Pigs do require time and money and are a big commitment, but they are a great addition to any barnyard. The smaller breeds especially can be easier to manage and a good choice if you are considering raising animals for their meat. I hope this section has painted a picture of what having pigs could be like, and I wish you luck on your hog journey.

Educator and Goatherd

SALLY VANDERKAR

I met Sally VanDerKar years ago when I worked as an assistant in her Waldorf classroom. Throughout the years, she has combined her two passions—education and goats—by taking her preschool students on field trips to the farm to milk and make cheese. My own children love to visit Sally and her goats and chickens. She often gives them cheese, and sometimes even surprises them with a puppet show. Sally's loving relationship with her goats was what inspired me to get my own pet sheep.

Sally has lived on the Central Coast of California most of her life, and found her love of goats on a whim. One Sunday morning in 1969, while attending college and living in Santa Barbara, she was looking through the classified ads and happened to see two goats for sale. Randomly, she decided to see them. They were two beautiful Saanens, and she couldn't resist. She returned home with her new purchases, named them Valerie and Brumel (after an Olympian high jumper from Russia), and then

began a life surrounded by goats. Valerie was a super milker, had a well-attached udder, and gave 10 quarts a day. The first night of milking, overwhelmed by how much milk she had, Sally learned to make cheese.

Eventually, Valerie, Brumel, and Sally moved a little east into the Los Padres Mountains, where she inherited more goats and a geodesic dome structure for their shelter. Besides being a teacher at the Waldorf School of Santa Barbara, she officially became a goat lady. She gained so much knowledge about goats by helping them thrive. One year, both of Valerie's babies were born with navel ill, which is when she learned to always dip the umbilical cord in iodine right after birth. Sally would take the babies to the preschool class she was teaching in order to take care of them throughout the day, and she started to feed them leftover Malt-O-Meal, which helped their growth.

In 1972, she moved to Sunburst Farms in the foothills of Santa Barbara, and the herd grew to 14 and then eventually to 65! With a few Australian Shepherd herding dogs, she had a routine taking the herd to and from water while spending most of the day taking care of simple necessities. One of her favorite places to take the goats was called Everlasting Meadow. In the winter and spring, it was a green meadow with a small creek that ran through it. One of her smartest goats was named Hannah, and she became Sally's lead goat. Hannah would walk at the front of the herd, especially on trails, and look out for rattlesnakes, poisonous mushrooms and plants, and other dangers. One day, she stopped and put her ears and front legs forward in a warning stance. Up ahead, Sally saw two mountain lions scuffling with each other. Luckily, they were too far away and busy with each other to notice the herd. They were able to turn around and head home safely—thanks to Hannah.

HERBALISM

Power and Beauty of Plants

ASHLEY

I SPENT MUCH OF MY TIME AS A CHILD AT NURSERIES WITH MY DAD AND BROTHERS, picking out eclectic edible plants for our gardens. We foraged at every opportunity, finding unlikely snacks along the sidewalks of San Diego, California, where I grew up. My dad would point out natal plums (*Carissa macrocarpa*), fennel (*Foeniculum vulgare*), and eugenia berries (*Syzygium smithii*) for us to try as we walked a few blocks back to our car after a dinner out or explored the abandoned lots near our home. I got my first book on herbal medicine from the library when I was a little girl, and from that moment on I was hooked. I found recipes for making dry shampoo, salves, and magical spells that removed freckles. I read the book cover to cover, over and over again.

My interest grew, and I went on to study herbalism at the Avicenna Institute with Kristie Karima Burns, Mh, ND, PhD, and, for years after that, I read every herbal book I could find and took every available course at the Herbal Academy. At the same time, I studied at Susun Weed's Wise Woman Center with an herbal apprenticeship in yarrow (*Achillea millefolium*). Last, I completed my certificate in the science and art of herbalism at Rosemary Gladstar's Sage Mountain Herbal Center. Over the years, I've also enjoyed attending the Northern California Women's Herbal Symposium and many other classes and workshops on foraging, plant identification, and herbal medicine. One of my local teachers and all-around favorite people is Lanny Kaufer of Herb Walks. He has taught me so much about the local native plants in our area. I've been fortunate to have such wonderful, experienced mentors and teachers throughout the years, and I am so grateful to them and the knowledge they so freely and generously shared with me.

With this book, it is my hope that I, too, can generously share any knowledge I have been fortunate enough to come by. I am grateful for my teachers and mentors, the authors of every single herbal book I've read, and this opportunity to share. I do not feel that any of these recipes are mine to hoard; like all herbal recipes, they are variations on centuries-old remedies that continually evolve over time. By sharing with one another, we can grow together, and that is a beautiful thing. Enjoy these recipes, change and improve them as you see fit, and share them with others whenever you can.

FORAGING

Foraging is the word I use when talking about searching for food in the wild. That might mean mushroom hunting, berry picking, weed gathering, pollen collecting, or flower plucking. It's sometimes hard to justify why someone would forage when delicious, fresh food is so readily available at the local supermarket. Why make the extra effort to look for food out in nature? I forage because I enjoy spending time outside. It makes me feel like I'm tapping into an ancestral part of myself, and it feels meaningful to feed my family with food I have harvested myself.

One of the things I love most about foraging is learning to see and find a use for things growing nearby in abundance, especially things that might be considered a nuisance. Every edible weed in the garden is a perfect example. I am inspired by the usefulness of plants, but also by how overlooked most of them are. Each plant has a purpose and is a valuable part of the ecosystem. I make food, drinks, beauty and personal care products, clothing dyes, and medicine, all from the plants growing around me.

In this chapter, you'll find recipes that call for common weeds from your property or the surrounding wilderness. Some plants easily self-propagate in the garden or the wild areas near you. Identifying and using backyard plants is another way to connect with the land, save money, and help you see the value in everything, no matter how small or plain. I hope you'll be inspired to try using the plants that grow around you in new ways—adding them to your skincare regimen, making home remedies, dyeing yarn or clothing, or cooking new foods.

Safety and Ethics

There are some rules to know and things to learn before running out and eating every plant in sight. You can't just take whatever you want without restraint or knowledge; that could cause serious damage to both the environment and your body. The number one rule when foraging is do it with respect. Remaining respectful to yourself, the plants, the earth, and the law is essential when foraging.

First, respect your body. Some plants are toxic or even deadly. Never touch or ingest a plant you can't confidently identify with 100 percent certainty. If the flowers look the same, but the leaves are a little different—or the other way around—stop and do not proceed. It is probably an entirely different plant. An ideal way to learn how to forage is to take an herb walk with a local plant expert. If you can't find an expert, sign up for an educational hiking class. Another option is to bring a friend and a bare minimum of two plant identification guides specific to your area on your forage. This book, while full of beautiful plant pictures, does not replace a plant identification guide. You can find excellent, comprehensive books at your local museum of natural history, or consult the resources section at the back of this book for reputable titles.

Second, be respectful to the plants. Never take more than you will use, and never take so much that it negatively impacts the plant population. On the website of United Plant Savers, you will find lists of plants in the "at risk" and "to watch" categories. I never forage plants from either of these lists. A good rule of thumb for plants that are not on these lists is to never take more than 10 percent of any plant or harvest from more than 10 percent of a stand of plants. For example, if there are 100 purple sage

TOOLS FOR FORAGING

- Large, easy-to-carry open basket for holding your foraged plants
- Small shovel or hori-hori knife if digging roots
- Good pair of garden shears
- Camera or cell phone for taking pictures of plants you'd like to identify later
- Minimum of two plant identification guides
- Appropriate clothing for exploring the outdoors (this might include a hat, shorts or pants, and comfortable and sturdy shoes)
- Sunscreen and possibly mosquito repellant
- Bucket and a small broom brush or tongs (and tweezers!) if foraging prickly pear

plants, harvest from 10 or fewer of those plants and take less than 10 percent of each plant. Treat it a little like pruning, which can help the health and regrowth of the plant. A person coming down the trail 15 minutes after you should never be able to tell that someone was foraging there, because the plants should be left in integrity. Digging roots does end the life of the plant. In the case of root harvesting, never take more than 5 to 10 percent of a stand of plants and be sure to fill in all the soil you've dug.

Third, be respectful to the earth. This involves leaving the land in the same or ideally better condition than when you found it. If you see garbage on the trail, pick it up. Don't harvest directly on the trail or in a place that others enjoying the space will be frequenting. Remember, someone coming along after you should not be able to notice that you have taken any plants. Some people, including myself, like to leave an offering of song or tobacco as a symbol of appreciation and respect to the land and plants.

Last, respecting the law means making sure you have permission to harvest plants before doing so. In some places, you may have permission to pull invasive, nonnative plants that are considered weeds, such as fennel or plantain, but may need to leave native plants like black sage alone. Check local regulations to make sure.

FAVORITE PLANTS TO FORAGE

FOR FOOD: prickly pear, fennel, nasturtium, dandelion, sow thistle, nettle, chickweed, lamb's-quarters, sage blossoms, miner's lettuce, bay laurel, elderberry, kumquat, loquat

FOR MEDICINE: fennel, horehound, yarrow, dandelion, elderberry, sages, yerba santa

FOR DYE: toyon, fennel, nettle, elderberry, prickly pear, golden yarrow, ironbark eucalyptus, sour grass

Plant Identification

TOYON (*Heteromeles arbutifolia*) | This plant is an evergreen shrub that grows to 15 feet. The leaves have sharply toothed margins, and are oblong to lance-shaped, stiff, and leathery. The flowers are clusters of five-petaled white blossoms, and the bright red fruit ripens in the winter. The fruit has a mealy consistency, and in my opinion is only tasty when dried before eating. Once it has been dehydrated, it makes a tasty snack.

FENNEL (*Foeniculum vulgare*) | This plant is a perennial that grows to 6 feet. The leaves are feathery, and the yellow flowers are in umbellets arranged in flat-topped umbels. The oblong, ribbed fruits smell strongly of licorice when crushed. All parts of the plant are eaten. The base is especially tasty when peeled and then roasted. I make a syrup of the seeds or aerial parts of the plant and pour it over sparkling water for a refreshing beverage. The seeds can be chewed for an upset stomach, flatulence, or to stimulate milk flow in nursing mothers.

MINER'S LETTUCE (*Claytonia perfoliata*) | This annual weed is in the purslane family. It grows up to a little more than a foot and has rounded leaves sitting at the top of the stem from which tiny, white flowers protrude. It is so delicious. I like to eat it in salads or as is as a trail snack. You will often find miner's lettuce growing under oak trees in the moist shade.

CALIFORNIA MUGWORT (*Artemisia douglasiana*) | This beautiful, aromatic plant grows taller than I am in ideal conditions, but often is only waist-high. The leaves look like tiny hands and are white-silver underneath. The flowers are whitish to yellowish. Used in similar ways as common mugwort (*Artemisia vulgaris*), it has a large range of uses. For safety, tinctures prepared with alcohol are not recommended due to the presence of the neurotoxic compound thujone. My family and I predominately use mugwort externally—as a wash for skin exposed to poison oak, dried and sewn into dream pillows (small square pillows about 6 by 6 inches that are placed under pillows to encourage vivid dreams), or as incense (the lower leaves, which have dried on the stalks).

HOREHOUND (*Marrubium vulgare*) | This plant grows up to 2 feet. It is a whitish, woolly perennial in the mint family. The leaves are opposite, round to ovate, with deep wrinkles on each leaf. The stems are square and the margins are scalloped. The small, white flowers grow in dense whorls. Horehound has been used all over the world as a tea, syrup, and candy to ease coughs and colds. It does not taste great, but it works well for me, and I make a strong horehound tea with honey every time I have a cough.

NASTURTIUM (*Tropaeolum majus*) | All parts of this plant are edible—leaves, stems, flowers, immature seeds, and ripe seeds. The large, round leaves can be harvested most of the year, and the flowers in the late spring to early summer. The seeds ripen in the late summer to autumn. Nasturtium is pretty spicy, especially plants that have been in full sun. My family eats the flowers, stuffed with cashew cheese, and the fruits, pickled in seasoned vinegar. We also use the showy hot orange, red, and yellow flowers to decorate salads, quiches, and other dishes.

DANDELION (*Taraxacum officinale*) | A common garden weed, dandelion is a hairless perennial. The bright yellow flowers grow in a single head from each hollow, leafless stem. The oblong leaves are deeply lobed, jagged, and toothed, and they grow in a rosette around the stalk. Dandelion is another medicinal plant of many uses historically. I use the leaves in salads and soups, the flower petals in baking, and the roots (roasted and simmered) as a coffee substitute. I also tincture the fresh root and use it along with burdock root tincture as a liver cleanser and toxin expeller.

SOW THISTLE (*Sonchus oleraceus* and other species, such as *S. arvensis* and *S. asper*) | The dandelion's cousin, sow thistle, is not as medicinal as dandelion, but is much less bitter. It makes for a tasty green to add to salads. It grows up to 6 feet and the base of each leaf clasps on the stout stem. Like the dandelion, a milky latex is released when the stem is broken. This plant is commonly mistaken for dandelion, but there is an easy way to tell them apart: many flower heads come from a single stem of the sow thistle, whereas only one flower grows from each dandelion stem.

FIELD NETTLE / DWARF NETTLE (*Urtica urens*) | Growing to 2 feet, this plant is a much smaller cousin to stinging nettle (*Urtica dioica*) and has similar uses. The leaves are ovate and opposite, with coarsely toothed margins. The green flowers grow in drooping clusters. Both plants are covered with tiny stinging hairs and should be handled with care. Most folks choose to use gloves when harvesting, but an experienced nettle-gatherer can grasp the plant in a respectful, deliberate way and not get stung. (All three of my children have this impressive skill!) There are numerous medicinal and culinary uses for this plant, but I predominantly use nettle as a nourishing tea, in soups, or steeped in vinegar and honey as a general spring tonic. The seeds can be harvested and added to salads and soups. It is not recommended to ingest the leaves when the plant is in flower.

HUMMINGBIRD SAGE (*Salvia spathacea*) | The showy, fuchsia-colored flowers of this plant do seem to attract bees and hummingbirds! The long, wrinkled leaves are resinous and sticky. I think the whole plant smells like candy. I drink it as a sun tea, and it has also been used to reduce fevers.

BLACK SAGE (*Salvia mellifera*) | This is an aromatic plant that grows in the coastal sage scrub and chaparral. The green lance-shaped or oblong leaves are small, resinous, and sticky. The flowers are usually purple-lavender to lavender-blue. I simmer sprigs of this plant on the stove to give my home a wonderful smell, and my family eats the flowers on salads and decorates baked goods with their beauty rather than using candy sprinkles.

PURPLE SAGE (*Salvia dorii*) | Found in the same habitats as black sage, purple sage is also highly aromatic and has delicious-tasting flowers. Overall, it is lighter in color than black sage. The leaves have a silvery color, and the margins are without teeth. The flowers are lavender. In addition to eating the flowers and using them as edible decorations, I simmer the leaves and inhale the fumes to treat headaches.

WHITE SAGE (*Salvia apiana*) | Because this plant is irresponsibly overharvested, I do not harvest it in the wild. I grow my own in my garden, and use only that, and I respectfully ask that you consider doing the same. The flavor is very strong, so I may throw one leaf—or more likely just one small part of a leaf—into a dish to give it that strong white sage flavor. Alternatively, I may eat some of the small, white (or very light lavender with light lavender dots) flowers, or burn a dried leaf as incense.

YARROW (*Achillea millefolium*) | This aromatic perennial grows to 3 feet and has finely divided, fernlike feathery leaves. The white flowers grow in dense, flat-topped clusters. This famous medicinal plant has been used for nearly every ailment, but I mostly use it as a tea to bring down a fever (not to be used on an alarmingly high fever, as it is possible there will be a temporary spike in temperature before it brings the fever down). I also use the fresh leaves or dried, powdered blossoms to stop a scrape or cut from bleeding. I make a tea of the leaves and flowers to wash a wound. It is not recommended to use large doses internally over a long period of time, as it could be potentially harmful.

WOOD SORREL (*Oxalis spp.*) | This plant is also commonly referred to as sour grass because of the tangy, sour taste. Eating excessive amounts could cause a buildup of oxalic acid, which could be problematic for people susceptible to kidney stones. Most wood sorrel in my area has bright yellow flowers, although there is also a little redwood sorrel, which has pink-lavender flowers. The leaves each have three heart-shaped leaflets and are edible, along with the flowers and stem. I mostly use just the flowers in spring rolls, salads, and as an edible garnish.

PRICKLY PEAR *(Opuntia spp.)* | Prickly pear is kind of thrilling to forage. The tunas, or fruits, are bright pink-red and have a fresh, mild taste. The hard, black seeds are best strained out before making jams, jellies, pies, or juice from the tunas. The paddles of the cactus are called nopales, and they are so delicious fried and wrapped in a corn tortilla with some cilantro. To forage this food, though, you will need some special tools. The tunas are covered in glochids, which will easily prick your skin like a hair splinter. For this reason, please bring tweezers. I almost always get just one of the glochids in my hand, and they are basically impossible to remove without tweezers. Before picking the tunas, use a small brush in all directions, over all sides of the fruit. Then, gather it in a bucket. To harvest the nopales, choose just one or two of the young pads per plant. Use gloves and a sharp knife to cut the pad, and put it in a separate bucket from the fruit. Once home, use a knife and tongs to cut the skin and spines off of the nopales. Some foragers like to remove the spines before bucketing the nopales. Either way, be careful!

MALLOW *(Malva parviflora and M. spp.)* | This incredible weed grows to more than 5 feet tall in ideal conditions. The large palmate leaves have five to seven lobes and can be as big as your hand. The flowers are a sweet light-pink color, and the round, somewhat flat fruit splits into several pieces like a pie. They are sometimes called cheesewheels or cheeses, and the mallow plant also goes by the common name cheeseweed. The young leaves and flowers are tasty on salads, and the cheesewheels are delicious.

FILAREE *(Erodium cicutarium)* | This plant is another weed that grows in abundance. It has tiny pink flowers and its seedpods are said to resemble a stork's bill, which is, fittingly, another of this plant's common names. Because I have so much of this plant, I try to use as much of it as I can. My chickens love to eat it, and my kids will tolerate a little on a salad. Before splitting, the seedpods can be made into a pretend pair of scissors by inserting one into a spot toward the base of the other, which is a fun party trick for very young children.

PLANTAIN *(Plantago lanceolata and P. major)* | Plantain is easy to identify by its ribbed basal leaves, which grow in a rosette. The variety pictured (*Plantago lanceolata*) has very long, narrow lanceolate leaves. The ribbed flower stalk ends in an inflorescence of tiny white flowers. Plantain is a staple in my home. I make a tea of the leaves with honey to calm a cough, a simple syrup for the same purpose, and a salve for scrapes. On the trail, if someone is stung by a bee or scrapes a knee, I crush up the leaves and put them on the affected area. The leaves can also be added to salads, although I'd recommend chopping them finely first.

CHICKWEED *(Stellaria media)* | This plant is a low-growing, sprawling weed with beautiful, tiny white flowers. The flowers appear to have 10 petals (but there are actually five petals, each with a deep cleft). The ovate leaves grow opposite on a short petiole on the weak stem. A thin line of hairs travels up the stem, alternating sides with each pair of leaves. Some toxic lookalikes to chickweed are spurge and scarlet pimpernel, but they can easily be distinguished from chickweed. Scarlet pimpernel has five orange, red, or sometimes blue petals (*not* white) with a purple center, and the stalk has a milky sap when broken. Spurge is in the euphorbia family and also emits a milky sap when the stem is broken. Chickweed has no white fluid in the stem. Chickweed is delicious in salads, spring rolls, wild pesto, and many other recipes. Its flavor is mild, and most children love it. Medicinally, I use it as an eye wash for pink eye, as a spit poultice (chew up the leaves and then spread on the affected area) on scraped knees, or in combination with plantain, St. John's wort, and comfrey in all-purpose salves.

WILD MUSTARD *(Brassica spp.)* | Bright yellow, four-petaled flowers are the telltale sign of wild mustard. The two most common species are *B. nigra* and *B. rapa*. Their basal leaves are deeply lobed, and their seedpods are elongated and angle upward. Wild mustard has a spicy taste, as you might guess, and the flowers are a delightful addition to spring salads. I also use the aerial parts of the plant as a footbath (a strong, hot tea of the plant is poured into a small tub, where I put my feet and soak them for 15 minutes or so) whenever I feel a cold or flu coming on.

LAMB'S-QUARTERS *(Chenopodium album and C. ssp.)* | A relative to quinoa, both the leaves and seeds of this plant are edible. I use the young leaves chopped finely in omelettes and quiches.

BLUE ELDERBERRY *(Sambucus nigra ssp. caerulea,* formerly known as *Sambucus mexicana)* | This plant is generally referred to as a deciduous shrub, although some grow so large I think they have to be called trees. Many lack a central, main trunk. The leaves are pinnately compound, with five to nine ovate to elliptic leaflets with pointed tips and toothed margins, and smell like peanut butter when crushed. The whitish-yellow flowers smell like honey and grow in flat-topped clusters, usually blooming in the spring. In summer, when the white film is wiped off the berries, they are dark purple. Although all parts of this plant have been extensively used as medicine throughout the world, the leaves, stems, bark, and unripe berries have been known to cause diarrhea and nausea. There are no known deaths from consuming any part of this plant. My family and I enjoy the flowers and ripe berries often, and we dry the surplus so we can have tea and syrup all year long. Elderflower tea has a delicate, honey-like taste, and I give it to my children when they have a fever or whenever they feel like a yummy cup of this golden yellow drink.

NOT ALL PLANTS ARE EDIBLE!

While it's fun and exciting to get outside and forage, I cannot emphasize enough how important it is to properly identify a plant before you even touch it. Here in California there are a handful of poisonous plants—including castor (*Ricinus communis*), poison hemlock (*Conium maculatum*), and poison oak (*Toxicodendron diversilobum*)—and some can cause serious harm if they are even slightly grazed. This book will be helpful for plant identification, but in order to be safe, you need a minimum of two other plant identification guides specific to your region.

CASTOR
(*Ricinus communis*)

POISON HEMLOCK
(*Conium maculatum*)

POISON OAK
(*Toxicodendron diversilobum*)

Food and Drink

Herbalism certainly has its place on the dinner table. I think the best kind of medicine is a healthy diet full of nutritious foods and herbs. These recipes are a fun way to incorporate healing herbs and wild, foraged foods into your everyday life.

Elderberry Soda

SERVES 1

This is the drink the kids in my house always ask for. It not only tastes good, but also is a remedy for colds and flu. It tastes even better when you make it yourself.

2 tablespoons elderberry syrup (see page 341)

Sparkling water

1. Add the elderberry syrup to an 8-ounce glass and then fill it with sparkling water.
2. Stir and serve.

Wild Salad

This recipe is different every time I make it depending on what I have on hand. Even with alternating ingredients, it always makes a beautiful, vibrant spring or summer salad. You can make whatever size salad you'd like—from a single serving to a large bowl to take to a potluck.

1. First, make your favorite garden salad with your desired lettuce. This will serve as a base and should take up only half to three-quarters of the final size of the salad.
2. Next, top it off with edible weeds. (Don't include nettle, of course, since it must be cooked, dried, or otherwise crushed before being eaten.) Some of my favorite salad weeds are chickweed, mallow buttons or cheesewheels, young mallow leaves, lamb's-quarters, dandelion greens, and sow thistle greens.
3. Last, sprinkle edible flowers on top. My favorite edible flowers are chamomile, calendula petals, mallow flowers, violets and pansies, nasturtium, sweet alyssum, sage blossoms, and cornflower (pull the individual flowers from the tough flower head first).
4. If using, top the salad with sunflower, sesame, or hemp seeds and your favorite dressing.

Lettuce

Edible weeds

Edible flowers

Sunflower, sesame, or hemp seeds (optional)

Salad dressing (optional)

Forager's Gin

This gin is my husband's favorite drink, and I like it too! It has a potent, woodsy flavor and is fantastic on its own or poured over tonic water. All of the ingredients can be adjusted for taste, and everything is optional other than the juniper berries. Sometimes I let my gin infuse and mellow for 6 months or more. It will be strong and herby, and it's surely not for everyone, but personally I think it's great.

Handful of ripe juniper berries

3 teaspoons yarrow blossoms

1 teaspoon dried orange peel (or 1 teaspoon chopped fresh orange peel)

1 teaspoon dried lemon peel (or 1 teaspoon chopped fresh lemon peel)

Vodka

1. Add the juniper berries, yarrow blossoms, and citrus peels to a 1-quart jar.
2. Fill the jar to 1 inch from the top with vodka.
3. Cover, shake, and let the jar sit for 4 weeks.
4. Strain out the solids and drink.

Making a Forager's Garden

If you don't have anywhere to forage, you can grow plants in your own yard! It is also the very best way to get to know them and be sure of their identity. Buy seeds or starts from a reputable nursery that sells organic plants that have not been sprayed. Many of my favorite weeds grow in my veggie patch, and I let them grow wild until I use them. If they are crowding the other plants in the garden, my chickens are thrilled to gobble them up. As you watch your new plants grow and change throughout their life cycles, you will begin to recognize them growing in the wild or between the sidewalk cracks in urban areas. How exciting it is to discover chickweed spilling out of someone's window garden, dandelions in the sidewalk, or elderberry waving in the breeze on the roadside! You will get "new eyes" for plants.

FAVORITE PLANTS FOR A FORAGER'S GARDEN

- Chickweed
- Purslane
- Horehound
- Elderberry
- Dandelion
- Plantain
- Fennel
- Hummingbird sage
- Yarrow
- Violets and pansies
- Chamomile
- Gooseberry
- Nasturtium
- Honeysuckle
- California hedge nettle
- Sweet alyssum

A Home-Grown Garden

Having a garden is really important to me as an herbalist. I grow many of the plants I use in my remedies and dye recipes, and I love being outside tending to my flowers. Growing my own plants helps me get to know them in an intimate way by observing the changes they make throughout their life cycles, and with the seasons. Another perk of having my own garden is being able to harvest each plant at the most optimal time, making it very convenient for plant medicine. I also don't risk making a negative impact on the plant population of rare plants like I would if I harvested them from the wild.

Nearly everyone can have a garden. A small box in the window counts if there isn't space outside for a large garden. Make it work for you and the space you have. If you have a truly tiny space, hanging small cooking herbs near the kitchen window will be fabulously rewarding. Other options include finding a community garden near you, having a garden entirely in pots of various sizes, or even tending to the wild, taking on the role of steward in the wild spaces near you.

Carpinteria Garden Park

ALENA STEEN

Alena Steen grew up in North Carolina, roaming the woods around her suburban house. She chose to spend almost all her time outside as a kid, and joined a community garden in college. A deepening interest in food systems and food security inspired her to find work on organic animal, vegetable, and fruit farms for almost a decade on both the East and West Coasts.

Farming changed her life, affirming the connection to the other-than-human world she had cherished since she was a kid. Alena's work at the Carpinteria Garden Park is a meaningful

way to facilitate relationships between people and plants, with an eye for social justice and environmental sustainability. Watching first-time gardeners cherish their growing space and learn how to build healthy soil while conserving water and feeding their families is a source of never-ending pleasure for her. Community gardens connect neighbors of all different ages, backgrounds, and life experiences in the shared work of tending land and building greater food security. They are dense hubs of life and health in urban spaces, especially important for those without other access to fresh food or nature.

The Carpinteria Garden Park is a newly established community garden nestled in the heart of downtown Carpinteria, California. More than 100 community members and households grow their own organic fruits, vegetables, flowers, and herbs in individual raised beds. The garden's objective is to empower the diverse community through access to affordable organic gardening space and public education.

The community garden is a vital connection to Carpinteria's long history of agriculture, where temperate summers and rich soil nourish many farms just outside of town. The garden is home to a large composting operation, several honeybee hives, worm bins, a dense and biodiverse landscape of edible and native plants, and an orchard of 50 dwarf and semidwarf fruit trees. The gardening practices are completely organic. Gardeners are encouraged to build soil fertility and reduce water needs throughout the growing season by adding compost, fertilizing with compost tea, and mulching with organic material.

Many folks are first-time gardeners who do not have access to yards, so there are free classes on beginner gardening skills, such as seasonal

planting, companion planting for biodiversity and pest management, composting, whole foods cooking, and more. The garden also provides classes on broader topics of home-scale sustainability, including landscaping with native plants for urban wildlife, rainwater and greywater catchment, beekeeping, and more.

Community gardens are springing up across the country. Particularly in areas where food resources are limited (aka "food deserts"), these community gardens are a powerful way to reclaim food sovereignty and good health. There are many resources available for those interested in learning more. A good place to start is the American Community Gardening Association's website (communitygarden.org).

Transforming an empty lot into an abundant food oasis takes time, money, and community

support. The possibilities for a nourishing relationship to food and community are endless, and can include creating a local plant nursery or farmers market, building a commercial kitchen to create value-added local food products, or developing school gardens and garden-based curriculum.

The Carpinteria Garden Park is a project of the city of Carpinteria, funded by a generous grant from California's Environmental Enhancement and Mitigation Program. If you do not have the support of your city or town, there are many other funding opportunities available, including federal and state money via urban greening and forestry programs, a community garden grant organization called SeedMoney, community impact grants from various for-profit organizations, donations from local plant nurseries and hardware stores, and more.

BEAUTY AND PERSONAL CARE

I first began making my own skincare and beauty products because I have very acne-prone, sensitive, difficult skin. I also wanted to avoid the toxic ingredients that are in practically every commercial product. Additional bonuses to making my own skincare include saving money, tailoring it to my wants and needs, and having the products I put on my body be as fresh as the food I eat. Making many of the products that I use on a daily basis also creates a wonderful self-care routine.

My favorite plants for beauty and personal care are calendula, rose, helichrysum, and orange blossom for topical applications. I also grow plants that I use internally for beauty, in teas and tinctures. These plants include burdock, calendula, and dandelion.

Homemade vs. Store-Bought

Most of the skincare options out there, even items at health food stores, are full of toxic ingredients. Many of the ingredients are preservatives, the benefit of which give the product a long shelf life, but only at the expense of your health. I like to compare skincare to food. The food that is best for your body is not the food that lasts the longest, but rather the food that is freshest, that must be consumed relatively soon. If you pump your food with all kinds of toxic preservatives, you can have it look the same and last longer, but you lose the nutritional value and also ingest poison.

If you consider this same approach when buying skincare, you will no longer be impressed at the lotion that still looks and smells new after 6 months of sitting in the hot car. You have to wonder why it has not gone bad in those conditions. The skincare I prefer is the kind that does get moldy after 6 months or a year, especially in conditions that are not ideal—just like the food I buy at the farmers market or harvest from my garden, which goes bad if I don't eat it within a few days. Shelf life comes at a cost, and I think it's important to realize what that is.

Unfortunately, the word *natural* on a label means very little and is not protected at all. Any company can use it however it wishes. The word *organic*, however, is very protected and regulated; it cannot be slapped on any label. This can be a disservice, though, because many small companies (such as mine) cannot afford the prices and process of becoming certified organic and thus cannot put those words on the front of the label. Always check the ingredients list. There, any organic ingredients may be noted, even for the small companies that have not yet become certified. That said, it's better to make your own skincare. That way you can be sure the ingredients are safe and pure, and you can make it just the way you like it.

Drying Herbs

You can purchase already dried herbs to use in your skincare recipes, but truthfully they will never compare to your own freshly dried herbs. Drying your own herbs is remarkably easy. Most herbs will dry well if they are scattered in shallow baskets with plenty of airflow. Giving them a gentle stir or shake every few days will help discourage any chance of mildew.

You could also use a dehydrator on a setting at or under 100°F, checking them a couple of times a day. You will know when they are done because they will crumble in your fingers.

Another option is to hang herbs or flowers in small rubber-banded bundles upside down until they crunch and crumble a little in your fingers. I tie my herbs with string, but before I do, I use rubber bands to bind them because they lose their water content as they shrink. Without the rubber bands, many of them will fall out of their bundles as they dry.

As soon as your herbs are dry, store them in glass jars with tight-fitting lids. Their color, taste, and medicinal qualities will last much longer if you store them in a dark, dry, cool place, always out of any direct light from the sun. With proper storage, your herbs should stay in fresh, usable condition for at least a year.

Herbal Oils

Herbal oils can be used as is or as the base of many homemade personal-care products. There are two main techniques to making an herbal oil: solar and Crock-Pot. The solar technique is generally preferred over the Crock-Pot technique because the plants have time to give their healing gifts to the oil without losing strength due to heat. Oil also has the potential to go rancid if it becomes too hot. The only time I use the Crock-Pot method is if I need the oil quickly and cannot wait the 4 weeks it takes to let it infuse in sunlight. All oils are unique. Before you choose one, you should consider the qualities of each oil and compare them to your desired effects (see page 310).

SOLAR-INFUSED HERBAL OIL

The solar-infused method is by far the preferred method among herbalists to make an herbal oil. This method not only prevents the carrier oil from overheating, but also imbues the oil with the beautiful rays of the sun.

Dried herbs of choice
Base oil of choice

1. Fill a jar one-quarter to one-third full with your desired dried herbs. My favorite herb for skincare, hands down, is calendula (*Calendula officinalis*).
2. Fill the jar the rest of the way with your base oil of choice, leaving a 1-inch space at the top.
3. Cover the jar with a lid and give it a gentle shake.
4. Leave the jar in a sunny window, shaking once a day to keep the plant material covered in oil.
5. After 4 weeks, strain out the solids, reserving the oil. Now your infused oil is finished and ready to use in recipes or as is!

CROCK-POT HERBAL OIL

In very dark and cold climates, it just might not work to make a solar-infused herbal oil. Or perhaps you need your oil right away and can't wait the 4 weeks it takes to fully infuse in the sun. In either case, you can still make a lovely herbal oil using a Crock-Pot.

Dried herbs of choice
Base oil of choice

1. In a small Crock-Pot, add a ratio of ¼ to ⅓ part dried herb to 1 part oil.
2. Set it on the lowest heat setting and let it infuse for 24 to 48 hours.
3. You may need to periodically turn your Crock-Pot off to keep the oil from getting too hot and going rancid. Do not let it smoke or simmer. If your oil has gone rancid, you will know by the characteristic, waxy smell.

Favorite Oils for Skincare

Base Oils

The following oils can be used as the base oils for skincare recipes. Each oil can be used by itself, as the only oil in the recipe, or blended together with other oils.

JOJOBA OIL: Similar to skin's sebum; highly penetrative; absorbs very well; noncomedogenic; very helpful and regulating for acne-prone skin; helpful for sunburned or inflamed skin

OLIVE OIL: High in fat-soluble vitamins; repairs and rejuvenates damaged and dry skin; soothes inflamed skin; can feel heavy and greasy; slightly antifungal

ALMOND OIL: High in vitamin E and other fat-soluble vitamins; light texture; protective and nourishing; not too greasy; good for all skin types; often used in baby skincare

RAW (NOT TOASTED) SESAME OIL: Nourishing for dry and dehydrated skin; high in vitamin E; used to prevent sun damage and treat inflamed or sprained joints

SUNFLOWER OIL: Noncomedogenic; light texture; nongreasy; great for a variety of skin types

HEMPSEED OIL: Heavy but nonclogging; reduces size of pores; clears blackheads and acne; anti-inflammatory; reduces redness

APRICOT KERNEL OIL: Similar feel and use as almond oil; light and nongreasy; good for all skin types, especially prematurely aged, dry, or inflamed skin; astringent and toning

AVOCADO OIL: Fortifying and regenerating; one of the heavier fixed oils; more readily absorbed than olive oil; good for extremely dry, cracked skin, dehydrated skin, wrinkles, and premature aging caused by sun damage; high in vitamin E

COCONUT OIL: Solid at room temperature; light protection from the sun; greasy but very moisturizing; good for prematurely aged skin

ARGAN OIL: Typically used in haircare recipes, but also used on the face and body; high in vitamin E; antiaging and wrinkle-fighting; useful for acne-prone skin

Specialized Oils

These oils are used in combination with base oils and generally make up 15 percent or less of the final recipe.

CASTOR OIL: Not for use during pregnancy; anti-inflammatory; medicinally used externally in packs for heavy and congested periods, gastrointestinal cramping, and constipation (*Please note that the castor plant is highly toxic, and the store-bought oil has been processed to remove the toxin ricin.*)

ROSEHIP SEED OIL: Excellent antiaging properties; very high in vitamin C and other free radical scavengers; reduces scar tissue and damage from sun exposure; regenerates tissue

SEA BUCKTHORN OIL: High in vitamins, nutrients, and antioxidants; regenerates tissue; helpful for healing scar tissue; improves skin elasticity; anti-inflammatory

Face

I love making my own face-wash blends, and usually they don't require a lot of ingredients. Water is very important in any skincare routine, as it brings moisture to the skin, plumps it, and reduces the appearance of wrinkles. Even if you use an oil-based cleanser, it's important to wet a washcloth with very warm water and hold it over your face to open your pores and moisturize your skin. Follow the cleansing with a few sprays of hydrosol or flower water, four to five drops of serum, and lotion.

Aloe-Honey Face Wash

This face wash is so simple, and it works wonders for sensitive, dry, aging, and acne-prone skin. For an extra treat for your skin, make a mask of pure honey and leave it on for 10 to 20 minutes before rinsing it off with warm water.

¼ to ½ teaspoon aloe vera

1 teaspoon honey

1. Mix the aloe vera and honey, either in a small bowl or right in your hand, and massage into damp skin.
2. Rinse off gently with warm water, pat dry, and follow with a hydrosol, serum, and lotion.

Calendula Oil–Based Cleanser

This is an excellent choice for all skin types. Oil-based cleansers remove excess oil, makeup, and dead skin cells without stripping moisture or disturbing the skin's balance. While it seems counterintuitive to use oil to remove oil, it's actually a wonderful tactic. Think of it like removing tar from the bottom of your feet after a day at the beach—olive oil does the job. Oil-based cleansers are really excellent when used properly.

½ cup calendula-infused olive oil (see page 309)

⅓ cup calendula-infused almond oil

⅓ cup calendula-infused sesame oil

⅓ cup castor oil

15 to 20 drops rosewood essential oil

15 to 20 drops geranium essential oil

1. Combine all the ingredients and store in an amber glass bottle with a pump for easy application. For a longer shelf life, store in a dark cabinet or closet away from light, heat, and moisture.
2. To use, pump about 1 teaspoon of the cleanser into your hand and massage onto your face. Wet a washcloth with warm water, and hold it to your skin for 10 to 15 seconds. Wipe the oil-based cleanser off gently, re-wet the washcloth, and hold it to your face for another 10 seconds.
3. Pat your face dry and follow with hydrosol, serum, and lotion.

TIP: It's tempting to skip the washcloth in your nightly skincare routine, especially when using oil-based cleansers, because dirt and makeup wipe off easily with a tissue after massaging in the cleanser. My advice is don't skip the washcloth step. It helps your skin get even cleaner, and it plumps it with much-needed moisture.

Chamomile-Rose-Lavender Cleansing Grains

Another face wash I use often is cleansing grains. As with the calendula oil–based cleanser and aloe-honey face wash, it leaves the skin's natural protective barrier—the acid mantle—intact. The cleansing grains exfoliate without stripping moisture. A bonus feature is they can also be applied and used as a mask. I use bentonite clay in my cleansing grains, along with gluten-free oats and my favorite skin-nurturing herbs.

1. Grind all the ingredients in an herb grinder. You can also use a coffee grinder that hasn't been used for grinding or a mortar and pestle.
2. Mix together, and store in a glass jar with a tight lid. If stored properly, cleansing grains will last a few months.
3. To use as a cleanser, put a scoop of the cleansing grains in your hand and mix with a little water or hydrosol. Massage onto your face, and then wash off with warm water or a warm, wet washcloth. Follow with hydrosol, serum, and lotion.
4. To use as a face mask, apply as described in the previous step but leave it on until it is dry. Once completely dry, wash it off with warm water or a warm, wet washcloth. Follow with hydrosol, serum, and lotion.

1 cup organic, gluten-free oats

½ cup bentonite clay

½ cup dried herbs (any combination of calendula, chamomile, lavender, and rose)

HONEY CLEANSING MASK

If I have a little extra time, I like to mix up my cleansing grain mask with organic, raw, local honey and some hydrosol. This is the ultimate treat for your face. Blend a scoopful of cleansing grains with a tablespoon of honey and enough hydrosol to make it the right consistency— not too runny but not too dry to spread. Leave it on for 10 minutes before rinsing it off.

Herbal Facial Steam and Tea

Facial steams help keep your complexion glowing and vibrant. All the herbs can be used fresh or dried. This recipe is balancing and especially helpful for acne-prone skin. It can be used as a facial steam, or you can make it into a tea to drink. For best results, I would suggest doing both the steam and the tea.

Small handful of fresh calendula petals

Small handful of burdock root

Small handful of dandelion root or leaves

Small handful of peppermint leaves or yarrow blossoms for oily skin or violet flowers, comfrey leaves, or mallow leaves for dry skin (optional)

Filtered water

Honey (optional)

1. Add the herbs to a medium-sized bowl.
2. Boil enough water to cover all the herbs in the bowl by 2 inches, and then pour the water over the herbs.
3. Position your face a comfortable distance away from the steam. (Careful: it can be hot.) For the most effective treatment, put a towel over your head and shoulders to keep the steam in. Breathe deeply and enjoy the fragrant steam for 2 to 8 minutes.
4. To drink this as a tea, combine 1 teaspoon of each herb. Boil 8 ounces of water, pour it over the herbs, and let it steep. Sweeten with honey if desired.

Hydrosol (Flower Water)

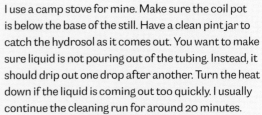

A hydrosol is the by-product of making essential oils. It is often called "flower water," and it makes the perfect toner. It also smells amazing! As essential oils and hydrosols gain popularity, more and more people are investing in glass or copper stills to make their own. I chose copper for my still because the metal is not only an excellent conductor of heat—making for very even distilling—but also wonderfully beneficial to the skin. While it might feel intimidating at first, using a copper still is actually very simple. Before you use it, wash and dry every part well. You may also want to do a scrub with vodka or another strong alcohol to really clean the surfaces.

Next, do a round of distilling with only water (no plant matter), which is an essential step to really clean your still before you begin. I do this extra step every time I use my still to make sure it is completely clean and remove any potential residue. Put only water in your still, attach the "onion" to the base, and fill the condenser (the pot with the coil of metal inside) with ice and water. As the ice melts, keep replenishing it. Your kit should have two bits of tubing. (If you purchased your still independently rather than as a set, you will need to purchase two.) One is for draining the condenser (coil pot). The other is for collecting what comes out of the coil—your hydrosol and the essential oil. Put the base of the still on a low flame.

I use a camp stove for mine. Make sure the coil pot is below the base of the still. Have a clean pint jar to catch the hydrosol as it comes out. You want to make sure liquid is not pouring out of the tubing. Instead, it should drip out one drop after another. Turn the heat down if the liquid is coming out too quickly. I usually continue the cleaning run for around 20 minutes.

After your still is completely clean, you are ready to begin. Fill the base with your desired herb no higher than the rivet line (the line of dots you can see from the outside) or no more than three-quarters full. (In the accompanying photos, I've used rosemary.) Cover your herbs with warm distilled water, clean spring water, or rainwater. Make sure you don't have too much plant matter in there, and that it can move freely in the water. This is very important to make sure none of it scorches or burns. Then, repeat the process you just completed with plain water— put the base on a very low flame, make sure the condenser (coil pot) is filled with ice, and replenish it as needed so there is always plenty of ice in there. After a few minutes, you will notice drops coming out of the tubing leading from the condenser (note that water will be flowing out of the other tube as ice is added, so it does not spill out of the top). Make sure the hydrosol is coming out drop by drop, and not pouring out too fast. This is an art. It should sound like *drop, drop, drop*—not *trickle, trickle, trickle*, with many drops coming out all together. In other words, you should be able to see actual drops, not a trickle, coming out. When in doubt, turn the heat down.

Once you have collected no more than half the water you initially started with, it is time to stop. Let your hydrosol settle. If you have made a lot, and from a plant with a high volatile-oil content, you will be able to use a dropper to collect the essential oil, which will settle at the top. As a final step, I use a coffee filter to strain the hydrosol, because I like mine crystal clear. At this point you may bottle it. If you store it in a cool, dry, and dark place, it should keep for at least a year, often much longer.

Antiaging Serum

Serum is my favorite part of my skincare routine. It helps my skin retain balance and moisture, and it fights the signs of aging. I use it at night after cleansing and spraying my face with hydrosol, but before I apply lotion.

¼ cup (2 ounces) jojoba oil

1 tablespoon rosehip oil

1 tablespoon sea buckthorn oil

10 to 15 drops helichrysum essential oil

5 drops jasmine or rose essential oil

1. Mix all the ingredients together in a small container. (I use a glass measuring cup with a spout.)
2. Store the serum in amber dropper bottles away from sunlight, heat, and moisture.
3. To use, after cleansing your face and spraying with hydrosol, apply four to seven drops of this serum to your face and massage until absorbed. Follow with lotion.

Age-Reverse Face and Body Lotion

A good lotion is an essential step in any skincare routine. It will help the skin retain moisture without clogging the pores and penetrate deeper layers of the skin rather than just floating on the epidermis. I learned how to make lotion many years ago from one of my teachers, master herbalist Rosemary Gladstar. This recipe is inspired by her wonderful lotions, and I encourage you to read her many books on skincare, as they are all truly excellent. I created this lotion to address the issue of my aging, sun-damaged skin, which is also quite sensitive and still very acne-prone. Please note that helichrysum is incredible at preventing and reversing signs of aging, but the essential oil is very expensive, so feel free to omit it if the cost is prohibitive. You will still get many antiaging benefits from the hydrosol.

1. Add the infused jojoba oil, sesame oil, sunflower seed oil, coconut oil, and beeswax to a double boiler on very low heat.
2. When melted, wipe all the water from the bottom of the top pan and set it aside.
3. In a high-powered blender, add the hydrosol, aloe vera, essential oils, and vitamin E, keeping the blades going at medium speed.
4. Carefully pour the melted oils and wax mixture into the blender. Blend until the two are fully combined, and then turn the blender speed down to low. You may see some drops of hydrosol on top, and some of the mixture may not have fully incorporated, remaining on the sides of the blender. This is all fine. Don't try to mix it in.
5. Quickly pour the lotion into very clean dark-colored glass jars. It will become more firm as it cools. (See the resources section in the back of this book for suggested jar vendors.)
6. After you've poured all you can into separate jars, scrape out whatever is left in the blender. This last jar of lotion is not ideal for your face, as it's not evenly incorporated, but it will work just fine as a body lotion. I try not to waste a drop of this liquid gold! Store all of your jars in a cool, dark place away from moisture. If the jars are sterile, they will last a minimum of several months.

¼ cup jojoba oil, infused with dried calendula petals

¼ cup sesame oil, infused with dried helichrysum blossoms

¼ cup sunflower seed oil, infused with dried calendula petals

⅓ cup coconut oil

2 tablespoons (½ ounce) beeswax pastilles

1 cup helichrysum hydrosol

2 tablespoons aloe vera gel

20 drops helichrysum essential oil

20 drops rose, geranium, or ylang ylang essential oil

20 drops jasmine essential oil

1 teaspoon vitamin E

TIP: You can combine the jojoba, sesame, and sunflower oils and infuse them with dried calendula petals all in the same jar if you prefer. I often go this route, as it saves time and I have fewer dishes to do in the end. However, if I am also making other things with each infused oil, I infuse them separately.

Body

Water is the best moisturizer for your skin. The problem is, water quickly evaporates and leaves your skin drier than it started. In order to get the longest-lasting effects, moisturize after a bath or shower while your skin is still just barely damp. This will help keep the plumpness of your skin and reduce the chances of dry, scaly-looking skin. Good choices for body moisturizers are my age-reverse face and body lotion (see page 323) or an herbal-infused body oil.

Calendula-Rose Body Oil

This body oil is wonderful for dry or itchy skin. It smells lovely and feels divine. For the best results, massage into your skin immediately after bathing.

Dried calendula petals

Dried rose petals

Sweet almond oil

Sesame seed oil

Essential oils of choice
(I love rose and jasmine or a combination of frankincense, lavender, and sage)

1. Fill a jar one-third full with a combination of dried calendula petals and dried rose petals. Then fill the jar half full of sweet almond oil and half full of sesame seed oil.
2. Put on the lid, and place the jar in a sunny window.
3. Give the jar a gentle shake every day for 1 week.
4. Keep the jar in the sunny window for 1 to 3 weeks after that, and then strain out the petals. Add a few drops of your desired essential oils to give it a lovely scent.
5. To use, massage approximately 2 tablespoons of the oil into towel-dried skin immediately after bathing while skin is just slightly damp.

TIP: A good rule of thumb for essential oils is one percent dilution for face products and two percent dilution for body products. For 1 cup of herbal-infused oil, add no more than 48 drops total of essential oil if it will be used on your face. If you will only use it on your body, you can add up to 96 drops of essential oil per cup of herbal-infused oil—although personally I prefer a one percent dilution even on my body.

Lemon-Eucalyptus Body Scrub

Exfoliation is a very important part of every health and beauty routine. Your skin is the body's largest organ, and one of its major jobs is to help the body eliminate toxins. A buildup of dead skin cells makes this elimination difficult. Dry brushing is a really effective method of exfoliation. To do this, a special brush is used in long strokes on the body in the direction of the heart. Body scrubs are another wonderful way to exfoliate and enliven the skin.

1. Fill a half-pint jar one-third full with the eucalyptus leaves.
2. Pour the sweet almond or olive oil up to ½ inch from the top, put on the lid, and give it a shake.
3. Place the jar in a sunny window and shake it every day for 1 week.
4. After 1 week, strain out the leaves.
5. Next, put the sea salt in a large bowl. Add the eucalyptus-infused oil to the bowl.
6. Grate the skin of one to two lemons into the bowl and add the lemon or eucalyptus essential oil. Mix well.
7. Fill 4-ounce jars with your scrub and screw on the lids.

⅓ cup eucalyptus leaves, broken into small pieces (optional)

1 cup sweet almond or olive oil

1 cup finely ground sea salt

10 to 15 drops lemon or eucalyptus essential oil

1 to 2 organic lemons

Toothpaste

Toothpaste from the store is full of all kinds of toxins that are incredibly bad for you, including fluoride (yes, fluoride is bad for you), sodium lauryl sulfate, triclosan, and artificial sweeteners and colors, just to name a few. Some of these ingredients have been linked to canker sores and other unpleasant health concerns. Luckily, there are a couple of natural brands on the market that avoid most of these toxins. Another way to avoid putting anything poisonous in your mouth is by making your own toothpaste. It's fun and really simple, and with a few minor tweaks you can make it exactly how you like it.

1 cup bentonite clay, French green clay, or arrowroot powder

2 teaspoons sea salt

2 tablespoons baking soda

Filtered water

2 to 3 drops peppermint essential oil (optional)

1. Grind the clay, salt, and baking soda to a fine powder. It is very important to grind your ingredients very, very well so they do not scratch your teeth. An electric coffee grinder reserved for grinding herbs only or a mortar and pestle are both good options.
2. Mix the dry ingredients together, and then add enough water to make a paste.
3. If desired, add the peppermint oil. Peppermint is antibacterial, antifungal, and antiviral, and it will make your mouth feel fresh after brushing.
4. You can store your toothpaste in a glass jar with a lid, or even buy some refillable toothpaste tubes to keep it in.

TOOTHPASTE VARIATIONS

← If you want to give your toothpaste extra shelf life, you can leave out the water, making what is known as a "tooth powder." Store it in a jar, and then when you are ready to brush your teeth, simply dip a wet toothbrush in the powder and brush as usual. Alternatively, you can mix a teaspoon of powder with some water to make toothpaste on the spot as you need it, and then apply it to your brush.

← If you like some sweetness to your toothpaste, you can add a little vegetable glycerine to your mix. Start with a small amount and add to taste. This does not work for tooth powders, but is a great option for the toothpaste version with water.

← To address specific mouth concerns and make your toothpaste work even harder, you can add herbs to your tooth powder or paste. Calendula and sage are two of my favorite herbs for the mouth. Licorice root is another good one to try. These herbs are anti-inflammatory, antimicrobial, and vulnerary (wound healing). To incorporate these herbs, finely powder a small amount (start with 1 teaspoon or less) and then add to your tooth powder or paste.

Foxen Canyon Soap Company

ELLOWYN ISAACSON

Ellowyn Isaacson is such a gift to the community of women who create. Extremely humble, she empowers others to connect back to their roots, leading by example. What inspires me most about Ellowyn is her wealth of knowledge. She is constantly learning and sharing and enriching the community.

She was born in San Jose, California, and grew up surrounded by animals. Her mom was an avid gardener who raised birds for a wildlife foundation. She spent years traveling and studying in France, and spent time in Corsica, where she learned about pastoral goat and sheep raising and sausage and cheese making.

For most of her adult life, Ellowyn has explored everything from cooking with homegrown foods to making cheese from her hand-milked goats, sewing and quilting, building animal pens, and raising animals. In 2015, Ellowyn, her husband, and their six children moved into an old remodeled Pacific

Coast Railway weigh station on a half-acre in Sisquoc, California. It was built in 1909 and converted into a home in the 1970s. Just a few weeks after moving in, her goat had two kids. With all the excess milk, she learned how to make cheese, yogurt, and kefir, which she used for baked goods. Then, she started to make goat's milk soap for Christmas gifts. For Ellowyn, soapmaking is the culmination of following her passion for homemaking skills.

Her hobby became her business, and Foxen Canyon Soap Company was launched in 2018. Success and sales were instant, and her business quickly outgrew her home-produced ingredients. Ellowyn still uses only local, natural, and sustainable ingredients from small agricultural businesses, and specific native plants and herbs are used to bring the soap colors and beneficial properties. She even partners with local butchers to purchase unwanted animal fat that would otherwise be discarded, which she renders herself to ensure no chemicals or preservatives are added. The organic coconut oil she uses is from a small, family-run co-op in Oregon that sources from a small, fair-trade, sustainable producer in the Philippines. Every detail is of the utmost quality. For her packaging, she found a local company that manufactures clamshell soap boxes made with 100 percent recycled material that are also 100 percent compostable. Ellowyn's soaps are sold in retail shops around the Central Coast of California, and in national grocery stores under private labels. The intention behind artisan soapmaking is to keep things local and reduce carbon footprint.

In her spare time, she teaches classes and helps other people discover the joy of living a sustainable, natural lifestyle. Today, she is one of 30 soapmakers around the world who were chosen based on their soapmaking, leadership, and teaching skills to moderate the Soapmaking Natural Ingredients Forum.

HOMESTEAD MILK SOAP

Homemade soap isn't as difficult to make as you might think, and the result is so gratifying. It's another way to preserve the gift of your animal's milk that is so precious, and you can enjoy it for months. For best results, it's important to use a kitchen scale to measure each ingredient by weight.

11 ounces lard or tallow (rendered)
1 ounce honey (raw, melted)
2 ounces fresh milk (raw or pasteurized)
1 ounce sodium hydroxide
1 ounce distilled water

1. In a stainless-steel saucepan, combine the lard or tallow and honey and melt together over low heat. Remove it from the heat as soon as the two are melted. Do not overheat. Add the fresh milk and, using an immersion blender, mix until well incorporated.
2. Using gloved hands, carefully combine the sodium hydroxide and the water. Stir gently until it is completely dissolved.
3. Carefully pour the lye solution into the saucepan. Using the immersion blender completely immersed in the mixture, begin to pulse. The mixture will begin to thicken. Continue until you can trace a visible line across the surface of the mixture with the blender. When this happens, immediately stop mixing.
4. Pour the mixture into a soap-safe mold. Gently tap the mold against the table a few times to release any bubbles or air pockets. Allow the soap to sit undisturbed for 24 hours.
5. After 24 hours, carefully remove the soap from the mold and cut it into bars. Set the bars on a nonaluminum drying rack, out of the sun, but in an area with good air circulation. The bars will remain here for the next 4 to 6 weeks to cure.
6. After curing, the bars are ready to be used. Allowing the bars to dry completely between uses will extend the life of the soap.

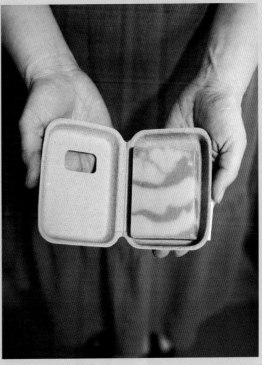

Hair

I stopped using conditioner a long time ago, but I used to be a conditioner junkie. I have fine hair, and I would search out the heaviest conditioners to slather on to prevent tangles and split ends. What I didn't realize was that the same product I was using to prevent those tangles and split ends was actually causing them. It was also weighing my thin hair down, and making it appear even thinner. When I stopped using conditioner, my hair also had much more body. Then I started using hair rinses instead, which gave my entire hair and scalp an upgrade. The vinegar rinses kept my hair shiny and healthy, and it had more body because I didn't have any heavy conditioner weighing it down.

Herbal Hair Oil

Just like your skin, sometimes your hair needs a little moisturization. Conditioner is not the answer, since it can weigh down your hair and cause split ends. Hair oil, on the other hand, works nicely. I usually only use hair oil on the ends of my hair. I alternate between argan oil and olive oil, both infused with stinging nettle.

Dried stinging nettle

Argan or olive oil

1. Fill a glass jar a quarter full with dried stinging nettle.
2. Pour the argan oil, olive oil, or a mix of both over the nettle.
3. Let the jar sit for 1 week, shaking once a day.
4. Let the jar sit for another 1 to 3 weeks, and then strain out the solids.
5. Store in a dark-colored bottle away from heat, sunlight, and moisture.
6. To use, put a few drops in the palm of one hand. Rub your hands together, and then run them over the ends of your hair. Rinse out in the morning if needed; if not, leave it in for extra moisture.

Rosemary Hair Rinse

Rosemary is an excellent herb when it comes to hair, especially for those with dry scalps. Hair rinses can bring a shine to your hair and health to your scalp. They nourish the hair with the nutrients in the herbs and normalize the pH of the scalp, which can be helpful for anyone prone to dandruff.

Handful of rosemary sprigs

Apple cider vinegar

1. Fill a jar with the rosemary sprigs.
2. Pour the vinegar to cover the rosemary.
3. Top with a plastic lid or wax paper under a metal lid.
4. Let the jar sit for 4 weeks, shaking once a day.
5. Strain out the solids, and reserve the infused vinegar.
6. For ease of use, I keep the infused vinegar in a bottle. When I'm ready to shower, I pour some into a big cup, about one-quarter full. I fill the cup the rest of the way with water. While in the shower, after shampooing, I pour the vinegar-water mixture over my head and massage it in. Then, I rinse it out and towel dry.

HAIR RINSE VARIATIONS

CHAMOMILE HAIR RINSE
Chamomile also makes a good rinse. It is said to bring out the golden tones of blonde hair. Follow the directions explained here, but substitute chamomile for the rosemary.

WILD AND WEEDY HAIR RINSE
Weeds are nutrient- and mineral-dense, and I love incorporating them into my life in as many ways as possible. I fill a jar with mallow root and leaf, nettle, and chickweed, and cover it with apple cider vinegar. After a few weeks, I strain off the weeds and feed them to my chickens. I then dilute the infused vinegar with water and use it as a hair rinse.

HERBAL MEDICINE

There are endless combinations and recipes when it comes to herbal remedies. For the sake of keeping things simple, I've included just a few of my favorites. If you find yourself hungry for more, you might consider purchasing more books on the subject or maybe even pursuing training as an herbalist. It may sound daunting, but there are many excellent schools that have made obtaining an herbal education convenient through distance programs. Some of the schools I have personally attended and recommend can be found in the resources at the back of this book.

It is important to note that while I have studied herbalism and health for many years, I am not a doctor. Although herbal medicine is the oldest and most widely used form of medicine worldwide, it is not recognized as a legal form of health care in the United States. Neither licenses nor certifications are recognized in this country. It is recommended that you seek guidance from a licensed health-care professional before taking any of these remedies, especially if you are on any medication or are pregnant or breastfeeding. These recipes are the remedies I use in my own house, and although my experience with them has been very positive, every human body is different and unique. I do not make any claims to treat, prevent, or cure any disease.

Herbal Medicine Basket

An herbal medicine basket is an at-home herbal first-aid kit. It is especially useful with young children in the house. In fact, my children each have their own self-care basket with age-appropriate items for them to use. My oldest is 11 and responsible enough to have some glycerides and tinctures in her kit, along with her salve, toothbrush, and toothpaste. My youngest is only five, so he has only a salve, toothbrush, and toothpaste, along with some floss and Band-Aids. We also have a family medicine basket, which includes all of the tinctures and other remedies that are more safely administered by a parent. Your medicine basket should include a selection of remedies tailored to your specific needs. It has been so empowering to replace my existing drugstore items one by one with the remedies I make myself.

FAVORITE PLANTS FOR A MEDICINE GARDEN

- Elderberry
- Comfrey
- Burdock
- Dandelion
- Valerian
- Yarrow
- Sage
- Oregano
- Gotu kola
- Horehound
- Borage
- Peppermint
- Echinacea
- Lemon balm
- Ashwagandha
- Clover
- Chamomile
- Rose

HERBAL PREPARATIONS

TEA OR INFUSION: A water-based extraction of flowers, leaves, and stems, usually made by pouring very hot water over the herbs and letting them steep

DECOCTION: A water-based extraction of the tougher parts of the plant, such as berries, bark, and roots, usually made by simmering these parts in water on the stove for a minimum of 20 minutes before steeping

TINCTURE: An alcohol-based extraction of herbs

GLYCERIDE: An extraction using vegetable glycerine and water

HERBAL VINEGAR: A vinegar extraction often used for nutritive herbs rich in minerals

ELIXIR: An extraction of herbs using honey and alcohol

HERBAL OIL: An extraction of herbs where the oil is heated gently

SALVE OR OINTMENT: A topical remedy made with an oil extraction of herbs

Elderberry Syrup

Elderberry is the favorite herb in my house to fight the cold and flu. The local variety here in Southern California is Mexican or blue elderberry (*Sambucus nigra ssp. caerulea*). There has been some buzz about this plant being toxic, but it is important to clarify that no one has died from consuming this plant. However, it is not uncommon to get an upset stomach, sometimes lasting a couple of days, after consuming the green parts of the plant, such as the leaf and stem, the unripe fruit, and also the bark. The flowers and ripe fruit do not cause this reaction. Use only ripe berries and remove and compost all green parts of the plant. If you have a sensitive stomach, however, you may want to dry and then cook your berries rather than juicing them fresh. I make a syrup of the fresh or dried berries and take it by the spoonful, drizzle it on pancakes, or add it to sparkling water to make a wild soda. This is one of my favorite herbs, and I enjoy it year-round. I dry the fruit I gather throughout the summer and early fall to use throughout the winter and spring.

1. Fill a pot with the elderberries and any combination (or all) of the star anise, vanilla bean, orange peel, astragalus slices, and cinnamon stick, and then cover with the water. If you are using dried elderberries, use 1 part elderberries to 4 parts water.
2. Let the berries simmer until they are broken down a bit and the liquid is reduced by half.
3. Turn off the heat and mash everything carefully with a potato masher.
4. Add a handful of elderflowers (blossoms only, no stems) and let the mixture sit, covered, while the flowers infuse for 5 to 10 minutes.
5. Strain out all of the solids, reserving the liquid.
6. Mix the liquid at a one-to-one ratio with the honey. Add the brandy if using. (It is optional, but it will help preserve the syrup, giving it a longer shelf life.)
7. Store your syrup in clean glass bottles in the fridge. It will last for at least a couple of months, but it is so delicious it will likely be gone long before then.
8. To use, take a teaspoon of elderberry syrup every hour at the first hint of a cold or flu. I also use it like maple syrup, for a treat, or as a wild soda (see page 294).

2 cups fresh elderberries (or 1 cup dried elderberries)

2 star anise pods (optional)

½ vanilla bean, sliced lengthwise (optional)

1 tablespoon chopped fresh or dried orange peel (optional)

3 to 4 astragalus slices (optional)

1 cinnamon stick (optional)

Filtered water (about 4 cups if using dried elderberries)

Handful of elderflowers (blossoms only)

Raw local honey

¼ cup brandy (optional)

Horehound Candy

This recipe is a convenient spin on an old-timey remedy. Horehound is one of my favorite herbs because it fights chest congestion like nothing else, thinning and expelling mucus, and quickly heals an aggressive cough. Horehound candy is bitter but effective. In a pinch, if I don't have any fresh, I use a teaspoonful of dried horehound. I drizzle the honey on top, mix it up, and eat it as is. You can even make it into an herbal tea, and I have tried to drink it a few times. I won't lie—it tastes awful! But it works wonders for a phlegmy cough and chest congestion, and if I am really sick, I try to sip a little at a time throughout the day. Please note that horehound is contraindicated during pregnancy.

Fresh horehound

Honey

Powdered mullein, slippery elm, ashwagandha, and licorice (optional)

1. Finely chop the fresh horehound.
2. Drizzle the honey over it and mix to form a paste.
3. Spread this paste in little dabs on wax paper. Put the paper in a dehydrator and dry on low (110°F) until it is the consistency of the inside of a dried fig.
4. This is optional, but I like to roll the candy in powdered mullein (*Verbascum thapsus*) or a combination of powdered slippery elm, ashwagandha, and licorice, which also keeps the pieces from sticking together. (Slippery elm is overharvested, so please take care to source it from an ethical distributor or omit it from this recipe.)
5. Store the candy in a clean glass jar with a lid.
6. To use, eat approximately 1 teaspoon at a time whenever you have a rattly, wet cough.

Eucalyptus Chest Rub

A eucalyptus-based chest rub is great for relieving congestion. Sometimes I call it "Victoria's vapor rub" to be cheeky. Eucalyptus is acclaimed for its ability to clear the sinuses, relieve congestion, and help you breathe more easily. It is antibacterial and antiseptic, and it helps relax and relieve respiratory upset. It's a common ingredient in many cough and cold syrups, as well as chest rubs. Personally, I love chest rubs when I am really congested and having trouble breathing through my nose, especially right before bed. I like to make my own with eucalyptus-infused olive oil, and I sometimes include other health-promoting and antiseptic herbs, such as lavender, rosemary, peppermint, sage, or wormwood. This also makes a great all-purpose salve if you limit the essential oil to 2 or 3 drops.

1. In a double boiler, combine the eucalyptus-infused olive oil with the beeswax pastilles.
2. Heat on low until everything is melted together.
3. Turn off the heat. Add the vitamin E oil and eucalyptus essential oil, stir to mix, and pour it into small jars.
4. To use, rub a little on your chest whenever your sinuses are clogged to ease congestion.

½ cup olive oil infused with eucalyptus leaves or herbs

2 tablespoons beeswax pastilles

¼ teaspoon non-GMO vitamin E oil

30 to 45 drops eucalyptus essential oil

Fire Cider

The name fire cider refers to a traditional recipe that has deep roots in herbal medicine. This name was originally coined by Rosemary Gladstar, and the remedy itself is centuries old. This folk recipe is used to boost the immune system, as well as put an end to oncoming symptoms of a cold or flu. Everyone's version is a little different, but all are made by infusing a few immune-strengthening herbs and vegetables in apple cider vinegar, straining, and then adding honey. This is the recipe I use, but try making your own version by adding a few sprigs of rosemary, oregano, or a bay leaf.

1 large horseradish, grated

1 whole hand fresh organic ginger, grated

1 onion, chopped

4 to 8 heads of garlic, pressed

Powdered cayenne

1 organic lemon, sliced

Apple cider vinegar

Honey

1. Put the horseradish, ginger, onion, garlic, cayenne (to taste), and lemon in a large glass jar, or divide between several smaller jars.
2. Pour the apple cider vinegar over the vegetables and herbs until it reaches 1 inch from the top.
3. Put on the lid, and shake the jar once a day for 1 week.
4. Let the jar sit for 3 to 5 weeks on the counter.
5. Strain out the solids and add honey using a one-to-one ratio of vinegar mixture to honey.
6. Store your syrup in clean glass bottles in the cupboard. Once open, store in the fridge for freshness. It will last this way for many months without spoiling.
7. To use, take a spoonful a day during flu season, or a teaspoon six to eight times a day if you feel like you are coming down with something.

IMMUNE-BOOSTING INGREDIENTS

HORSERADISH: Antibacterial, nutritious, and diuretic; traditionally used to clear congestion, boost immune system, and aid digestion

GINGER: Digestive aid, carminative, expectorant, antiseptic, pain reliever, and anti-inflammatory; traditionally used to treat stomach problems, nausea, respiratory problems, indigestion, and inflammation

ONION: Antioxidant, anti-inflammatory, blood tonic, antibacterial, nutritious, and antifungal; traditionally used to relieve a sore throat and cough symptoms

GARLIC: Antimicrobial, antibiotic, anti-inflammatory, expectorant, diaphoretic, and diuretic; traditionally used as an immune system stimulant and as support for respiratory issues, treating a cold, and thinning mucus

CAYENNE: Carminative; traditionally used to relieve congestion, sore throat, cold, and digestion

LEMON: Antihistaminic, anti-inflammatory, and diuretic; traditionally used to boost immune system

HONEY: Antibacterial, antihistamine, and antioxidant; traditionally used to ease allergies, boost immune system, and calm a cough

Echinacea Tincture

Tinctures are probably the most convenient form of herbal medicine. They are easy to travel with and take only seconds to administer. Alcohol is excellent at extracting the medicinal compounds in the plant and will preserve them almost indefinitely. Echinacea tincture is my favorite remedy to combine with elderberry syrup at the first sign of a cold or flu. It is a potent antiviral immune booster and powerful, stimulating antiseptic. It increases bodily resistance to infections. It is quite strong, so I don't use it as a preventative, nor do I take it for extended periods of time. Rather, I use it at the onset of a cold or flu, and for the first few days.

Echinacea root, chopped or dried

Vodka

1. Fill a small jar three-quarters full with cleaned, chopped echinacea root (*Echinacea purpurea*) or one-quarter full with dried echinacea root.
2. Pour the vodka over it to completely cover the echinacea, up to ½ inch from the top of the jar.
3. Put on the lid, and shake the jar once a day for 1 week.
4. Let your tincture sit for a minimum of 3 more weeks. Strain out the solids (you can use a coffee filter to capture all of the tiny pieces), and then pour your tincture into 1-ounce dropper bottles.
5. To use, take half a dropperful every 2 hours at the onset of a flu for up to 3 days. Often I mix that half a dropperful with a tablespoon of elderberry syrup.

GENERAL WELL-BEING

The most common thing I turn to herbalism for is general well-being. Taking small amounts of nourishing, gentle herbs feels good to my whole system, keeps my skin looking healthy, and helps me feel my best. Herbs are powerful and work differently for each person. Explore which herbs work best for you and listen to your body as you discover their health benefits.

Herbal Tea

Herbal tea is my favorite form of herbal medicine. It's calming, relaxing, and most of the time delicious too. Most people are used to drinking teas made with commercial tea bags, but growing your own herbs for tea is more effective as medicine and much tastier. Even purchasing freshly dried herbs and making your own tea from them is preferable to the store-bought variety.

To make a tea with fresh herbs, such as peppermint, simply fill a heatproof jar at least halfway with loosely packed herbs. (I use a glass measuring pitcher or jar.) Then pour just-boiled water over the top. After a few minutes of steeping (letting the plants infuse into the hot water), strain out the solids, sweeten with honey or stevia, and enjoy.

To make a tea with dried herbs, put 1 heaping teaspoon of the herbs per 8 ounces of water into

a heatproof vessel, pour just-boiled water over the top, and steep for a few minutes. Then strain out the solids, sweeten if desired, and enjoy. Alternatively, you could use a mesh tea strainer, French press, or make your own tea bags.

TISANE

Tisane is the proper name for an herbal tea. The word *tea* is only technically correct when talking about the beverage made from the leaves of the tea plant. White tea, green tea, or black tea are all from the same plant (*Camellia sinensis*). The term *herbal tea* refers to a tisane, or infusion of plant matter from any other plant. Because I didn't grow up using that word, I usually refer to my tisanes as teas, even though that's not technically correct.

Fresh vs. Dried

I will always choose fresh tea rather than dried if it's available. The taste is unbeatable, and the herbs themselves are more potent. I only know of two medicinal herbs that must be dried before you use them because they are toxic when fresh: cascara sagrada and orris root. Everything else is better fresh when it comes to herbal teas. That said, it's not always possible or convenient to have fresh tea. Fresh herbs will quickly go bad if they are not used or dried. Freshly dried tea is the next best thing, especially when it's grown in your own backyard or by a local farmer. The recipes in this chapter all call for freshly dried ingredients, but if you have the fresh version on hand, feel free to use that instead. It will taste even better. The only benefit of using dried herbs is they can be made in larger batches and stored.

Herbal Tea Recipes

For each of these recipes, simply mix all the dried ingredients together, transfer the herb mixture to a glass container, and store it away from light and heat. These recipes are given in parts, or ratios, so they can be made in any size quantity, depending on how much you need and how much of each herb you have on hand. A good starting point is designating 1 cup as 1 part. Then you have a decent amount of tea, but not so much that it goes stale before you can use it. If you only want to make a little, you could even designate 1 tablespoon as 1 part. The choice is yours.

Love Tea

This tea tastes wonderful, and uses aphrodisiac herbs like rose petal (*Rosa spp.*), peppermint (*Mentha piperita*), and damiana (*Turnera diffusa*). To be honest, I never actually measure these herbs, and I use any combination of the three. If I'm out of peppermint, I'll use rose petal and damiana alone, and if I'm out of damiana, I'll use rose petal and peppermint.

1. Combine the rose petal, peppermint, and damiana.
2. To use, add 1 to 2 teaspoons to a tea infuser, French press, or heatproof glass pitcher. Pour 8 ounces of just-boiled water over the herbs and cover.
3. Let steep for a couple of minutes, strain, and then sweeten if desired.

1 part rose petal

1 part peppermint

1 part damiana

Pregnancy Tea

I drank this tea throughout all three of my pregnancies, sweetened with a little stevia. Red raspberry (*Rubus idaeus*) is *the* pregnancy herb. It is a uterine tonic, improves blood supply, and prevents postpartum hemorrhage. Alfalfa (*Medicago sativa*) is a blood builder and is full of nutrients. Nettle (*Urtica dioica*) is extremely nutritious, and is helpful for anemia as well as thyroid deficiency. Oats (*Avena sativa*) are also nutritious, and are used to treat insomnia and nervous system irritation from exhaustion or stress. I add rose petals to surround the mama-to-be with love. This is a great tea to drink from the second trimester on, all the way until the end of breastfeeding.

1 part red raspberry leaf

¼ part alfalfa

1 part nettle

½ part milky oat tops

Handful of rose petals

1. Combine the red raspberry leaves, alfalfa, nettle, oats, and rose petals.
2. To use, add 1 to 2 teaspoons to a tea infuser, French press, or heatproof glass pitcher. Pour 8 ounces of just-boiled water over the herbs and cover.
3. Let steep for a couple of minutes, strain, and then sweeten if desired.

DRINKING VINEGAR VARIATION

You can make a delicious drinking vinegar (pictured) out of these herbs as well. Mix up enough to fill the bottom quarter of a glass jar, and then fill it the rest of the way up with apple cider vinegar. Put on a nonmetal lid, such as plastic or glass. (If all you have is a metal lid, put a piece of wax paper over the top before putting the lid on. This will keep the vinegar from reacting with the metal and making it rust.) Shake the jar once a day. After 2 to 4 weeks, strain out the solids. Mix your infused vinegar with equal parts honey and store it in glass bottles. When you feel like a refreshing, nourishing drink, add 1 or 2 tablespoons to a glass of water. It is so good!

Sweet Mountaintop

MARY GONZALEZ

Mary Gonzalez is a dear friend of mine and a fellow plant lover. She is endlessly inspiring me with her music, her style, and the beautiful, artistic way she lives her life. The connection she has to her land and to the plants she grows is both genuine and palpable. A short while back, she decided to follow her dreams and create a medicinal plant business. On her mountaintop land, she grows, harvests, dries, packages, and sells her favorite medicinal flowers in the form of teas and medicinal bouquets at the local farmers market. We are always swapping our latest herbal remedies with one another.

MARY'S TEA FOR CALMING THE NERVES

Mary's special tea blend is the best I've ever tasted. It's my favorite tea, and I drink it often for its delicious taste and gentle but effective calming qualities. It combines four soothing ingredients: tulsi (*Ocimum tenuiflorum*), lemon balm (*Melissa officinalis*), anise hyssop (*Agastache foeniculum*), and chamomile (*Matricaria recutita*). I'm so grateful she generously shared it in this book.

1 part tulsi, also known as holy basil
1 part lemon balm
1 part anise hyssop
⅓ part chamomile

1. Combine the tulsi, lemon balm, anise hyssop, and chamomile.
2. To use, add 1 to 2 teaspoons to a tea infuser, French press, or heatproof glass pitcher. Pour 8 ounces of just-boiled water over the herbs and cover.
3. Let steep for a couple of minutes, strain, and then sweeten if desired.

Other Recipes for Well-Being

In addition to herbal teas, I also make tinctures, elixirs, and syrups to support overall health. The benefit of these forms of herbal remedies is that they have a much longer shelf life than tea, which only stays fresh for around 24 hours. Syrups last for a minimum of 30 days, and tinctures and elixirs last for many years, if not indefinitely. Once they are made, they can be quickly and conveniently administered.

Gotu Kola Tincture

This truly amazing tincture is one of my favorites. It reduces stress, increases energy and endurance, boosts hair and nail growth, and accelerates the healing time for wounds. I think it's so amazing that I grow the herb in my garden so I always have access to it. As a tincture, I take half a dropperful once a day. Please note that gotu kola is contraindicated during pregnancy.

1. Chop up the fresh gotu kola, and fill a jar two-thirds full. If using dried, fill your jar one-quarter full.
2. Pour the vodka over it to about ½ inch from the top.
3. Put on the lid, and shake the jar once a day for 1 week.
4. Let the jar sit for 3 more weeks, shaking occasionally, and then strain out the solids.
5. Bottle the tincture in 1-ounce dropper bottles.

Fresh or dried gotu kola

Vodka

Calming Hops Elixir

The cone-shaped fruits of the hops plant (*Humulus lupulus*) are used for this elixir. I use it for anxiety, a nervous tummy, and insomnia. I take half a dropperful one to three times per day for up to 2 weeks at a time. For this recipe, you can grow your own hops plant or order the dried strobiles from a local farmer or reputable online source.

1. Fill a jar two-thirds full with the strobiles.
2. Pour the vodka or brandy over them to cover.
3. Put on the lid, and shake the jar once a day for 1 week.
4. Let the jar sit for at least 3 more weeks. Strain out the solids, and then mix the tincture at a one-to-one ratio with local honey.
5. Bottle the elixir in 1- or 2-ounce dropper bottles and label them.

Dried hops strobiles

Vodka or brandy

Honey

Rose Hip Syrup

Every year in November or early December, I make rose hip syrup. Rose hips are one of the most concentrated sources of vitamin C, and I like to give a spoonful to each member of my family in lieu of vitamin tablets. This recipe also uses the petals of the rose and a few leaves of garden sage (*Salvia officinalis*). These add-ins are optional, but I love the extra complexity of taste they bring to the syrup. Honey is another main component of the recipe, and another one of my favorite medicines. I use it on cuts and scrapes, to soothe a sore throat, and as an ingredient in cough syrups. It is antimicrobial, making it an excellent preservative, and also contains important vitamins, minerals, and antioxidants.

You can order dried rose hips from reputable online companies, such as Mountain Rose Herbs. If you decide to use fresh, you will first need to prepare them. With a sharp knife, cut each rose hip lengthwise, scraping out the seeds and fine hairs and reserving the fruit. Once all the fruit is cleaned and seeded, you are ready to begin.

Sometimes I like to make the syrup extra special by infusing the brandy with rose petals. If you choose to do this step, fill a small jar with rose petals. Cut them up if they are fresh, or use a mortar and pestle to grind them up if they are dried. Then, cover the petals with the brandy. Put the lid on the jar, shake, and let it infuse for at least 24 hours or up to 1 month—or more if you'd like. When you are ready to make your syrup, strain out the petals and reserve the brandy.

4 cups filtered water or rainwater

2 cups cleaned rose hips (or 1¼ cups dried)

A handful of fresh or dried rose petals (optional)

2 or 3 garden sage leaves (optional)

1 to 2 cups honey

A splash of brandy (or rose petal–infused brandy)

1. Place the water and rose hips in a pot. Let it simmer until the water reduces by half.
2. Turn off the heat. Add the rose petals and sage leaves (if using), cover, and let steep for 5 to 10 minutes.
3. Strain out and compost the solids, reserving the liquid. Return the liquid to the pot.
4. Add the honey and brandy to the pot and stir until combined.
5. Pour your syrup into sterilized bottles, and keep them in a cool, dry place or the fridge. Any leftover rose hips can be cleaned and dehydrated, and then stored in a glass jar with a tight lid. You can use these in your tea, or to make more syrup next time.

TIP: Easily harvested by holding a hip in your fingers and giving it a small twist, the rose hip is actually the fruit of the rose. It develops as a red, roundish seedpod after the petals drop off. You can use the hips off of your garden roses if they are not sprayed with any pesticides, or you can forage for wild rose hips in the late summer through autumn.

NATURAL DYES

I use natural dyes for three reasons: out of consideration for the environment, for the extra connection to the project and my land, and for the range of color. There are three main types of natural dyes. One is substantive (or direct) dye, which requires nothing to get the color on fiber. A good example of this is coffee. (How hard is it to get that coffee stain out of your shirt?) Another type of dye is mordant, which requires a preparation of the fabric in order to accept the color from the dye. And last, there are vat dyes, which require a special procedure. Dyes in this category include indigo (see page 372), shellfish purple, and woad.

Many factors can alter the color of the dye bath—the type of water, the type of pot, the type of mordant, the type of material you are dyeing, the concentration of the plant material, the time of year the plant was harvested, and the amount of water and sun the plant had. Different plant materials and different mordanting processes will give you colors with different levels of permanence. Many plant dyes are what is called fugitive, which means they do not last long. You can increase the permanence of these dyes by making a very concentrated dye bath, by taking care to mordant properly, and by being very careful when washing. Generally, protein fibers such as silk and wool are the best when using natural dyes. Dyeing cellulose fibers such as cotton is still a lot of fun, but the colors usually do not turn out as strong and may not last as long.

My own style of natural dyeing has evolved to be very free-flowing and casual. The fun of natural dyes for me is the mystery of color in the plants, the ways it can be altered with different water and other modifiers, and sharing this whole process with my children. I love experimenting with different plants I find, and using parts of plants I would otherwise just throw on the compost heap. Some great examples are carrot tops, onion skins, and avocado pits and skins. If you love natural dyeing and decide to take your craft to the next level, the resources section in the back of this book lists some fantastic works that I consider to be must-haves in any natural dyer's library.

Preparation

When beginning a dye project, the first thing to consider is what type of material you will be dyeing. You also need to decide if you will use a mordant. A mordant is something that helps the dye bind to the fabric, making the color last longer without fading and often making it darker or more vibrant. I think it is optional (although many others would disagree with me), but if you are dyeing cotton it is especially helpful so the color doesn't wash right out of the fabric. I like to pre-mordant my fibers, if I choose to mordant at all, but you can also do the mordanting process during or even after the initial dye process. Most dye recipes call for alum mordant. If you are dyeing protein fibers, such as wool or silk, you would use alum sulfate; if you are dyeing cellulose fibers, such as cotton, you would use alum acetate. There are also ways to mordant your fibers with soy milk. There are endless ways to experiment, which keeps things interesting in your journey with natural dyes.

Before you mordant, you should scour your material. This is basically a fancy way of saying "wash." Scouring is an important step because it removes residue from the fabric and helps the dye work better. To get the best results, you

FAVORITE PLANTS FOR A DYE GARDEN

- Calendula
- Fennel
- Lobelia
- Elderberry
- Blackberry
- Onion
- Sour Grass
- Pansy

may want to use a special scouring solution determined by the type of fiber you are dyeing. My style is pretty casual; I usually just wash my fabric the regular way with the rest of my clothing in the machine.

After you scour, while the fibers are still wet, you can mordant. Use approximately 10 to 15 percent of the weight of your fiber in alum. Mix it into water and then put it in a big pot with your fabric. Heat, and then simmer for an hour. I sometimes like to turn the heat off and let the fiber sit in the mordant overnight, and then I rinse it out and dye the next day. I also like to prepare my dye bath the night before, letting the plant material sit in the water overnight, and then the next day I bring it up to temperature for 30 minutes before straining out the plant material.

Sourcing Materials

You might find recipes, especially older ones, calling for the use of chrome, copper, or tin. Please do not use any of these. They are incredibly harmful to your health and to local wildlife, and you can create a beautiful rainbow of colors without using these dangerous additives. Another consideration is how you source your materials for dyeing. Please make sure to respectfully and ethically harvest anything you source from the wild. Growing the plants you use is an excellent way to source material. Using invasive plants, such as abundant fennel, or repurposing what would otherwise go in the compost heap, such as the onion skins, carrot tops, or avocado pits I mentioned, is also an ethical way to dye.

Tools and Supplies

You don't need many tools to use natural dyes at home. Probably the most expensive items will be stainless-steel pots to use exclusively for dyeing. For health and safety reasons, it is not recommended to use the same pots you cook with for your dye projects. You also need some wooden spoons or dowels for stirring, an apron or some old clothes to wear while you dye, gloves if you do not wish to have colorful fingernails for a week after your project, goggles if you wish, a mask if you will be using powders in your dyeing, and a scale if you like to be very precise. I do not use a scale, but if you are hoping to repeat exactly the same colors, a scale is helpful in replicating your process.

If you're brand-new to natural dyeing, the following recipes are a great place to start. They are simple and don't require special equipment.

Sour Grass Natural Dye

This is an excellent first natural dye recipe because you don't need any special equipment, and the sour grass (also called wood sorrel) yields a really gratifying and striking color. The end result is a shocking yellow that is very similar to the blossoms. You can try out natural dyeing without having to buy anything other than some wool yarn or silk squares to dye, and you can use the same pots you use for cooking as long as you don't use any modifiers that could be harmful. Before dyeing, consider tying your yarn in two places so it doesn't tangle in the pot.

Sour grass flowers

Filtered water

1. Pick enough sour grass flowers to fill a pot halfway.
2. Boil some water, and then pour it over the flowers until the pot is half to three-quarters full of water.
3. Leave it to soak overnight.
4. The next day, strain out the flowers and heat your dye bath to a gentle simmer.
5. Add your white wool, yarn, or silk fabric.
6. Let it simmer gently for 10 minutes.
7. Turn the heat off, and let your yarn sit in the dye bath until it has cooled.
8. Once cooled, carefully remove your yarn, squeeze out the extra liquid, and hang it to dry.
9. If you'd like to try a modifier, sprinkle a little wood ash in the pot to get an orange color. Some of my yarn came out a deep orange-red when I did this, and some a very gentle, muddy orange. The silk, while it looks vibrant, dried to a very pale orange.

Elderberry Solar Dye

This is another easy dye recipe that doesn't require any special equipment. It's also an ideal project to do with children, since you don't have to worry about anyone getting a burn, which is an important consideration with stovetop dyeing methods. I've had success with this recipe using elderberries, blackberries, black pansies, lobelia blossoms, calendula petals, and more. Have fun with solar dyes! Experiment with different berries and flowers for a whole range of color.

1. Fill your jar to 1 inch from the top with elderberries, and then pour water on top to cover them.
2. If you're using wax paper, put it over the top of the jar, and then screw on the lid. (This will ensure rust does not get on your material.)
3. Place your jar outside in a sunny spot for 3 days.
4. After 3 days, open your jar and strain out the berries, squishing them a bit to release the color.
5. Return this dye liquid to your jar, and add a teaspoon of alum powder. This is optional, but it will help the fabric resist fading.
6. Screw on the lid and give it a shake to mix it.
7. Get the fabric you wish to dye. You may want to get it wet first so the color will be more even, but it's not necessary. Put it in your jar with the dye.
8. Put the lid back on and leave the jar in the sun for 3 more days, turning upside down or shaking every now and then.
9. After 3 days, remove your fabric, give it a rinse with water, and hang it to dry.

Glass jar with lid

Elderberries (enough to nearly fill the jar)

Filtered water

Wax paper (optional)

1 teaspoon alum powder—alum sulfate for silk or wool or alum acetate for cotton (optional)

Cotton, wool, or silk fabric (note that wool and silk will hold the color much better than cotton)

Modifiers

Changing the pH of the dye bath will change the color, sometimes dramatically. Some of my favorite modifiers are iron, vinegar, and wood ash. Iron will deepen the colors. I like to use it with fennel dye baths, as it brings a nice, natural green to the wheat color. Vinegar enhances red, orange, and yellow dyes and increases the permanency in some. Wood ash makes a dramatic difference in the color of the sour grass dye (see page 366). It turns the lemon-yellow dye into anything from a muted, gentle orange to a shocking orange or sometimes a deep orange-red. You can use modifiers at any point in the dye process. I usually use mine at the end.

IRON

1. Fill a glass jar with a handful of rusty nails.
2. Fill the jar with one-quarter white vinegar and three-quarters water. Let it sit for 1 week. The color will deepen, and the water will turn orange.
3. To use, add a little of this mixture to a bowl with some water in it, and dip your fabric in it.
4. Add more if the color isn't deep enough for you.

VINEGAR

1. Fill a bowl with 1½ cups of water and 1½ cups of white vinegar.
2. Fabric can be dipped or swirled in this bowl.
3. This can be used right away. Vinegar can also be added directly to the dye pot.

WOOD ASH

1. Wood ash can be purchased or you can make your own. Place some wood ash in a nut milk bag (a very fine-mesh bag used for making nut milks, available at most natural food stores).
2. Submerge the bag in a pot of water, and let it sit for a few days. You can give the bag a squeeze every now and then to release more of the wood ash into the water.
3. Remove the bag, and your liquid modifier is ready to use.
4. For best results, heat your liquid until hot, and then dip or soak your freshly dyed fabric in the pot for up to 10 minutes. Alternatively, you can pour a little dry wood ash right into your pot.

Quick and Simple Natural Dye

This is a basic recipe that can be used successfully with fennel, onion skins, avocado pits, and many other plants. It is not as simple as the sour grass or elderberry solar dye recipes, but it is easier than it first appears. I encourage you to try it once you are feeling confident with the other techniques. I like this basic recipe because it works with so many plants. Try using what you have an abundance of. Saving onion skins in a jar over time will make a dye bath that is rich, strong, and warm golden yellow, and you can compost the skins when you've finished (as long as you haven't used a modifier that has altered the pH). More excellent plants to try are toyon leaf and bark, golden yarrow, blackberries, coreopsis, and ironbark eucalyptus.

1. Weigh the dry fabric (unless you plan on winging it, like I often do).
2. Put between one to two times the weight of your fabric in plant matter in the pot, cover it with plenty of water, and simmer for an hour.
3. Turn off the heat, and let it sit overnight.
4. Scour the fabric.
5. If desired, pre-mordant your fabric by heating a big pot of water with 10 percent of the dry fabric weight in mordant. Use alum acetate if you are dyeing cotton, hemp, or linen, and alum sulfate if you are dyeing silk, wool, or alpaca. (If you choose not to mordant, skip to step 8.)
6. Add the wet fabric to the pot and simmer for an hour.
7. Rinse in warm water. You can save the water and alum for next time, as it will contain half the metals you need and reduce waste, cost, and environmental impact.
8. The next morning, remove some or all of the plant material from the dye pot you left to steep overnight.
9. Bring your dye bath up to a simmer, wet your fabric, and add it to the bath.
10. Simmer your fabric in the dye bath for an hour or until you are happy with the color—sometimes 5 minutes is plenty. (Remember that the color will be lighter once the fabric is rinsed and dried.)
11. Take the fabric out. Without rinsing it first, hang it until it is completely dry.
12. Rinse out the fabric, and then hang it to dry again.

Fabric to dye, such as wool yarn, silk scarves, cotton napkins, or a T-shirt

Water (preferably rainwater, as tap water will often alter the color of the dye bath)

Alum acetate for cotton, hemp, or linen; alum sulfate for silk, wool, or alpaca

Fresh dye plants of your choice (enough to loosely fill the pot at least one-third full)

Abuela Quilts

CAITLIN MCCANN

Artist, seamstress, and naturalist Caitlin McCann lives in California with her husband and son. She was raised in Alabama, where her interest in sewing was birthed when her mother sewed ribbons on her ballet shoes. Eventually, Caitlin's mother taught her to use a sewing machine, and from then on Caitlin made and altered her own clothes, including her prom dress! Creating costumes and clothes continued until her nephew was born, which is when she started making him a quilt for his birthday every year. When she was pregnant with her own son, she felt a deep ancestral desire to create and share items from generation to generation, so she started her business, Abuela Quilts.

As her business grew and expanded into pillows and other home goods, Caitlin became more interested in working with natural and organic materials. She attended Rebecca Burgess's natural dyeing workshop at the Ojai Valley Grange, which inspired her to dye organic cotton fabric with plants harvested from her area. She realizes how important natural dyeing is in order to protect the environment, which is also the reason she only uses organic cotton.

INDIGO FERMENT VAT

I have been fortunate to sample the indigo vats Caitlin has made on several occasions, and every time I've achieved lovely blues that fade just right over time. It's a fun activity to do together with friends, and I'm so pleased to share her recipe here. In addition to a large vat, you will need a heat blanket or heat lamp for this recipe.

10 gallons filtered water
1 pound indigo
½ pound madder root
½ pound oat bran
3 pounds soda ash

1. Mix all the ingredients together in a large vat.
2. Cover and wrap with a heat blanket or place a heat lamp over the vat.
3. Slowly stir around the edge of the vat once a day, being careful not to disturb the "indigo flower" in the center.
4. Maintain a temperature of 100 to 110°F for about 1 week and then the dye is ready.

HERBS AND CHILDREN

Kids are easily excited by herbalism, and there is so much for them to learn and enjoy. Ever since my oldest started toddling around, my family and I have prioritized being in wild open spaces, foraging for food, making teas and remedies, and identifying potentially harmful plants. It gives me joy to watch their own journeys with plants develop. My oldest is mostly interested in remedies and magic, and she spends time communicating with the plant spirits. My middle child enjoys cooking with herbs and weeds and making her own face paint, tinctures, snack recipes, and healing salves. My littlest is an avid forager, and he loves nothing more than munching on mallow cheesewheel snacks, loquats, and wood sorrel as we hike and play.

Getting Started

Some parents feel overwhelmed when first introducing their kids to herbs, and it can be hard to know where to start. I find that if I go out into wild places with children, they will lead the way. Watch your child. Maybe he or she begins collecting acorns under the oak trees at the park. Collect them too! Look for acorns without wormholes. Bring them home, do some research, and make something together with them (acorn cakes are a favorite around here). Or maybe he or she picks a dandelion. Admire it! Pick one too. When you head home, look it up in some of the resources listed in the back of this book and make some dandelion fritters, or simply add the flowers to your salad or muffin mix.

CHILDREN'S GARDEN

Take note that many of these plants grow a lot and will take over a garden bed. For example, most mints are best grown in containers so they don't choke out all of the other plants. Take some time to learn which plants are best in separate pots or containers versus which are better planted in the garden bed.

Medicinal Plants

- Calendula
- Viola
- Pansy
- Peppermint
- Oregano
- Chamomile
- Lemon balm
- Valerian

Edible Flowers

- Chamomile
- Calendula
- Violet
- Pansy
- Guava blossom
- Starflower/borage
- Wood sorrel/sour grass
- Sage blossoms
- Nasturtium (edible but spicy)
- Wild mustard (edible but spicy)
- Sweet alyssum (edible but spicy)

Children have a natural curiosity, and they delight in doing projects with their parents and siblings. It's fun for the whole family. Starting small and simply is the surest way to success. You can then go to the plant nursery and buy some starts of edible plants. As the flowers bloom, try adding them on top of pancakes or

making flower ice cubes. When you point a plant out to your child (or maybe you choose a plant because your child is pointing it out to you), sit with it for a while. You might make up a story or song about it to sing. There are many ways to help herbalism come alive for your little ones.

When it comes to foraging with kids, safety is the most important thing. As a beginning forager, it's ideal to grow your own plants as a way to learn about them and make sure the plants you're foraging are safe. You can buy small starts from a plant nursery and create a children's garden. Every garden will be different. You'll find you and your children are drawn to certain plants and not as interested in others. That's the beauty of it. Just be sure to get your plants from a reputable, organic source, and always double check with the specialist at the nursery that everything in your cart is edible and safe.

Kids often have a lot going on with their growing bodies. Whether it's tummy aches, fevers, itchy skin, or just irritability, I prefer to soothe my kids with natural ingredients for minor ailments. Here are some of my go-to home remedies that have worked well for my kids.

Tincture for Upset Tummies

When I make tinctures for kids, I generally make glycerides. A glyceride uses vegetable glycerine and water rather than alcohol for the menstruum. It does not extract the medicinal constituents as well as alcohol, but it tastes sweet and children are more likely to take the medicine this way.

Fresh lemon balm leaves, finely chopped

Vegetable glycerine

Filtered water

1. Fill a half-pint jar three-quarters full with the lemon balm leaves.
2. Cover with a mixture of two-thirds vegetable glycerine and one-third water and put on the lid.
3. Shake the jar once a day and make sure the leaves are staying below the surface of the liquid.
4. After 4 weeks, strain and then bottle in tincture bottles.
5. Give a quarter dropperful as needed, up to three times per day.

Oat and Comfrey Bath for Itchy Skin

This is one recipe I turn to more than I ever would have guessed before having children. My kids get itchy for all kinds of reasons. Sometimes it's over something as seemingly benign as playing in the grass or swimming in a pool with too much chlorine. Other times it's something more serious. All three of my children have had chicken pox, and I gave them each this bath to help soothe their skin. I've made it with both fresh and dried comfrey, and both ways work well, though I will caution you to remove the comfrey right away when you drain the tub. Otherwise, it may leave a stain.

1. Fill a nut milk bag (a fine-mesh bag used for making nut milks, available at most natural food stores) with the oats and comfrey leaf and root.
2. Put the bag in a medium-sized pot with freshly boiled water. Think of the herb-filled bag as a giant tea bag, and the pot as a giant tea cup.
3. Let the herbs infuse in the hot water for a few minutes.
4. Carefully put all of this (the bag and the liquid from the pot) into the bathtub. Keep the nut milk bag tied closed. If you open it, the herbs will go into the tub and make a big mess.
5. Mix this hot, infused tea with the bathwater. Make sure the temperature is comfortable before getting in or putting any children in the tub.
6. Soak for at least 20 minutes, and then gently towel dry and apply a good, natural lotion.

1 cup oats

1 cup comfrey leaf and root

All-Purpose Salve

Generally, I prefer to use honey on small cuts and scrapes, but I often use a salve instead because it is so much easier to travel with. Making an all-purpose salve is very simple and fun to do with kids. First, make an herbal oil, and then turn it into a salve.

Dried plantain

Dried calendula

Olive oil

¼ cup beeswax pastilles

1 teaspoon vitamin E
(optional)

10 to 20 drops lavender oil
(optional)

1. Fill a jar one-third full with equal parts dried plantain (*Plantago major* or *Plantago lanceolata*) and dried calendula (*Calendula officinalis*).
2. Pour the olive oil to cover the herbs, leaving 1 inch of space at the top.
3. Screw the lid onto the jar, give it a shake, and set it in a sunny window.
4. Shake the jar a few times a day for the first week, and then every once in a while for 3 weeks after that.
5. Strain out the solids and reserve the oil.
6. When ready to make the salve, add ¾ cup of your herbal oil to the beeswax pastilles in a double boiler.
7. Heat on low until melted, and then remove from the heat.
8. This is optional, but for a natural preservative, add 1 teaspoon of vitamin E and 10 to 20 drops of lavender oil.
9. Pour the mixture into small jars or salve tins and let it cool. It will last 6 months or more under normal conditions.

Herbs don't need to be associated with medicines all the time. For kids, there are a lot of other fun activities that also involve herbs.

Flower Ice Cubes

Flower ice cubes add sweetness and spring vibrancy to every drink, and they are so simple to make.

1. First, fill an ice cube tray halfway full with cooled, boiled water (to make the ice cubes nice and clear). Then add edible flowers, such as calendula petals, chamomile, sage blossoms, borage, violets, or pansies.
2. Put the tray in the freezer.
3. The next day, you will notice the flowers have floated to the surface. Now, pour water over the floral ice cubes, and put the tray back in the freezer for another day.
4. The flowers will now be in the middle of the cubes. When they melt, they can even be eaten!

Edible flowers (calendula, chamomile, sage blossoms, borage, violets, or pansies)

Filtered water

Herbal Face Paint Sunscreen

This recipe is a spin on the Zinka sunscreen of my childhood and makes putting on sunscreen fun. For a nice variety of color, you'll want to use several different kinds of herbs. For green, I like nettle, spirulina, or spinach. For a purple-blue color, I use elderberry. I use red rose petals for a reddish color, and calendula or turmeric for yellow. All of these herbs have felt fine to my children on their skin. If you choose herbs outside of what I've listed here, please make sure they will not be irritating to your children's delicate skin. Even if you stick to this list, it is always advisable to do a mama test run first so your little ones don't get any upsetting surprises. It's also important to remind them to keep it out of their eyes.

Herbs of choice
(nettle, spirulina, spinach,
elderberry, rose petals,
calendula, or turmeric)

Natural sunscreen of choice

1. First, powder your herbs. You can use a coffee grinder reserved especially for herbs, a mortar and pestle, or even purchase herbs already finely ground.
2. Put each type of powdered herb in its own little dish.
3. Add a dab of natural sunscreen to each dish and mix.
4. Use the mixture as you would use Zinka—sunscreen that is meant to be seen. Make stripes down the nose and across the cheeks—the more, the better.

Resources

FOOD

PRESERVING

Sarah Marshall, *Preservation Pantry: Modern Canning from Root to Top and Stem to Core*

Kevin West, *Saving the Season: A Cook's Guide to Home Canning, Pickling, and Preserving*

Linda Ziedrich, *The Joy of Pickling: 300 Flavor-Packed Recipes for All Kinds of Produce from Garden or Market*

FERMENTATION

David Asher, *The Art of Natural Cheesemaking: Using Traditional, Non-Industrial Methods and Raw Ingredients to Make the World's Best Cheeses*

Sandor Ellix Katz, *The Art of Fermentation: An In-Depth Exploration of Essential Concepts and Processes from around the World*

René Redzepi and David Zilber, *The Noma Guide to Fermentation*

SOURDOUGH

Emilie Raffa, *Artisan Sourdough Made Simple: A Beginner's Guide to Delicious Handcrafted Bread with Minimal Kneading*

Peter Reinhart, *The Bread Baker's Apprentice: Mastering the Art of Extraordinary Bread*

Chad Robertson, *Tartine Bread*

RAW

Catherine Bretherton, *Sprouted!: Power Up Your Plate with Home-Sprouted Superfoods*

Rosalee de la Forêt, *Alchemy of Herbs: Transform Everyday Ingredients into Foods and Remedies That Heal*

Rita Galchus, *Homegrown Sprouts: A Fresh, Healthy, and Delicious Step-by-Step Guide to Sprouting Year Round*

Jerry Traunfeld, *The Herbal Kitchen: Cooking with Fragrance and Flavor*

Jerry Traunfeld, *The Herbfarm Cookbook*

COOKING WITH CHILDREN

Erin Gleeson, *The Forest Feast for Kids: Colorful Vegetarian Recipes That Are Simple to Make*

Nancy McDougall and Jenny Hendy, *300 Step-by-Step Cooking and Gardening Projects for Kids*

Mardi Michels, *In the French Kitchen with Kids: Easy, Everyday Dishes for the Whole Family to Make and Enjoy*

SEASONAL FOOD

Kendra Aronson, *The San Luis Obispo Farmers' Market Cookbook: Simple Seasonal Recipes and Short Stories from the Central Coast of California*

Pascale Beale-Groom, *A Menu for All Seasons: Autumn*

Pascale Beale-Groom, *A Menu for All Seasons: Spring*

Pascale Beale-Groom, *A Menu for All Seasons: Summer*

Pascale Beale-Groom, *A Menu for All Seasons: Winter*

Barbara Kingsolver, *Animal, Vegetable, Miracle: A Year of Food Life*

Alice Waters, *The Art of Simple Food: Notes, Lessons, and Recipes from a Delicious Revolution*

ANIMAL HUSBANDRY

THE BASICS

Gail Damerow, *Barnyard in Your Backyard: A Beginner's Guide to Raising Chickens, Ducks, Geese, Rabbits, Goats, Sheep, and Cattle*

Mark Fisher, *Animal Welfare Science, Husbandry, and Ethics: The Evolving Story of Our Relationship with Farm Animals*

Temple Grandin, *Temple Grandin's Guide to Working with Farm Animals: Safe, Humane Livestock Handling Practices for the Small Farm*

CHICKENS

Gail Damerow, *The Chicken Health Handbook: A Complete Guide to Maximizing Flock Health and Dealing with Disease*

Robert and Hannah Litt, *A Chicken in Every Yard: The Urban Farm Store's Guide to Chicken Keeping*

Eric Lofgren, *The Backyard Chicken Bible: The Complete Guide to Raising Chickens*

Rick and Gail Luttman, *Chickens in Your Backyard: A Beginner's Guide*

Harvey Ussery, *The Small-Scale Poultry Flock: An All-Natural Approach to Raising Chickens and Other Fowl for Home and Market Growers*

DAIRY COWS

MaryJane Butters, *Milk Cow Kitchen*

Joann S. Grohman, *Keeping a Family Cow: The Complete Guide for Home-Scale, Holistic Dairy Products*

Philip Hasheider, *The Family Cow Handbook: A Guide to Keeping a Milk Cow*

Dirk Van Loon, *The Family Cow*

Sue Weaver, *The Backyard Cow: An Introductory Guide to Keeping a Productive Family Cow*

PIGS

Philip Hasheider, *How to Raise Pigs: Everything You Need to Know*

Kelly Klober, *Dirt Hog: A Hands-On Guide to Raising Pigs Outdoors Naturally*

Kelly Klober, *Storey's Guide to Raising Pigs: Care, Facilities, Management, Breeds*

Jeremy N. Marchant-Forde, *The Welfare of Pigs*

Wendy Scudamore, *Small-Scale Outdoor Pig Breeding*

BUTCHERING

Adam Danforth, *Butchering: Poultry, Rabbit, Lamb, Goat, Pork*

Camas Davis, *Killing It: An Education*

Jamie Waldron and Angela England, *Home Butchering Handbook: Enjoy Finer, Fresher, Healthier Cuts of Meat from Your Own Kitchen*

HERBALISM

HERBAL EDUCATION

Herbal Academy, theherbalacademy.com

Rosemary Gladstar's The Science and Art of Herbalism, scienceandartofherbalism.com

Wise Woman Center, susunweed.com/Wise-Woman-Center.htm

FORAGING

Steven Foster et al., *Peterson Field Guides to Medicinal Plants and Herbs*

Nancy J. Turner and Adam F. Szczawinski, *Common Poisonous Plants and Mushrooms of North America*

BEAUTY AND PERSONAL CARE

Leslie M. Alexander and Linda A. Straub-Bruce, *Dental Herbalism: Natural Therapies for the Mouth*

Rosemary Gladstar, *Herbs for Natural Beauty: Create Your Own Herbal Shampoos, Cleansers, Creams, Bath Blends, and More*

Stephanie Tourles, *Organic Body Care Recipes: 175 Homemade Herbal Formulas for Glowing Skin and Vibrant Self*

HERBAL MEDICINE

Stephen Harrod Buhner, *Herbal Antibiotics: Natural Alternatives for Treating Drug-Resistant Bacteria*

Richo Cech, *Making Plant Medicine*

Zoë Gardner and Michael McGuffin, eds., *American Herbal Products Association's Botanical Safety Handbook* (2nd ed.)

Anne Kennedy, *Herbal Medicine Natural Remedies*

Tieraona Low Dog, *Healthy at Home: Get Well and Stay Well without Prescriptions*

JJ Pursell, *The Herbal Apothecary: 100 Medicinal Herbs and How to Use Them*

Dr. Jill Stansbury, *Herbal Formularies for Health Professionals, Volume 1: Digestion and Elimination*

Dr. Jill Stansbury, *Herbal Formularies for Health Professionals, Volume 2: Circulation and Respiration*

Dr. Jill Stansbury, *Herbal Formularies for Health Professionals, Volume 3: Endocrinology*

Michael Tierra, *Planetary Herbology*

Dr. Sharol Marie Tilgner, *Herbal Medicine from the Heart of the Earth*

Rachel Weaver, *Be Your Own "Doctor"*

GENERAL WELL-BEING

Juliette de Baïracli Levy, *Common Herbs for Natural Health*

Juliette de Baïracli Levy, *The Complete Herbal Handbook for Farm and Stable*

Rosemary Gladstar, *Herbal Healing for Women: Simple Home Remedies for Women of All Ages*

Rosemary Gladstar, *Herbal Recipes for Vibrant Health: 175 Teas, Tonics, Oils, Salves, Tinctures, and Other Natural Remedies for the Entire Family*

Rosemary Gladstar, *Rosemary Gladstar's Family Herbal: A Guide to Living Life with Energy, Health, and Vitality*

Elson M. Haas, *Staying Healthy with the Seasons*

David Winston and Steven Maimes, *Adaptogens: Herbs for Strength, Stamina, and Stress Relief*

Matthew Wood, *The Earthwise Herbal Repertory: The Definitive Practitioner's Guide*

NATURAL DYES

Rita Buchanan, *A Dyer's Garden: From Plant to Pot, Growing Dyes for Natural Fibers*

Rita Buchanan, *A Weaver's Garden: Growing Plants for Natural Dyes and Fibers*

Rebecca Burgess, *Harvesting Color: How to Find Plants and Make Natural Dyes*

Rebecca Desnos, *Botanical Colour at Your Fingertips*

Chris McLaughlin, *A Garden to Dye For: How to Use Plants from the Garden to Create Natural Colors for Fabrics and Fibers*

HERBS AND CHILDREN

Demetria Clark, *Herbal Healing for Children: A Parent's Guide to Treatments for Common Childhood Illnesses*

Herb Fairies, learningherbs.com/herb-fairies/

Herbal Roots Zine, herbalrootszine.com

Anne McIntyre, *Herbal Treatment of Children: Western and Ayurvedic Perspectives*

Janet Zand, Robert Rountree, and Rachel Walton, *Smart Medicine for a Healthier Child*

DRIED HERBS, JARS, AND OTHER SUPPLIES

Bulk Herb Store, bulkherbstore.com

Mountain Rose Herbs, mountainroseherbs.com

Rosemary's Garden, rosemarysgarden.com

Specialty Bottle, specialtybottle.com

Acknowledgments

Many helping hands made this book possible. We would like to thank everyone who believed in and supported us while making this dream come true. We'd of course like to thank Carla Glasser from the Betsy Nolan Literary Agency and Rizzoli for having our back from the very beginning. We'd like to give a huge thanks to Lauren Ross for her beautiful photos and documentation of our adventures over the years. It has been an honor. Thank you also to Mikaela Hamilton, Sophie Haber, Brittany E. Smith, and Moira Tarmy for their incredible photo contributions. You made this book feel whole. We'd also like to thank Audria Culaciati for her hard work and the way she channeled our mission through words. What a joy it was to work together. Many thanks to all of the women who contributed features to this book (and their support teams, who made those features possible). We know photographing and writing contributions was not easy, and we're so appreciative of the time and effort. From the bottom of our hearts, thank you to the entire team. We are forever grateful for all you have done for us.

EMMA ROLLIN MOORE

I would like to thank my husband, Kevin, and our two children, Olivia and Liam, for their infinite patience, constant support, and unending love. After all, they are the inspiration and motivation behind my drive to create and cook whole, nourishing foods daily. I'd like to give special thanks to my parents, for always believing in me and being the most amazing human beings. Thanks also to Sandor Katz, for his endless knowledge and teachings, and Sally Fallon, for writing the book *Nourishing Traditions*, which influences how I cook and create food daily. I am thankful for my partners, Lauren and Ashley, for their inspiring ways and for being along for the journey. Last, I am grateful for the wisdom of countless people who have enriched my world over the years.

LAUREN MALLOY

I would like to thank my husband, Keith, for his proofreading skills, ideas, and patience, and our children, Milly and June (and baby number three on the way), for always being willing to try a new animal adventure and learning experience. A big thanks to my mom, Pam Coffield, for her help and support throughout my life as well as this writing process. A heartfelt thank-you to Vernie Bradway for all of her ideas, advice, and expertise. I am so grateful for the eternal inspiration I get from my partners, Emma and Ashley. Last, I am thankful for all who have mentored me throughout my animal journey. It truly takes a village.

ASHLEY MOORE

I would like to thank my husband, Ryan, and our three children, Isla, Lyra, and Jupiter, for their endless patience and abundant love. A heartfelt thank-you to all of my teachers along the way—Rosemary Gladstar, Susun Weed, Marlene Adelmann, Kristie Karima Burns, and Lanny Kaufer—for their generous sharing of knowledge and expertise. I'd also like to thank my first teacher, my father Dr. Geoffrey Smith, who instilled in me a love of both plants and the art of healing. I am grateful to my entire family, friends, and community for their encouragement and support. Last, I'd like to thank my two hardworking, dynamic partners, Emma and Lauren.

TO OUR CHILDREN

First published in the United States of America in 2020 by Rizzoli International Publications, Inc.
300 Park Avenue South • New York, NY 10010 • www.rizzoliusa.com

All photographs © Lauren Ross except for the following:
Sophie Haber: pp. 218, 220, 223, 260, and 261. **Mikaela Hamilton:** pp. 41, 43, 49, 54, 55, 69, 76, 77, 89, 100, 117, 118, 124, 127, 128, 131, 132, 135, 136, 139, 140, 143, 144, 147, 148, 151, 152, 160, 163, 166, 167, 171, 174, 177, 178, 179, 181, 182, 183, 184, 187, 188, 189, 190, 191, 193, 234, 236, 237 (both), 268, 272, 276, 277, 288 (bottom two), 289 (all), 290 (all), 291 (bottom three), 292 (top three), 296, 299, 302, 303, 304, 311, 312, 315, 319, 322 (both), 325, 326, 329, 339, 340, 343, 352, 358, 362, 367, 370, 372, 373, 374, 379, 380, 383, and 384. **Brittany E. Smith:** pp. 196–197, 203, 211, 216, 238, 242, 259, 267, 300, and 301. **Moira Tarmy:** pp. 214, 218, 220, and 223.

The goal of Women's Heritage is to bring elements of the homestead into everyday life. We understand in today's world women are extraordinarily busy, and making things from scratch or even learning a new skill can seem daunting. We hope to inspire women to explore, discover, and learn new passions and skills. For more information, please visit womensheritage.com.

Publisher: Charles Miers
Associate Publisher: James Muschett
Managing Editor: Lynn Scrabis
Editor: Candice Fehrman
Design: Susi Oberhelman

Printed in China

2020 2021 2022 2023 / 10 9 8 7 6 5 4 3 2 1

ISBN: 978-1-59962-155-5

Library of Congress Control Number: 2019950384

Visit us online:
Facebook.com/RizzoliNewYork
Twitter: @Rizzoli_Books
Instagram.com/RizzoliBooks
Pinterest.com/RizzoliBooks
Youtube.com/user/RizzoliNY
Issuu.com/Rizzoli